Discovering the Bible

ARCHAEOLOGISTS LOOK AT SCRIPTURE

Edited by Tim Dowley

Marshall Pickering/Eerdmans

First published in the UK by
Marshall Morgan & Scott Publications Ltd.
3 Beggarwood Lane,
Basingstoke,
Hants RG23 7LP

ISBN 0 551 01372 9

First published in the USA by
Wm. B. Eerdmans Pub. Co.
255 Jefferson Ave S.E.
Grand Rapids
Michigan 49503

Created and designed by
Three's Company
12 Flitcroft Street,
London WC2H 8DJ

Book Designer: Peter M. Wyart MSIAD
Typesetting by
Creative Editors & Writers Ltd,
Hampermill Cottage, Watford WD1 4PL
Printed in the United States of America

Authors

Dr LaMoine F. DeVries, Campus Minister/Teacher, Southwest Missouri State University, Springfield, Missouri

Dr John McRay, Professor of New Testament and Archaeology, Co-ordinator of Biblical Studies, Wheaton College Graduate School, Wheaton, Illinois

Dr Victor H. Matthews, Associate Professor of Religious Studies, Southwest Missouri State University

Dr James Moyer, Professor and Head of the Department of Religious Studies, Southwest Missouri State University

Dr John Wilson, Dean of Seaver College, Pepperdine University, Malibu, California

Contents

The Bible and Archaeology

Archaeological milestones
Since early in the Christian era, people have been fascinated by the history of the eastern Mediterranean countries, regarded by Jews, Christians and Moslems as the Holy Lands. Helena, mother of Constantine, the first Roman emperor to be a Christian, visited this part of the world in about AD 328, and built churches over some of the holiest places. Her visit is recorded by a contemporary historian and friend of the family, Eusebius of Caesarea[1], and is discussed in the church histories of Sulpitius Severus[2], Rufinus[3], Socrates[4], Sozomen[5] and Theodoret[6], all written within a century of her death. These records are confusing, some of them claiming that Helena alone constructed the churches, and others that they were built by both Helena and Constantine. But they all agree that the churches were built during the reign of Constantine, a view supported by the archaeological evidence.

Holy places Eusebius himself made a careful search for the holy places, and left a record of more than one thousand place names in his book *Onomasticon*, which we have today. In the centuries that followed, pilgrims went to the Holy Lands largely for religious purposes, although occasionally study visits were made, prompted largely by an interest in history, art, architecture, sculpture or coins. Efforts to obtain antiquities of this kind amounted to little more than treasure hunts, having very little scientific value for the archaeologist.

Probably the earliest recorded attempt at what we might properly call archaeological excavation was made on 1 October 1738 at Herculaneum in southern Italy by the Spanish engineer, Rocco Giocchino de Alcubierre, assisted by the Swiss architect, Karl Weber, and later by Francesco La Vega, although these were not excavations in the modern sense of the term.

Herculaneum, like Pompeii, which was first excavated on 23 March, 1748 by Alcubierre and Giacopo Martorelli of Naples, was covered when Mount Vesuvius erupted in AD 79. The 'excavations' consisted of tunnelling operations into the hardened mud lava, which was more than fifteen metres (fifty feet) thick

Opposite: The Church of the Holy Sepulchre, Jerusalem, founded in AD 326 by the Emperor Constantine.

Below: Entrance to the 'Holy Sepulchre' inside the Church of the Holy Sepulchre, Jerusalem.

7

in some places. In this way the excavators gained access to underground streets, buildings and passageways, through which they removed many of the precious treasures of the buried city. There was none of the systematic, scientific removal of layers of earth, carefully recorded, measured, drawn and reported, which characterizes modern archaeological excavations. Pompeii, unlike Herculaneum, rested beneath layers of soft pumice, ash and earth.

Precious stones The continuing search for ancient treasure was extended to the Middle East in 1799 by the unexpected discovery, by an officer of Napoleon, of a stone with a trilingual inscription. This was the famous 'Rosetta Stone', which, once deciphered, proved to be the key which could unlock the language and history of ancient Egypt, written in previously undecipherable hieroglyphics on the walls of its buildings and tombs. Throughout the nineteenth century, entrepreneurs filled the museums of Europe and the private collections of wealthy sponsors with antiquities taken from the Middle East.

The 'Rosetta Stone', the famous key to Egyptian hieroglyphics.

Expeditions were also sent to Mesopotamia. Paul Botta ravaged Khorsabad, ten miles north of Nineveh, in 1842, and filled the Louvre in Paris with antiquities from the reign of Sargon II, an Assyrian monarch. Sir Austen Layard, beginning in 1845, surpassed Botta, and filled the British Museum with still greater treasures from Nineveh, from the reign of another Assyrian king, Ashurnasirpal II.

Reading the tablets However a positive note amidst this plunder of the past was struck between 1846 and 1855 when Sir Henry Rawlinson deciphered the cuneiform script of the Old Persian language on the trilingual Behistun Rock, the 'Rosetta Stone of the East'. Soon the Elamite and Akkadian languages were also deciphered, and in this way the history of Assyria and Babylonia was opened to the world, through the translation of stone inscriptions and clay tablets, approximately 500,000 of which have now been discovered.

Since Palestine itself, the land comprising modern Israel, Jordan and Syria, seemed to be largely devoid of valuable artifacts, the first scholars there undertook geographical surveys and the identification of ancient sites. Prominent among those who performed this vital work were the Germans Ulrich Seetzen and Johan Ludwig Burckhardt (1805–12), the Americans Edward Robinson and Eli Smith (1838–52), and the Britons C.R. Conder and H.H. Kitchener (1872–78).

Palestinian excavation began in Jerusalem in 1850 with the Frenchman, F. de Saulcy, but his work was unscientific; he mis-dated the tomb of Helen of Adiabene by 600 years. The British archaeologist Charles Warren worked in Jerusalem from 1867, as did the Frenchman Charles Clermont-Ganneau; but their work was no more scientific than that of de Saulcy.

Above: Workers remove a gigantic bull with a human head from the mound at Nineveh, under the direction of the the nineteenth-century archaeologist Sir Austen Layard.

Below: The human-headed bull from Nineveh is now in the British Museum, London.

Throughout the Middle East archaeologists have found mounds, or tells, which mark the site of ancient cities. This is Tell el Husn at Beth Shan.

Homer's Troy It remained for Heinrich Schliemann, the German excavator of Homer's Troy and Mycenae, to introduce scientific methodology into archaeology. At Troy, in 1870, Schliemann discovered that the mounds which appear like truncated cones dotting the countryside of the Middle East are in reality the accumulated layers of ancient cities which have been destroyed and rebuilt time and again over the centuries. Beneath each mound (or *tell*, as they are now called in Hebrew and Arabic) lay an ancient city or portion of a city. By cutting through these layers, as one might slice a cake, the history of the site could be uncovered from the most recent period of occupation (at the surface) to the earliest (at the bottom).

Twenty years later the English Egyptologist Sir Flinders Petrie worked briefly at Tell Hesi in Palestine and observed that each layer in the tell contained its own unique type of ceramic pottery. By carefully recording the pottery in each layer one could observe the changes in cultural occupation. He saw that some of the pottery had different forms, which he recognized from his work in Egypt. There he had found similar pottery in contexts which could be dated from inscriptions found at the levels in which the pottery was discovered. In this way originated 'ceramic typology', the most important technique in modern Palestinian archaeology for dating stratigraphic levels which do not contain inscriptions or coins. More often than not the pottery had been broken, and the potsherds had to be carefully extracted from the debris and studied for identification and possible reconstruction.

Pots and dates The importance of Petrie's discovery was almost immediately acknowledged as revolutionary. Since ancient people often made their own pottery, when they moved from one place to another they did not bother to take it with them because it was so inexpensive. Since pottery was virtually imperishable, every layer of a tell contains an abundance of potsherds. Once this was recognized, a chronology based on ceramic typology had to be established so that more precise dates could be given to the changes in pottery styles, which could be distinguished as precisely as changes in car models today.

The man who recognized and met this need was the pre-eminent Middle Eastern archaeologist, William Foxwell Albright. Working at Tell Beit Mirsim in southern Palestine from 1926–32, he was fortunate enough to excavate a well-stratified mound with enough pottery in each stratum to record scientifically the typological and chronological evolution of their major forms. His work remains the basis of all modern ceramic typology, which is constantly being refined by continuing excavation.

Some of the largest excavations in Palestine were carried out before this method of dating had matured, and were for this reason less effective than if they had been conducted later. This is true, for example, of the original excavations at Jerusalem, Samaria, Jericho, Tanaach, Megiddo, Gezer, Lachish and Hazor. Most of these have been re-excavated since World War II by British, American and Israeli archaeologists, using not only a highly-refined pottery chronology but also the scientific techniques discussed below (p. 17).

Diagram showing how archaeologists investigate a tell.

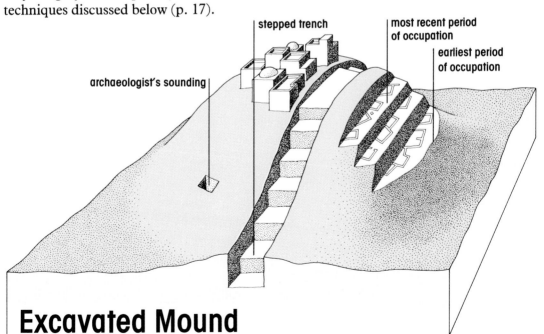

archaeologist's sounding

stepped trench

most recent period of occupation

earliest period of occupation

Excavated Mound

Biblical archaeology

Much of the work done in the early surveys and excavations of the Holy Lands was prompted by the religious convictions of men impressed by the positive influence of the Bible on human history. Some were churchmen, others were teachers in religious institutions, all were dedicated to the essential trustworthiness of the Scriptures.

In more recent times, the great contribution of science to archaeology has been accompanied by an increased interest in scientifically and historically based excavation by people whose primary concern is not the Bible. They have a geographical rather than a religious perspective, and talk about Syro-Palestinian rather than biblical archaeology; they dig 'Syria-Palestine' and not the Holy Lands.

Diagram showing how different styles in pottery help date strata at a dig.

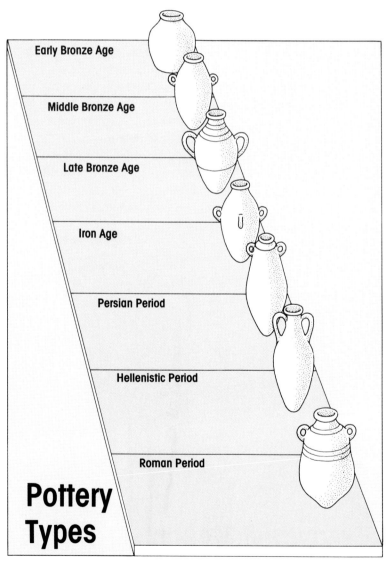

Early Bronze Age

Middle Bronze Age

Late Bronze Age

Iron Age

Persian Period

Hellenistic Period

Roman Period

Pottery Types

Heinrich Schliemann gives an account of his discoveries to the Society of Antiquaries at Burlington House, London.

What is biblical archaeology? Certainly there are no special methods for biblical archaeology. All reputable archaeology is done in essentially the same way, with the greatest care to excavate in a responsible scientific manner according to the latest and best methods. Archaeology becomes 'biblical' in the same way that it becomes 'classical' – when the process of excavation uncovers something relating to biblical or classical history.

Presuppositions are normally involved in the choice of a site: Schliemann chose Troy and Mycenae because of his classical interests; Yigael Yadin chose Hazor because of his biblical interests. However, there is no reason to assume that an archaeologist is less objective or scientific if he has biblical rather than classical interests. It was Schliemann's utter confidence in the Greek poet that led to his spectacular discovery of Homer's Troy; but it was also his presuppositions which caused him to identify erroneously the gold death masks he found in the tombs of Mycenae, and to cable King George I of the Greeks: 'I have gazed on the face of Agamemnon'.

Thus, in methodology, an archaeologist is an archaeologist. But the historical perspective from which he works, and the ultimate interest he has for using the discipline, labels him as biblical, classical, prehistorical, New World and so forth.

Three legendary archaeologists Three of the greatest archaeologists of the twentieth century were regarded as biblical archaeologists. W.F. Albright, of Johns Hopkins University, is legendary as perhaps the greatest archaeological mind in history. The son of missionary parents, his work was often directed against radical German critics who attacked the historical credibility of the Bible. In his later years Albright became increasingly conservative in his theological outlook.

Nelson Glueck, one of Albright's students, was president of Hebrew Union College–Jewish Institute of Religion, and an ordained rabbi. He became one of the best-known figures in the history of Middle Eastern archaeology, especially for his work in the nomadic areas of that part of the world. He often spoke of the way he used the Bible as a map when making his extensive archaeological surveys.

Another of Albright's students, G. Ernest Wright, was professor of Old Testament and Archaeology at Harvard University. His book, *Biblical Archaeology*, has been a standard work since its publication, and he trained many of the eminent archaeologists now working in the field. One of the world's greatest authorities on archaeological methodology, Wright considered himself to be a biblical archaeologist in the best sense of that expression, and made no apology for it. Most Israeli archaeologists today are biblical archaeologists in terms of their major concerns.

Armchair archaeology What, then, is biblical archaeology? In the first chapter of his book Wright calls it 'a special "armchair" variety of general archaeology', and points out that the biblical archaeologist 'must be intelligently concerned with stratigraphy and typology, upon which the methodology of modern archaeology rests ... yet his chief concern is not with methods or pots or weapons in themselves alone. His central and absorbing interest is the understanding and exposition of the Scriptures.' The limitations of non-professional archaeologists are recognized by all who take part in archaeology in the field. Interest in the biblical dimensions of Syro-Palestinian archaeology, however, is not one of these limitations. On the contrary, it is an aid to the more efficient application of archaeological methods in the lands of the Bible.

However there are also limitations inherent in the discipline of archaeology. Too much can be expected from a relatively young science – or is it an art? Perhaps it is a scientific art! By the very nature of the enterprise, the data extracted from an excavation can often be interpreted in a number of different ways, and can be dated only within relative degrees of certainty. Absoluteness and unequivocation are rare.

Much has been achieved since Heinrich Schliemann dug at

Map of Israel showing main places named

Tyre

Tel Dan

Hazor

Chorazin ● Bethsaida Julias

Capernaum

Magdala-Taricheae ● el Kursi

Tiberias

River Kishon

Sea of Galilee

Hippos

Nazareth ▲

Mount Tabor

Gadara

Megiddo

Caesarea

MEDITERRANEAN SEA

Beth Shan

Samaria

Jerash

River Jordan

Amman

Ai

Jericho

Gezer

Gibeah

Jerusalem

Qumran

Lachish

Dead Sea

Gerar

Masada

Beersheba

Troy, but archaeology remains an inexact science. It may illuminate us, excite us, challenge us, even disturb us, but rarely, if ever, does it completely satisfy us. While we wait for archaeology to mature as a discipline, we must also remember that our knowledge of the Bible is similarly imperfect. Critical approaches to the problems of the biblical text come and go, often with little or no permanent contribution to the solution of such puzzling questions as: How old is man? How old is the earth? When did Abraham live? What was the date of the Exodus? Was the Conquest of Canaan an invasion or just a social upheaval within the land itself? Did Moses write the Pentateuch? Neither Biblical criticism nor archaeological excavation has been able to answer these and other issues conclusively.

The Bible and history At times archaeology and biblical scholarship seem to work against each other. For example, archaeology has decisively altered the radical presuppositions of the Tübingen School of theology's evolutionary approach to the history of Israel. But it has only clouded the issue of the date of the Exodus and Conquest, providing evidence of a late date (thirteenth century BC) whereas the biblical text seems to support an early date (fifteenth century BC).

Part of the problem lies in a failure adequately to understand the biblical text, and part in a misunderstanding of the archaeological evidence. Some of the sites may be wrongly identified, while others may be inadequately dug or erroneously evaluated. What must be kept in mind is that we are in the process of developing our scientific understanding of both the Bible and archaeology. Archaeology can often help us understand something more clearly, but it rarely injects certainty into biblical uncertainties. To claim too much for it is to diminish its contribution and to weaken its potential for further enlightenment.

The acts of God The Bible is a collection of many books written over hundreds of years and from a particular theological viewpoint – that of Judaistic monotheism. Its authors never intended to write history in the way that modern historians such as Arnold Toynbee write it. Biblical authors wrote as historical theologians. Their purpose was to demonstrate the acts of God in Jewish history. G. Ernest Wright asked: 'What is biblical faith but knowledge of life's meaning in the light of what God did in a particular history?' It is precisely here that archaeology has made its contribution to the study of the Bible; not as an apologetic but as an important means of clarifying and dramatizing the history in which the biblical faith originated and by which it is sustained.

The Bible was not written in a vacuum, nor did the events it records take place in a vacuum. The Jews interacted with the ancient cultures with which they came into contact. The Bible is a record of those interactions, both good and bad. Biblical archaeology is a particular use of the broader discipline of general archaeology to penetrate and clarify that area of ancient history which gave birth to the Bible.

Archaeology from the earth

The methods of extracting evidence from the buried past have come a long way since human moles first burrowed their way into the heart of ancient Herculaneum and Pompeii. Much progress has been made since the early part of the twentieth century, when well-meaning but ill-equipped diggers attacked sites with spades, wheelbarrows and hundreds of hired labourers operating on a baksheesh system, paying each worker at the current market price for every artifact he found.

A scientific approach The techniques of excavation have evolved into what is now a highly scientific, carefully controlled and very expensive operation. It is not uncommon today to spend 100,000 dollars on a six-week dig. The cost, and the growing demand from the academic community for greater accuracy and control in the production of materials which must be published, have both helped transform excavation from a supervised quarrying of antiquities into an organization of highly-specialized experts pooling their skills in an expedition resembling an outdoor scientific laboratory.

Workers open a new square during a recent dig at Capernaum, Israel.

In this picture of the recent excavations at Capernaum the systematic division of the site into squares can be seen clearly.

Lachish has been re-excavated to take advantage of modern archaeological techniques.

There are five major tasks in modern archaeological expeditions: surveying, excavating, recording, interpreting and publishing. First, every new site must be approached by undertaking a general survey for miles around to discover as much as possible about the geographical and historical setting in which the site evolved. What cities were nearby? What sources of water were available? Where was their food grown and where were their livestock kept? What kind of food did they eat? What were their defensive capabilities? Where were the main roads? What may be discovered about settlement patterns?

The grid method Following the survey of the surrounding area, the site chosen is plotted from an aerial perspective, on a grid divided into five metre (fifteen foot) squares, and if possible tied into the overall grid of the country, using established points of reference and bench marks set by the government of that country. This is standard procedure, for example, in Israel. Each square will be numbered, and excavation will progress within selected squares. Only a representative number of squares are dug – not the whole site. This will allow later excavators to check and correct errors, if need be, as archaeological methods continue to improve. Many sites have been 'redug' in this way, including Gezer, Jericho, Hazor and Lachish.

The squares will be dug in successive strata, peeling off one layer at a time, including any pits that penetrate into lower levels. This method is known as the Kenyon-Wheeler method (after the British archaeologists Dame Kathleen Kenyon and Sir Mortimer Wheeler) and is standard in most Middle Eastern digs today. The method provides the greatest possible degree of control, according to currently-known excavation techniques. The work is done under the watchful eye of area supervisors, one to each square, who keep careful and detailed records of everything that happens in that square. Soil samples are taken and compared with the Munsell Colour Chart. Elevations are shot for all structures that come to light, and for the beginning and end of each day's work, as well as for any artifacts discovered or new *loci* encountered.

A *locus* is any object or small area that needs to be separately identified and recorded by itself. It may be nothing more than a change in the colour of the soil, or something as large as a stone floor or wall. Each locus is given a number, and all the data relevant to that locus will be recorded under that same number – elevations, photographs, pottery, coins, soil samples and so forth. All this information is kept in the area supervisor's notebooks, which he always keeps with him in the field.

Recording the dig Top-plans are drawn on graph paper on a

The area supervisor at the dig at Caesarea, Dr John McRay, records finds at his site desk.

Volunteers draw the baulks during recent excavations at Caesarea Maritima, Israel.

scale of 1:50, showing the square from a bird's-eye view as it appears at the end of each working day, and listing all the loci visible at that time. The plan changes, of course, from day to day as digging progresses, and in this way the area supervisor's daily diary is easily illustrated. Polaroid photos are taken when necessary to clarify the daily diary and, when needed, official dig photos in colour and black-and-white are taken of important stages in the process. This can later be used for publication.

When the digging is finished, the baulk, or exposed wall of a square, is carefully drawn to a scale of 1:25 and becomes the guide to the analysis of the chronological history of the square. By putting all the baulk drawings together, the archaeologist has the basis for making the same kind of analysis of the entire excavated site. Just as the number of layers in a cake can be determined by cutting a slice and thus getting below the covering layer of icing, so the history of a site exists in its stratigraphy. This is the single most important index to the site, and for this reason the baulks are kept trimmed and their loci identified by sticking baulk tags containing locus numbers onto their walls with long nails.

Nothing is more important than keeping careful records on a dig. By its very nature, archaeology is systematic destruction, and nothing will ever be seen again exactly the way it was when it was dug. The context is gone forever. Thus photography, elevations, scale drawings, supervisors' observations and impressions kept in their diaries are essential elements in modern excavations.

Understanding the dig All of this is necessary for the next step in the process – interpretation. This is, of course, the ultimate purpose of any dig, and always the most difficult part of the process. It is most uncommon for supervisors, volunteer diggers and excavation directors to interpret the data differently. For publication purposes, the right to the official interpretation of the dig resides with the archaeological director. Others may, of course, publish dissenting opinions, and ought to do so if they feel it necessary. Once the data is published – the next and extremely important step in the process – the material belongs to the public and may be challenged by those who evaluate it. This is, after all, the purpose of publication. Yadin challenged the reports of Aharoni at Beersheba, and Aharoni challenged Yadin's reports at Megiddo. Older publications, such as those on Hazor, Gezer, Megiddo, Jericho and others, are routinely challenged and corrected. Without this final stage, the vast expenditure of time and money on a excavation is largely wasted.

Part of the impressive remains at Megiddo, Israel. The archaeologist Yigael Yadin's reports on this site were later challenged by Aharoni.

Coins are vital for dating purposes.
Top: A coin of the Procurator Pontius Pilate, AD 30;
Bottom: Coin of the Procurator Antonius Felix, AD 59.

The 'new archaeology' Recent decades have seen the use of many advanced scientific techniques in field archaeology: ground and aerial photogrammetry, magnetometers and resistivity instruments, laser-guided and computerized transits for shooting elevations and making surveys, microfiche libraries that can be taken into the field and contain thousands of books, infra-red photography, neutron activation analysis of pottery, thin section and petrographic analysis of temper and clay, thermoluminescence, flotation of pollen samples, settlement pattern analysis, and the use of specialists such as anthropologists, palaeoethnobotanists, civil engineers, draughtsmen, architects, surveyers, numismatists, stratigraphers, linguists and historians. All are part of the evolving 'new archaeology' and have helped transform excavation techniques.

It is now possible to date discoveries with considerably more accuracy than was true years ago. In addition to noting the stratum in which an artifact or structure appears (the successively lower strata are progressively earlier under normal conditions, that is, if the strata are sealed and undisturbed) we are now able to place that object in a related pottery chronology which dates the stratum for us.

Dates and coins The discovery of coins is an extremely important contribution to dating, because coins carry names, and often dates, on them. Carbon 14 may be applied to organic matter, which once a portion is burnt, gives off radio-active carbon 14 at a rate which may be measured by a type of geiger counter. Under ideal conditions a dating accurate to plus or minus 200 years may be obtained from the amount of carbon detected. Potassium argon dating may be used for much older inorganic materials. For sites later than the Hellenistic period we are developing a chronological typology for glass similar to that for ceramic pottery. Though archaeology is not an exact science it is constantly becoming more exacting!

Interpreting the date The interpretation of archaeological data is most often done by parallelism, a phenomenon sometimes approaching parallelomania. This is an indispensible procedure, and one which requires vast knowledge of what has already been dug at sites with similar time frames to one's own. A particular find is compared to these parallel sites which hopefully will have been adequately dated, and may thus increase confidence in the interpretation given to that object at one's own site. Caution must be used, or one may end up in a fruitless cycle of circular reasoning and conjecture. Computers are increasingly being used to catalogue finds and will eventually make the retrieval of otherwise unknown parallels rapid and effective. The present writer's work in Caesarea, started in 1972, was one of the first to program pottery data into computers.

What mean these stones?

When Joshua crossed the river Jordan into Palestine, he erected a pillar of twelve stones, one for each of the twelve tribes, and said to the people that these stones would be a sign to them, so that when their children asked in time to come 'What do these stones mean to you?' they would tell them about the crossing of the Jordan by the power of God (Joshua 4:6–7). It is now time to ask ourselves what the stones we have been discussing mean.

What is the value of archaeological discoveries to the reader of the Bible? We must emphasize that archaeology's major contribution is not apologetic. To be sure, some difficulties are clarified by the results of archaeological work. For instance, there is the finding of stone inscriptions in Thessaloniki, Greece, containing the term *politarchs*, a term which Luke had used in Acts 17:6 in referring to Roman authorities, but which critics of the Bible had rejected as erroneous because no record of such a term existed prior to the discovery. On the other hand, attempts to find Joshua's Jericho or Solomon's Jerusalem have been largely disappointing.

This panel from the Black Obelisk of Shalmanezer shows King Jehu of Israel bowing before the Assyrian king, as he pays tribute.

The Cyrus Cylinder, which demonstrates the Persian ruler's assistance to exiled nations returning to their own lands.

This clay prism of King Sennacherib mentions Hezekiah, King of Judah.

Exciting discoveries Nevertheless, in the course of the legitimate excavation of ancient sites, many exciting discoveries have been made which illustrate the Bible beautifully: the Clay Prism of Sennacherib, mentioning the Judean king Hezekiah: the Black Obelisk of Shalmanezer portraying Jehu, the Jewish king, bowing before him; the Babylonian Chronicle, providing the basis for dating the destruction of the Temple in Jerusalem in 587 BC; the Cyrus Cylinder, showing the Persian monarch's policy of assisting nations like the Jews to return and rebuild their cities and temples; the inscription in the pavement of the theatre courtyard in Corinth containing the name of Erastus, the city treasurer, who is probably mentioned in Romans 16:23; the winter palace of Herod the Great in Jericho, and the site where he was buried in Herodium, to mention only a few. The rest of this book will focus on numerous such contributions that archaeology has made to our understanding of the Bible and its world.

We should pause, however, to remind ourselves of a warning issued by the eminent archaeologist, the late Roland de Vaux, in his article 'On Right and Wrong Uses of Archaeology': 'it must be understood that archaeology cannot "prove" the Bible. The truth of the Bible is of a religious order; it speaks of God and man and their mutual relations. This spiritual truth can neither be proven nor contradicted, nor can it be confirmed or invalidated by the material discoveries of archaeology. However, the Bible is written in large part as history ... it is concerning this "historical" truth of the Bible that one asks confirmation from archaeology ... what the Bible recounts is "sacred history"; it provides a religious interpretation of history, one that, again, archaeology can neither confirm nor invalidate. Archaeology can assist us only in establishing the facts that have been so interpreted.'

The value of archaeology The great value of archaeology to the student of the Bible lies in its ability to place our biblical faith in its historical setting, and to demonstrate clearly the cultural setting in which biblical events took place. For those who love the Bible, there is no experience comparable to standing on the Mount of Olives in Jerusalem and looking out upon the results of archaeological excavation in the Holy City: here is a part of Nehemiah's rebuilt walls; there are the steps leading up to the Temple during the days of Christ and the apostles; here is Hezekiah's tunnel leading to the Pool of Siloam, where Jesus made the blind man see; there are the beautiful and noble stones in the pinnacle of the Temple which the disciples pointed out to Jesus. And what a thrill to walk through the remains of the chariot city of Solomon and Ahab at Megiddo; to linger awhile among the ruins of Caesarea Maritima, Herod the Great's magnificent city on the Mediterranean coast; and to stroll among the huge pools built by the Essenes at Qumran, where the Dead Sea Scrolls were found. The aqueducts of Caesarea, the bath houses of Masada and Jericho, the synagogues of Galilee, the water tunnels of Megiddo, Hazor, Gezer and Jerusalem, the fortifications of Lachish, the altars of Beersheba and Mount Ebal, the fora and temples of Samaria and Jerash, the theatres of Amman and Ephesus, all create for us an indelible impression of the civilization that once inhabited these ruins. We are hence able to reconstruct in our minds these cities as they existed in the time of Abraham, Solomon, Jesus and Paul. We are able to walk down the marble street of Ephesus and sense the presence of the apostles Paul and John, who also walked here. As we pass the magnificent Graeco-Roman buildings, and look with wonderment at the skill of ancient craftsmen who could produce these magnificent Corinthian and Ionic capitals, we turn again and read with renewed interest and love the texts

This inscription, found on a pavement at Corinth, includes the name of Erastus, the city treasurer, and probably the official mentioned in Romans 16:23.

25

The Stoa which borders the Forum of ancient Athens has been restored to its supposed state in Paul's time.

that tell us of what took place here so long ago.

A historical context How can we stand beside the Parthenon in Athens and look across Mars Hill to the excavated market place the Greeks call the Agora and not turn again to Paul's sermon preached here, and read Acts 17 with renewed appreciation? What a thrill to be able to locate our Judaeo-Christian faith in the geographical and historical setting where God himself chose to bring it about in the fullness of time (Galatians 4:4).

The story of Jesus does not begin 'Once upon a time in a faraway land ...', but rather 'After Jesus was born in Bethlehem in Judea during the time of King Herod ...' (Matthew 2:1). What a thrill it is to traverse the hills of Judea and walk the streets of Bethlehem, to wander through Nazareth and take a boat-ride on the Sea of Galilee and walk the streets of Jerusalem's Old City. How exciting anxiously to watch each turn of the archaeologist's spade, knowing that it was here, in these very places, here in historical and geographical reality, not in mythological fancy, that the most precious heritage of human history was bequeathed to mankind. This is the value of biblical archaeology – its ability to locate the faith in the realities of ancient history.

ARCHAEOLOGY AND THE OLD TESTAMENT

Meeting at the Well

'Moses fled from Pharaoh, and went to live in Midian, where he sat down by a well' (Exodus 2:15). Such a scene of a traveller stopping at a well to refresh himself, and meeting a woman who later becomes important to him, is quite common in the Old Testament. Abraham's servant meets Rebekah at a well or spring (Genesis 24:15–22), and tests her suitability as a wife for Isaac. Jacob meets his future wife Rachel at what was probably the same well (Genesis 29:2–6). And, in the quotation above, Moses meets Zipporah, the daughter of Jethro, who later becomes his wife.

It is not surprising that these events are described as taking place at the well. This was the focal point of activity for almost every woman in the local community or regionally-based nomadic herding group.

Archaeologists have discovered layers of sediment deposited around wells, showing that water was frequently spilt here, as might be expected. They have also found deep grooves, worn into the stones around the mouth of the well by ropes used for hauling up jars of water. Excavation of the inside of wells has revealed fragments of jars from many different periods. These jars may have been shattered as they were drawn up by the women, or dropped accidentally into the water.

Women's work
Each woman was responsible for drawing water for her family, and also for the animals, when the men were busy elsewhere. Doubtless the women also expected to meet men from herding groups and travellers at the well, and by this means eventually find a husband. The repetition of such a scene in the Bible emphasizes the importance of this spot in the social as well as the economic life of the people of ancient Palestine.

The wells themselves were generally located in dry river beds, or wadis, where they were dug down to reach the underlying water table. Their location was often a deciding factor in setting up a permanent settlement in a particular area. Naturally, if the water ceased to flow, the settlement might have to be abandoned. Human and animal needs required a ready supply of water, and thus reliable wells would become cherished possessions; as a result many significant events took place in and around the wells.

Fighting for the well

An example of this can be found in the story of the conflict between the patriarchs Abraham and Isaac and the king of Gerar, over the use of the wells in the region between Beersheba and Gerar (Genesis 21:26). The value of water for herdsmen and farmers created a competition which forced the patriarchs to dig wells outside the political boundaries of Gerar, and then name them·

'So Isaac moved away from there and encamped in the Valley of Gerar and settled there. Isaac reopened the wells that had been dug in the time of his father Abraham ... and he gave them the same names his father had given them. Isaac's servants dug in the valley and discovered a well of fresh water there. But the herdsmen of Gerar quarrelled with Isaac's herdsmen and said, "The water is ours!"' (Genesis 26:17–20).

Two views of the well at Tell Beersheba.

Tell Beersheba.

The naming of wells, a common practice among ancient and modern bedouin peoples, was a key to their ownership, as well as a clue to later generations as to the location of these valuable resources.

Archaeologists have uncovered wells at Beersheba that were dug about 1000–900 BC. Some were dug into the bed of the wadi Beersheba, where they were filled like cisterns during the winter rains. The name of this site (Beersheba means well of seven, or the seventh well) is generally believed to originate from the existence of these walls.

The most striking of these wells is, however, located on the tell of the ancient city of Beersheba. Its shaft is approximately two metres (six feet) in diameter, with the upper section lined with hewn stone, and the remainder cut into solid rock over 30 metres (90 feet) deep. Pottery remains recovered from the shaft, although not representative of every period, since the well would have been dredged periodically in ancient times, demonstrates that it was dug in the eleventh century BC, and remained in continuous use until the Roman period.

Beersheba

This well's importance for the people of the community is shown by the fact that the earliest structures on the site were constructed around it. In at least one period of the city's existence, the wall was specially built to take account of the well. It is also interesting that the temple is situated on a mound near the well. When the temple was excavated, a remarkable horned altar was discovered, which had been dismantled, possibly in

Beersheba

The excavated area
of the ancient city.

dwelling houses

water system

governor's palace

storehouses

outer gate

well

Hezekiah's time. This altar had been incorporated into a wall of
a later period, but its existence close to the well demonstrates
the priests' need for water for use in purification rites and sacrifice, and adds to the well's significance in the life of the community. It is no wonder, then, that the well became associated
with major events in the history and tradition of the place.

Wells, then, were meeting places, sites for the taking of oaths
(as in the example of Isaac and Abimelech, Genesis 26:31), and
could be the source of conflict between different peoples needing the water to survive. Frequently, where archaeologists have
discovered the site of an ancient well, they have also discovered
evidence of the life of the people who depended upon it.

Signed and Sealed ...

When Jacob's son Judah asked his daughter-in-law Tamar 'What pledge should I give you?' and she answered: 'Your seal and its cord, and the staff in your hand' (Genesis 38:18), he thought he was talking to a common prostitute (she had veiled herself as a disguise). Judah promised Tamar a young goat if she slept with him, and she demanded a pledge from him until he paid. He imagined he was giving a prostitute the temporary loan of his seal; in fact the shrewd Tamar obtained from the patriarch his most intimate possession, by means of which she was later able to identify him: 'About three months later Judah was told, "Your daughter-in-law Tamar is guilty of prostitution, and as a result is now pregnant."

'Judah said, "Bring her out and have her burned to death!"

'And as she was being brought out, she sent a message to her father-in-law, "I am pregnant by the man who owns these," she said. And she added, "See if you recognise whose seal and cord and staff these are"' (Genesis 38:24–26).

The seal, usually of simple design, was carried round his neck on a string by a man of substance in an age when most people were illiterate. The seal would be pressed into clay writing tablets or onto possessions such as lamps and jars to show who owned them. When Judah recognized his seal, he admitted that Tamar was more righteous than he was, and did not sleep with his daughter-in-law again.

A personal mark
Archaeologists have found the impress of cylinder and ring seals on jar handles, on document seals ('bullae') and on cuneiform clay tablets, showing who owned the jars, or who was involved in a particular transaction. Sometimes such cryptic inscriptions provide us with information about people or nations who are otherwise unknown outside the text of the Bible.

Baruch and Jerahmeel

While we can never be completely certain that the names of people inscribed on these seals refer specifically to biblical characters, archaeologists can study the script, the style of carving and the vocabulary used to help them to identify the date of a seal and its probable original owner. For instance, two recently analyzed bullae (small pieces of clay used to help seal the string holding together a papyrus document) contain the names of Baruch the scribe and Jerahmeel the son of the king (a title which can mean either a police official or a member of the royal family). Both of these names are found in the episode in Jeremiah 36 in which the enraged King Jehoiakim burned a scroll which the prophet Jeremiah had instructed Baruch to

Top: Cylinder seals from Tel Dor, Israel.

Bottom: A cylinder seal from Tel Batashi, Israel.

Inscriptions from seals.
Top: 'Belonging to Berechiah son of Neriah the scribe.'
Bottom: 'Belonging to Jerahmeel, the king's son.'

read publicly in front of the temple. Jerahmeel was then commanded by the king to arrest the prophet and his scribe.

We cannot be certain that the names on the bullae refer to the characters in the book of Jeremiah, since both names are fairly common, and the bullae may in fact date from a different period. However, scholars have examined the bullae and found that they probably date from the late seventh century BC, and could therefore very well be evidence of the work of the Baruch and Jerahmeel mentioned in Jeremiah 36. Moreover, the fact that Baruch's bulla was found among a group of bullae from the royal archive suggests that he had served as a royal scribe before, or perhaps during, his service to Jeremiah.

Shema's seal

Another seal which has been identified with a specific person and time period was discovered in 1904 at Megiddo. It is inscribed as 'belonging to Shema, servant of Yarob'am (Jeroboam), which probably refers to Jeroboam II, king of Israel 786–746 BC, during the time of the prophets Amos and Hosea. The well-balanced carving of a roaring lion – a symbol of Judah, perhaps the original home or tribe of this servant of the king of Israel – is the work of a master craftsman. However, the lettering, rather cramped and unevenly written, appears to have been done by another, less skilled, hand.

Occasionally archaeologists discover a seal which throws light more widely than on personal names and vocabulary. One such seal, whose origin is as yet unknown, has been written up by Nahman Avigad, an Israeli expert on seal inscriptions. This seal is inscribed on both sides, the first with the name of its owner, Pela'yahu, and his father, Mattityahu. These are both names known from the Bible: Pelaiah (Pela'yahu) is the name of a Levite in Nehemiah 8:7, 10:11, who signed the covenant; and Mattithiah (Mattityahu) is the name of one of the sons of Nebo who had married a foreign wife in Ezra 10:43, and of one who stood at Ezra's right hand during the reading of the law in Nehemiah 8:4.

Forced labour

The other side of this seal impression is divided into three sections, with an inscription which reads: 'Belonging to Pela'yahu, who is in charge of forced labour'. The position of overseer of the forced labourers is only referred to twice in the Bible, and each time the officer named is Adoram, or Adoniram (2 Samuel 20:24; 1 Kings 12:18). The position is not mentioned in any other known text outside the Bible. The fact that it appears on this seal, dated by the script and ornamentation to the seventh century BC, shows that there was a continued use of forced

The magnificent seal of Shema features this well-designed roaring lion. It is inscribed 'belonging to Shema, servant of Yarob'am'.

labour gangs, and that there continued to be a special official in charge of these gangs.

It appears, in fact, from the evidence of this seal that the position of taskmaster over the forced labour gangs continued on into the period after the division of the kingdom. Certainly, the monumental construction projects undertaken by Ahab and other kings would have necessitated such forced labour to complete them. It may even be that the projects undertaken by King Jehoiakim, so roundly denounced by the prophet Jeremiah, are referred to by this seal: 'Woe to him who builds his palace by unrighteousness, his upper rooms by injustice, making his countrymen work for nothing, not paying them for their labour' (Jeremiah 22:13).

Since very few inscriptions have survived the humid climate found in much of Palestine, seal impressions also form the most extensive evidence we possess about early Hebrew writing. They provide a wealth of information about the language, writing styles and history of the biblical period, and even record for us the signatures of kings as well as the names of less exalted men of ancient times.

What Happened at the City Gate?

The city gate was of central importance to life in biblical times. Here were situated shops and stalls; here was a busy marketplace; public disputes were brought here for settlement; public pronouncements were made here; we even find the prophets speaking at the city gate. Given the obvious significance of the city gate, archaeologists have been anxious to try to discover and reconstruct imaginatively the city gates at such key Israeli sites as Hazor, Megiddo, Gezer, and Tel Dan.

We read in Genesis that 'Lot was sitting in the gate of Sodom' (Genesis 19:1). This conjures up a picture of massive wooden doors swinging open to let in businessmen and travellers, but closed and barred at night to protect the city. The fact that Lot is portrayed as sitting at the gate implies that he must have been trusted by the people of Sodom. Only people who were free citi-

The Damascus Gate into the Old City of Jerusalem bustles with life; many tradesmen cluster around it.

zens had the right to pass in and out of the city gates unchallenged; slaves and visitors, who could not be counted on to defend the city in time of danger, would have had to obtain clearance from the guards.

Business centre

Lot may have been sitting at the gate doing business, for the gate was not solely the entrance to the city, but often included side chambers, like those found by archaeologists in the gate at Gezer. Shops and stalls would have been crowded together around the gate, with hawkers competing for customers and shoppers looking for bargains or for the makings of that evening's dinner. Here, too, public disputes were settled in front of the elders, and legal matters duly witnessed. And, of course, the welfare of the community – symbolized by the gate's use as a business and legal centre – was physically protected by the strength and ingenious design of the city gate. All of this makes the reconstruction of the gate complex by archaeologists of prime importance in their attempt to discover patterns of life in the ancient city.

Signs of the significance attached to the gate in the Old Testament can be seen in the numerous encounters which take place here; for instance Saul met Samuel for the first time at the city

The gate at Gezer probably originally looked like this.

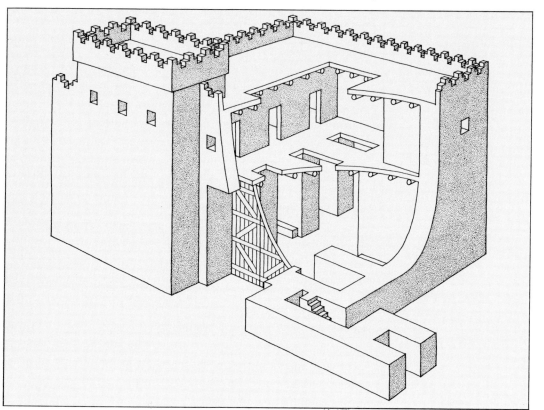

gate (1 Samuel 9:14), a meeting which signalled the beginning of the monarchy. The Old Testament refers repeatedly to people and groups going to the gate to lay a case before the elders (like Boaz who 'went up to the town gate and sat there ...' Ruth 4:1), or to see justice executed against the guilty (such as adulterers: 'You shall take both of them to the gate of that town and stone them to death' Deuteronomy 22:24). When corruption or injustice had become rife, the cry was for the re-establishment of justice in the city gate (Amos 5:15).

Kings at the gate

Occasionally the gate, which symbolized power and authority, was used by kings for political and military purposes. For instance, David used the gate as the backdrop for assembling his troops after the campaign against his rebellious son, Absalom: 'So the king got up and took his seat in the gateway. When the men were told, "The king is sitting in the gateway", they all came before him' (2 Samuel 19:8). King Ahab and King Jehoshaphat, preparing for war against Syria, consulted the prophet Micaiah in the gate of Samaria about the prospects for their adventure: 'Dressed in their royal robes, the king of Israel and Jehoshaphat, king of Judah, were sitting on their thrones at the threshing-floor by the entrance of the gate of Samaria, with all the prophets prophesying before them' (1 Kings 22:1).

Public announcements were also made here, and prophets found ready audiences near the city gate and in the Temple gate. One example is from the time of King Jehoiakim: 'From the room of Gemariah, son of Shaphan the secretary, which was in the upper courtyard at the entrance of the New Gate of the temple, Baruch read to all the people at the LORD's temple ...' (Jeremiah 36:10). Within and around the gate, life hummed with activity, demonstrating the prosperity of the community to travellers and merchants, and warning would-be enemies of the difficulties they would confront if they attempted to take the town.

The gate reflected both the character of the times and the physical environment of the city's site. The location was usually decided on the basis of physical features such as an easily-defended promontory, a reliable water supply or access to local trade routes.

Planning the gate

In planning the construction of a gate complex, several factors had to be taken into consideration. Since the gate formed the weakest point in the town's defences, towers, oblique turns and multiple gates had to be planned, in order to strengthen the gate against enemy attack. However, since the gate was also the

point from which soldiers and chariots could sally out to attack the enemy, attention had also to be given to offensive measures.

But offence and defence were not the only considerations. Planning the gate area was further complicated by the civil uses to which it was put, since it had to be wide enough to allow for caravans, shops and garrison posts.

With so much activity centred on this area, it is not surprising that archaeologists have spent a great deal of effort attempting to reconstruct the gate complexes of the cities they have excavated. They have had to deal with problems of stratigraphy, chronology and conflicting pieces of internal evidence as they begin to piece together a picture of the ancient city.

In this artist's impression of Sennacherib's siege of the city of Lachish the elaborate defences to the main gate can be seen clearly.

Tel Dan

New excavations have recently been carried out at Tel Dan (ancient Laish), mentioned in the Bible as the place to which Abraham pursued the five kings who had sacked Sodom and taken his nephew Lot captive. Archaeologists have discovered a gate complex constructed in the eighteenth century BC, but it was found to have been filled in shortly afterwards to make it into part of the city ramparts. It seems that the gate complex had only been used for a generation or two, and then, either because it proved too weak a link in the defences, or because the life of the city had shifted to another area of the mound, it was covered over and forgotten.

Archaeologists have also been able partially to reconstruct the

Steps leading from the north gate at Megiddo.

The gate complex at Tel Dan (ancient Laish) was soon filled in to form part of the ramparts.

history of some other Old Testament cities, by excavating the gates at Hazor, Gezer and Megiddo. Their work has revealed magnificent six-chambered gates with two outer towers, designed to strengthen the city's defences. Most scholars now agree that the gates discovered at Hazor and Gezer are those built by King Solomon, and mentioned in 1 Kings 9:15.

Megiddo

In order to compare the gates at Hazor and Gezer with the gate at Megiddo, the late Yigael Yadin, commander of Israel's defence force during the Arab War and late professor of archaeology at the Hebrew University in Jerusalem, decided to re-examine the excavations carried out earlier in the century at Megiddo. By following the plan of the gate complex of Solomon's times at Gezer and Hazor, Yadin's workmen were able to predict exactly where the walls and rooms of the distinctive casemate walls of Solomon's time would be found at Megiddo. Previous efforts to find these remains had been foiled by the covering layers from later periods, when the gate had been attached to a new style of offset-inset wall.

It is clearly important for archaeologists to attempt to reconstruct the gate complexes of such cities, discovering their style, artifacts such as pottery found on their floor, and the stages they

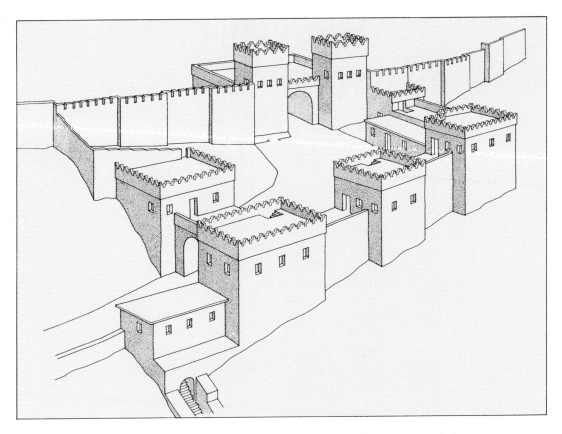

went through during the life of the city. The gate was the focal point – the means of access, the weak point that had to be defended in war, and the meeting place for the business and social life of the community.

An artist's reconstruction of the gate complex at Megiddo.

Weapons and Warfare

in the book of Judges

The book of Judges describes the period when the Israelites were settling into the Promised Land following the Exodus from Egypt. Because the conquest was not complete, warfare was frequent, and resulted in the hero stories preserved in Judges. These heroes were known as 'judges', meaning, not people who decided court cases, but military leaders who delivered Israel from her enemies. What weapons did these heroes use, and what was their strategy in defeating their enemies?

The Bible does not usually give a detailed description of weapons or of military strategy. Yet we have a good knowledge of weapons from archaeological discoveries and drawings, paintings and reliefs.

Offensive weapons

Offensive weapons in use at this time can be divided into three categories according to their range. Short-range weapons were used in hand-to-hand combat and included the sword or dagger and the spear. Medium-range weapons were designed to be thrown at enemies a short distance away. Occasionally spears were light enough to be thrown, but the shorter and lighter javelin was better suited for throwing. Long-range weapons could be thrown or fired at an enemy further away. Examples of long-range weapons include the sling, used to hurl stones, and the bow, for propelling arrows.

Armour was used to protect the foot soldier's body as far as possible. Armour included the helmet for the head, scale armour, coats of mail, the breastplate for the body and greaves to cover the shins. The foot soldier also carried a shield to cover any unprotected parts of his body. An armour-bearer or shield-bearer could also be employed to carry the soldier's weapons and his shield.

With this information, we can discuss the weapons and warfare described in the book of Judges, where we read '... not a shield or spear was seen among forty thousand in Israel' (Judges 5:8). Clearly weapons were in short supply, at least for the Israelites, an interpretation which is supported by the following lists of weapons mentioned in Judges:

Above opposite:
Spears and bows can be seen on this relief of Arabs fleeing Assyrian warriors, taken from Ashurbanipal's Palace, Nineveh.

Israelite weapons	Use
Double-edged dagger (3:16ff)	Ehud stabs Eglon
Ox-goad (3:31)	Shamgar kills 600 Philistines
Tent-peg and hammer (4:21, 5:26)	Jael kills Sisera
Trumpets, jars, torches (and shouts) (7:19)	Gideon surprises the Midianites
Thorns and briars (8:16)	Gideon punishes Succoth and Penuel
Sword (8:20)	Jether is told to kill two kings
Upper millstone (9:53)	Unnamed woman injures Abimelech
Sword (9:54)	Abimelech's armour-bearer kills him
Bare hands (14:6)	Samson kills lion
Fresh jawbone of a donkey (15:15)	Samson kills 1000 Philistines
Bare hands (16:29)	Samson topples the pillars of temple
Sling stones (20:16)	Benjaminite soldiers' accuracy

Enemy weapons	Use
Iron chariots (1:19)	People of the plain control plain
Iron chariots (4:3ff)	Jabin and Sisera control Hazor area
Swords (7:22)	Midianites kill each other

Deborah and Barak led their forces down the slopes of Mount Tabor to rout the armies of Jabin and Sisera.

This coin shows the Great King of Persia riding a chariot of the period.

These two lists of weapons reveal a striking contrast between Israel and her enemies. The Israelites used mostly 'primitive' weapons, such as farm implements and household articles, and had few metal weapons. By contrast, their enemies possessed metal weapons, particularly iron weapons. Iron was much harder and more durable than bronze or copper, and its manufacture took greater technological skill than the Israelites possessed. The Iron Age commenced in Israel during the days of the judges, or about 1200 BC, whereas the Philistines already had something of a monopoly of iron metallurgy: 'Not a blacksmith could be found in the whole land of Israel, because the Philistines had said: "Otherwise the Hebrews will make swords or spears!"' (1 Samuel 13:19). As long as the Philistines maintained this monopoly, Israel could not hope to dislodge them from the plain (Judges 1:19). On those occasions when the Israelites did prevail against their enemies, it was credited to divine help; some of their success must also have been the result of better strategy or tactics.

Iron chariots

Let us look first at the weapons of Israel's enemies. We learn that the men of the tribe of Judah could not drive out the inhabitants of the plain because they had iron chariots (Judges 1:19). Pulled by two horses, the chariot was in effect a moving platform for two or three soldiers. It was most valuable in making rapid flanking movements where the land was fairly flat and open. The coastal area of Palestine was relatively level, while the hill-country inland featured steep slopes and deep valleys. In ancient times the hills were heavily forested and Israelite guerilla tactics proved successful in this territory. However, in the coastal plain the Canaanite and Philistine iron chariots proved to be the tanks of their period, racing across the flat country. But chariots were ineffective on wooded hills.

Since the Iron Age had just begun in Canaan, iron chariots would have been the latest and best military weapon. Some scholars believe the iron would have been used to make part of the wheels and fittings of the chariot, while others think there was an iron plate to reinforce the wooden body of the chariot. In either case, the iron would have been superior to bronze, and would have made the chariot more durable.

Since Israel did not obtain chariots until the time of the monarchy, they simply could not dislodge the people of the coastal plain. But in one instance there was a strikingly different result. Jabin and Sisera, from the stronghold at Hazor, had a massive force of 900 iron chariots (Judges 4, 5). But Deborah and Barak, the Israelite leaders, were successful against this superior force because God routed the enemy. There is also the

implication that there was a late spring storm which turned the river Kishon into a raging torrent and rendered the iron chariots useless in the battle.

This relief from Calah shows Tiglath Pileser III of Assyria riding a chariot.

Apart from the chariots, the only other enemy weapon mentioned in Judges is the sword. The Midianites possessed them (Judges 7:22), but in their panic to flee from Gideon, killed one another (see below).

The assassination of Eglon

The Israelites also used some traditional weapons. The story of Ehud, who plotted a daring one-man assassination attack on King Eglon of Moab, is told in Judges 3:12–30. The standard sword of this period was curved, with one sharp edge used for slicing and slashing. It is sometimes called a sickle sword, and is the basis of the expression 'smite the enemy with the edge of the sword'. This type of weapon would not have served Ehud's need, since it could not easily have been concealed from the palace guards, nor could it be used to thrust or stab to death. So the text explains: 'Ehud had made a double-edged sword about a foot and a half long, which he strapped to his right thigh under his clothing.' Such metal weapons were still very rare in Israel.

Because Ehud was left-handed, he hid his sword on the right side; right-handed soldiers would wear their swords on their left side. This reversal may explain Ehud's success in getting past the king's guards. By implying that he was the bearer of a confidential message, Ehud got rid of all of Eglon's attendants.

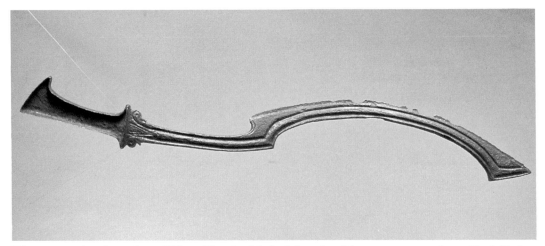

The strangely-shaped sickle sword was a characteristic weapon of the period. The single sharp edge was used for slicing and slashing.

When Ehud told the king that his message was from God, Eglon stood up and put himself in an ideal position for Ehud to stab him with the concealed sword. As the sword had been designed for stabbing, it probably had a relatively short hilt, which would have penetrated Eglon's fat body. Having accomplished his piece of treachery, Ehud fled, calling his waiting men into battle. With their king dead, the Moabites would have retreated hastily across the river Jordan to their homeland, or sought for reinforcements from Moabite territory. By taking control of the fords across the river, Ehud's men were able to win the ensuing battle decisively.

In another incident the judge Gideon told his son, Jether, to kill Zebah and Zalmunna with a sword (Judges 8:20). However, Jether was afraid because of his youth, and Gideon did it himself. This is one of the rare instances recorded in the book of Judges of an Israelite using a sword.

After Gideon's son Abimelech had been severely wounded, he asked his armour-bearer to kill him (Judges 9:54). The armour-bearer took the sword and killed Abimelech, as commanded. This was apparently one of the accepted functions of the armour-bearer in these times; later King Saul made a similar request of his own armour-bearer (1 Samuel 31:4).

There is no record in Judges of other individual Israelites using the sword, and the only other conventional weapon mentioned is the sling. We are told that 700 left-handed slingers from the tribe of Benjamin could sling a stone at a hair and not miss (Judges 20:16).

Alternative weapons

On the other hand, many other objects served as weapons when nothing better was available. We are told that Shamgar struck down 600 Philistines with an ox goad, in a tantalizingly brief reference (Judges 3:3). Perhaps he was ploughing with his oxen

Archaeologists have discovered a variety of metal weapons dating from Bible times, including a number of different types of spear-head.

when the Philistines appeared over the hill. The ox goad was a farm implement, about two or three metres (eight or ten feet) in length, with one end pointed, and sometimes metal-tipped, to prod the ox to plough. The other end was fashioned with a scraper to dislodge the clods that became entangled in the plough. Shamgar's heroic feat fits the pattern in the book of Judges of gaining victory with inferior weapons.

In Judges 4 and 5 we learn how Sisera fled the battlefield to avoid being killed or captured. He came to the tent of Jael, who seemed to offer him safety. However, while he was sleeping off his fatigue, she took a hammer and tent-peg and pounded the peg through his temple (Judges 4:1, 5:26). The hammer she used was probably made of stone, and the tent-peg a wooden object.

Gideon's surprise attack

Gideon was faced with the task of fighting the Midianites (Judges 7). They had large encampments, with women, children, cattle, camels and tents, which meant their greatest weakness was that they could easily be panicked by a surprise attack. This was exactly the strategy that Gideon chose to employ, which explains why he used such a small force of only 300 men. The smaller the force, the less chance there was of detection in a surprise attack. Gideon divided his troops into three companies and positioned one company on each of three sides of the Midianite camp. He probably left open the east side, where the terrain was most problematic, so that any survivors would have had a difficult time if they fled.

Gideon waited until the Midianites were all sleeping soundly, and until the new sentries, unaccustomed to the darkness and to night conditions, came on duty. Since co-ordination is absolutely essential in a surprise attack, he himself was to signal the attack, to ensure that nobody made a false start. At his signal, everyone smashed his jar, blew his trumpet and shouted. The noise panicked the Midianites; when they looked out of their tents they saw the flickering torches, which could easily have been used to set the tents alight, and so increase the panic. Fearing that they were surrounded by a huge enemy force, the

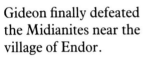

Gideon finally defeated the Midianites near the village of Endor.

Midianites rushed to escape, falling on each other with their swords in the confusion. The surprise attack had succeeded to perfection, and Gideon won the battle with ease.

Another unusual weapon was used by a woman against Abimelech (Judges 9:50–54). When he attacked Thebez, all the people fled to the city's tower. Safe in the tower, the woman waited till Abimelech was close to the entrance, then dropped a millstone on his head, mortally wounding him. A millstone was normally about five to eight centimetres (two or three inches) thick and 50 centimetres (eighteen inches) in diameter.

Samson's weapons.
Samson did not use orthodox weapons either. When he was met by a roaring lion, he had no weapons at all; using his bare hands and brute strength, he tore the lion apart as if it had been a tender young goat (Judges 14:6). On another occasion, he was weaponless because he had just been handed over to the Philistines. He picked up the fresh jawbone of a donkey (this must have been heavier and moister than an old, dried-out jawbone) and killed 1000 Philistines with it, wielding it like a club (Judges 15:15). On another occasion, Samson went to Gaza, in Philistine territory, to visit a prostitute. Since it was night, the Philistines closed the city gate on him. (The city would have had a thick wall surrounding it, and only one exit.) When the hero went to leave, he found the gate barred shut. Undeterred, he pulled up the gate-posts and the gate itself, and walked free from the city (Judges 16:1–3). Since a city would have taken great pride in its fortifications, his action would have been a great humiliation to the citizens, and left the place temporarily defenceless. Finally, at the end of his life, Samson used his hands and arms to topple the columns of the Philistine temple and thus kill himself and 3000 Philistines with him.

Final battle
The last battle recorded in the book of Judges, the attack on Gibeah, gives an interesting account of battle tactics (Judges 20:18–48). As the defenders, the people of Gibeah and the Benjaminites had an advantage since they were fighting to defend their home territory. Israel's two head-on assaults were successfully repulsed, as the town of Gibeah was well fortified and encircled by a thick, high wall.

On their third attempt, the Israelites set up an ambush out of sight of the city, and then pulled back their assault force as if in flight. The unsuspecting Benjaminites sallied out from the safety of the city to pursue the 'fleeing' army, leaving Gibeah defenceless. At this point the ambush party attacked the city, and set it on fire. The clouds of smoke from the burning city acted as a signal to the assault force to turn and counter-attack the Benjaminites, now trapped between the Israelites and their burning city. The clouds of smoke from the destroyed city further demoralized them.

This civil war disaster and its aftermath led the writer of Judges to conclude the book with a strong plea for kingship: 'In those days Israel had no king; every one did as he saw fit' (Judges 21:25).

Household Altars

Archaeologists excavating biblical sites in Palestine have discovered a large number of small altars, which are often known as 'incense altars'. These small altars reflect an important part of the life of the ancient Israelite. On these altars, offerings and sacrifices were made to God to thank him for his goodness to the family. Sometimes these offerings were made at a central sanctuary, such as Shiloh, or at the Temple in Jerusalem, after it was built, but other times the family would make their offering at home on such an altar.

These small altars were made of materials which were readily available and commonly used in that time. Some were made of pottery clay, others in bronze, and yet others were cut from limestone. Pottery altars were the most popular and most widely used. Two main types of pottery altar have been uncovered in excavations at biblical sites in Palestine: cylindrical altars, and altars made in the shape of a house. The cylindrical altars were often made in two pieces, consisting of a cone-shaped cylindrical base and a bowl or basin which sat on top of the base. The offering was placed in this basin. Cylindrical altars were often decorated, for instance with windows, with a row of stylized lotus leaves, serpents and doves, or with human-like figurines.

A Philistine incense-burner decorated with serpents, discovered at Beth Shan.

Windows of heaven

One of the most curious features of the cylindrical pottery altars is that they have windows in them. For example, cylindrical altars found at Beth Shan have triangular-shaped windows. Sometimes a small bird, possibly a dove, is found perched in the window. A large pottery altar found at the site of Ai has forty irregularly-shaped windows cut into its cylindrical wall. Other altars have square, rectangular or oval-shaped windows.

Why were these altars designed with windows? What purpose do the windows serve? Possibly for the ancient Israelites the windows served as a visual reminder of the dwelling place of God, or the 'windows of heaven', through which God sent forth his blessings (Malachi 3:10), or his judgment (Genesis 7:11).

Above: Philistine incense-burner discovered at Ashdod, on the Mediterranean coast.

Above right: Close-up of the incense-burner shown above. 'Musicians' are seen at the 'windows' in the burner's base.

Opposite: Philistine incense-burners discovered at Tel Kasila.

House-shaped altars

The house-shaped altars were formed in the shape of a two- or three-story house. The house-like design of such an altar was probably intended to remind the worshipper of the sanctuary or the worship centre, and was a symbolic reminder of the dwelling place of God, or of God's presence among his people. During the period of the Judges, when the Israelites were settling in the land of Canaan, altars of this type were probably widely used in worship ceremonies in the home. For instance, an account in the book of Judges relates the story of a man named Micah, from 'the hill country of Ephraim', who had a 'shrine' in his house (Judges 17:1–6). The 'shrine' (in Hebrew *beth elohim*, literally meaning 'house of Elohim', or 'house of God') was most likely a small house-shaped offering stand, used by Micah and his family in worship and offering rituals in their home. The house-shaped altars were often decorated with windows and doors, serpents and doves, lions, human-like figurines, sphinxes and various other animals and plants.

The Canaanite influence

Some of the decorations on the pottery altars reflect the influence of the Canaanite religion and culture on ancient Israel. This influence is referred to in the book of Judges: 'Then the Israelites did evil in the eyes of the Lord and served the Baals ...

They followed and worshipped various gods of the people around them' (Judges 2:11–13; see also Judges 3:7; 6:25–32). In many communities the Canaanites continued to live among the Israelites (Judges 1:27–33), as the Israelites moved into the land of Canaan and began the task of settling in and making it their homeland.

The Canaanite influence is reflected, for instance, in the ornamentation of a cylindrical pottery stand found at Megiddo, one of the sites where the Israelites and the Canaanites lived side by side (Judges 1:27). In addition to windows and painted designs, the stand is decorated with two female figurines in relief, each having the right arm bent at the elbow with the right hand placed between the breasts, and the left arm extended downwards with the left hand covering the pubic area. The symbolism is obvious; the two figurines were Canaanite fertility figurines. Such figurines were used by the Canaanites as symbolic reminders of the fertility they believed their gods, such as Baal and Asherah, provided for their flocks and their soil.

Bronze altars

The small bronze altars were made in two basic shapes, as tripod altars and as square open-work altars. The tripod altars have a tripod base supporting a central shaft, with a basin on top in which the offering was made. The square open-work altars have four sides, each side decorated with a bronze panel of silhouettes. The square offering stands have a ring-shaped top; the offering was placed in a bronze bowl on the ring-top. These square bronze altars are similar in design to the ten bronze stands which Solomon made for the Temple, though the temple stands were much larger in size (1 Kings 7:27–39) than those found in archaeological excavations.

Horned altars

Similarly the limestone altars were made in two basic styles, square and cylindrical. Some of the square limestone altars had a horn-like projection on each corner (see 'Meeting at the Well'), and were called 'horned altars', while others were made without horns. For the ancient Israelite, the horns on the altar reminded him symbolically of God's strength and power, that God was the ultimate source of refuge in time of trouble. In such times of trouble and distress, people would hold onto the horns of the altar to show symbolically that they were casting themselves on the mercy of God, in the hope that the ultimate source of help, God himself, would provide deliverance. For this reason Adonijah and Joab, both of whom opposed the anointing of Solomon as king, went to the sanctuary and 'caught hold of the horns of the altar' (1 Kings 1:50; 2:28).

The cylindrical limestone altars were frequently designed to look like miniature pillars. The top of the altar would be carved in the shape of a capital on the top of a pillar; in fact this capital-like top was a bowl in which the offering was made. One of the cylindrical limestone altars found at Megiddo has been of particular interest, since it has the same basic design – though in miniature form – as the two bronze pillars, Jachin and Boaz, which stood on each side of the entrance to Solomon's Temple (1 Kings 7:15–22). Like the small limestone pillar-like stand from Megiddo, the two pillars Jachin and Boaz were topped with capitals decorated with lily designs (1 Kings 7:19).

These small pottery, bronze and limestone altars must have been used extensivly during Old Testament times, since they have been found in excavations at biblical sites throughout the land of Palestine. They appear in layers of debris from all the major archaeological periods of ancient times. However, the largest number of altars comes from the Late Bronze Age, the period in biblical history when the Exodus and the Conquest of Canaan took place, and from Iron Age I, which in biblical history is the period of the Judges and of the beginning of the monarchy.

Small altars of this type were used in offerings by people throughout the ancient Near East. While small altars like this were frequently used by the Israelites, they were also employed by other groups in Palestine, such as the Philistines and the Canaanites. Each group decorated their altars in their own way, with distinctive symbols and motifs meaningful to them.

Burnt offerings
What kind of offerings were made on little altars of this type? Such altars were used for several different kinds of offering. First, they were used for incense offerings. Some of the altars discovered during excavations have been found to bear traces of burning, and bear a residue of ash on top. For this reason they are frequently labelled 'incense altars'. However altars of this type were also used for other kinds of offering; for instance the Israelites probably used them for cereal offerings, when the worshipper brought an offering of flour, which was mixed with oil and incense, and then offered to God (Leviticus 2:1–3). Sometimes the flour was made into cakes, and the cakes were offered (Leviticus 2:4–10). On other occasions the altars were used for libations, or drink offerings – that is, offerings of liquids such as olive oil or wine. In making a libation, the worshipper presented his offering to God by pouring the liquid into the bowl on top of the altar.

Keep the Lamps Burning

'Command the Israelites to bring you clear oil of pressed olives for the light, so that the lamps may be kept burning' (Exodus 27:20). Light is remarkable; it holds back the darkness and brings cheer to the faint-hearted; it banishes evil and, as in this quotation from Exodus, referring to the light in the Tent of Meeting, or Tabernacle, it symbolizes the continual presence of God. Today we think of light simply in terms of switching on an electric lamp, or, more rarely, lighting a candle. But in biblical times the best light available was that supplied by an oil lamp.

Archaeologists have discovered oil lamps from stratigraphic levels dating back as far as 4000 BC. They are almost as common as cooking pots, and were just as essential for the daily life of their original owners.

When lamps are mentioned in the Bible, they usually refer to the lamps involved in religious worship, such as those set on golden lampstands in the Tabernacle, or Tent of Meeting (Exodus 25:38; 37:23). Elsewhere the Bible refers to lamps metaphorically; for instance the prophet Jeremiah speaks of the coming time of destruction for the people of Jerusalem, when God 'will banish from them the sounds of joy and gladness, the voices of the bride and bridegroom, the sound of millstones and the light of the lamp' (Jeremiah 25:10).

Similarly, a family is said to become extinct in much the same way as a lamp is extinguished: 'The light of the righteous shines brightly, but the lamp of the wicked is snuffed out' (Proverbs 13:9). It is quite appropriate that such a common household item should come to stand for the family itself.

Dating levels with lamps
One of the methods which archaeologists use to date levels within an excavated site involves examining the lamps uncovered in each of these levels. There are distinctive lamp types, just as there are distinctive pottery types and architectural styles, all of which can signal that a new people moved into the area, or that an outmoded or unfashionable type of lamp had been abandoned.

The shape of a lamp, the materials used in its construction

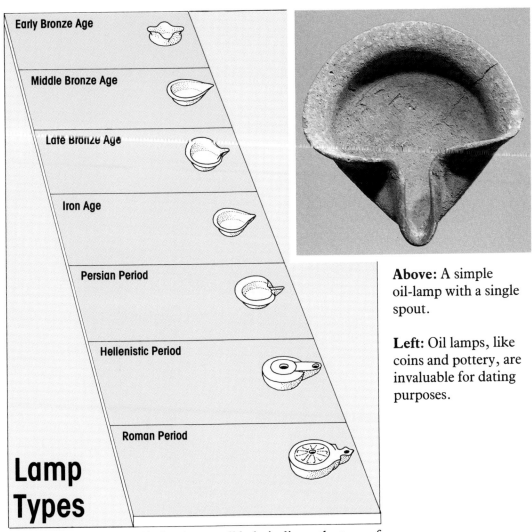

Early Bronze Age

Middle Bronze Age

Late Bronze Age

Iron Age

Persian Period

Hellenistic Period

Roman Period

Lamp Types

Above: A simple oil-lamp with a single spout.

Left: Oil lamps, like coins and pottery, are invaluable for dating purposes.

and the decoration applied to it, can all help indicate the type of use to which it was put in ancient times. The earliest lamps discovered were simply round bowls into which one or more flax wicks were placed. Once ignited, they were kept burning by adding more oil. Such bowls are known to have been used as lamps because of the soot marks which have been found on their rims.

Eventually potters became more adept at shaping lamps, and began to add a lip to hold the wick. This channelled the light, and made for the more economical use of the oil. Potters also began burnishing the lamps, which gave them a smoother surface, and also prevented oil seeping out through the porous clay. Burnishing also gave the potter a suitable smooth surface on which he could inscribe or paint some sort of pattern, giving the lamp a more decorative and personalized appearance. In some instances lamps became quite elaborate, possibly to serve some special religious purpose, or else simply to provide a 'curiosity' for the household.

Above: Olive oil was generally used as fuel in oil-lamps.

Right: A seven-spouted pottery oil-lamp on a small stand.

This relief of a menorah, or seven-branched lampstand, comes from the bath complex at Tiberias.

Different styles

Distinctive lamp styles appeared in each period. Changes in style were occasionally made with a view to giving more effective illumination, but usually simply reflected changing styles. For example, around 1400–1200 BC, we find there was a change in single-spouted lamps. Whereas previously the rims of such lamps had been pinched inwards, now we find that the rims are bent outwards, creating a flattened ledge, whose width varies according to period and local taste. From such variations in style, archaeologists can determine first the general period of a particular lamp, and then its more precise dating.

The fuel used in these lamps was generally olive oil. This commodity, used for cooking, as a medicine, as a cosmetic base and for illumination, was just as important as grain in the local economy. Olive groves were found wherever the tree could be cultivated, and on many ancient sites archaeologists have found evidence for an olive press used to extract the oil. This process involved crushing the olives and pressing the pulp to obtain the olive oil. In some cases it is thought that the pulp was also placed in water, when any remaining oil would rise to the surface, where it could be skimmed off.

The remains of an oil-press in the grounds of the Garden Tomb, Jerusalem.

Grades of oil

In the quotation from the book of Exodus which opens this chapter, clear oil was specified for use in the Tent of Meeting. Apparently several different grades of oil were available. Given the rather primitive extraction process, some of the resulting oil was inevitably of rather a coarse quality. Naturally, the best quality oil was set aside for use in the Temple and for the households of the wealthy. The poorer grades, which probably provided a smoky, sputtering light, would have been all that the impoverished could afford.

Lamps served an essential function in every household and building in ancient times. Their styles and types provide archaeologists with invaluable data from which to reconstruct the chronology of the biblical period. The lamps also serve to tell us something of the daily life of their owners.

The Farmer and his Implements

Once the people of Israel had settled permanently in Palestine, the main basis of their economy became agricultural. While there were some large urban centres, such as Jerusalem, most of the people lived in rural areas, and their lives were dominated by the changing seasons and the daily demands of the fields. Because farming was so much a part of their lives, many of the images depicted by the prophets are drawn from agriculture, and many scenes reflect agricultural activity.

The Gezer Calendar, probably a schoolboy's exercise, gives us a complete agricultural calendar.

Opposite: Women
reaping with sickles;
similar methods would
have been used in Bible
times.

Opposite below: An
Egyptian model of
oxen ploughing.

Seasons and calendars

Since agriculture is a seasonal occupation, a way of chronicling
the passage of time had to be developed from early times. A sign
of this is found in the Gezer calendar, which was discovered in
1908. This rare piece of Israelite inscriptional material is probably a schoolboy exercise, but it provides us with a complete agricultural calendar dating from the tenth century BC.

On the calendar, the year is divided up into periods: two
months for storage; two for sowing; two for spring growth; a
month for pulling flax and another for the barley harvest; a
month for harvesting all the other crops; two months for prun-
ing vines; and finally a month for the ripening of summer fruit.
Obviously life revolved around these events and periods, and it
would have been important for schoolchildren to learn about
this agricultural cycle.

The Old Testament itself contains a great deal of information
on such farming activities as planting, harvesting, threshing
and winnowing. Each of these tasks required some special implement to do the work. Archaeological excavations have uncovered the remains of some of these tools, but many were made
of wood and thus have not survived the centuries except in pictures and in the methods still practised in some Arab villages.

Clearing the ground

In biblical times, the first stage in preparing the land for planting was to clear it of stones. These were then stacked in piles,
many of which can still be seen today, forming boundary-mar-
kers and enclosures to prevent grazing animals from destroying
growing crops. In many areas of Palestine, however, the
amount of available level ground was limited. This necessitated
the construction of terraced fields on the hillsides, a craft which
became an art, and which is still taken advantage of today by
both Arab and Israeli farmers. There were some difficulties in
maintaining these terraces, due both to soil erosion and to the
constant need to keep them free of weeds.

Once the land had been cleared, or had been made available
through the construction of terraces, a wooden plough with a
metal sheath was used to help break open furrows. Elisha is said
to have been ploughing with twelve yoke of oxen when he was
called to be the companion of the prophet Elijah (1 Kings
19:19). His plough and yoke were probably more advanced in
style than those used in the Judges period. At that early period,
the Israelites had to go to the Philistines to have their
ploughshares sharpened, because they lacked the skill to do it
for themselves:

'So all Israel went down to the Philistines to have their
ploughshares mattocks, axes and sickles sharpened. The price

A threshing sledge in operation in recent times. A similar sledge, drawn by oxen, would have been in use in the biblical period.

was two thirds of a shekel for sharpening ploughshares and mattocks, and a third of a shekel for sharpening forks and axes and for repointing goads' (1 Samuel 13:20–21).

Flint sickles

Among the most common remains of agricultural implements found by archaeologists are sickle blades. These may have been used to reap the ripening grain, as mentioned in Joel 3:13: 'Swing the sickle, for the harvest is ripe'. Prior to the introduction of metal technology, flint was used to make the sickle blades. The flint was embedded into a wooden handle and held in place by bitumen. Since the method of construction of these stone blades can be traced to particular sources, they can be used (like pottery, see 'The Bible and Archaeology') to help date excavation sites and as evidence of trade. Harvesting knives were eventually made of bronze and iron, and some of these have survived as evidence of this activity.

Threshing was the next stage in the process of preparing the harvested grain for use. This involved transporting the sheaves to a central place, called the threshing floor. Here the stalks of grain were placed on a circular earthen floor, and cattle or other draught animals would trample on it. By doing this, they would separate the kernels of wheat or barley from the stalks so that

they could easily be collected. A further refinement of this procedure occurred when a threshing sledge, which had stones and bits of metal embedded into its underside, was hitched to the oxen and driven over the grain. A sledge of this type is mentioned in 2 Samuel 24:25, where Araunah sold David his threshing floor for use as the site of the Temple, and David burned a sacrifice on the spot, using as fuel the yokes of the oxen and the wood from the threshing sledges.

In the foreground, a labourer uses a winnowing fork to winnow the grain; in the background, four donkeys are used to thresh the corn. Similar methods were in use in Bible times.

The threshing floor

Because of its importance to the well-being of the entire community, the threshing floor eventually became associated with legal proceedings. This is graphically portrayed in 1 Kings 22:10, where the prophet Micaiah and his prophecies are judged before kings Ahab and Jehoshaphat, who were sitting on their thrones at a threshing floor by the gate of Samaria.

Once the kernels of grain had been separated from the stalks, what remained was then winnowed. This was done using a long wooden fork, which tossed the chaff into the air and allowed the evening breeze to blow away straw and other non-edible matter. Isaiah uses this common agricultural scene metaphorically: 'You will winnow them, the wind will pick them up, and a gale will blow them away' (Isaiah 41:16).

65

This imagery is also echoed in Psalm 1:4, where it is said that the 'wicked are ... like chaff that the wind blows away'. A further illustration of the legal overtones to the activity of preparing grain is found in Jeremiah 15:7, where the prophet describes God winnowing the people 'with a winnowing fork at the city gates of the land'. The gate, like the threshing floor (where winnowing would also take place), was a site often used for court proceedings (see 'What Happened at the City Gate?').

Sieving the grain

The final step in this process of separating the grain from the chaff was the use of sieves or screens. By sieving the grain, small stones or bits of pottery that had been swept into the heap of grain on the threshing floor would be caught in the mesh, while the smaller grains of wheat would fall through to the ground below, where they were collected. Amos uses this scene of final culling of undesirable elements in his prophecy, describing how God 'will give the command, and ... shake the house of Israel among all the nations as corn is shaken in a sieve, but not one ear will fall to the earth' (Amos 9:9).

With the grain now ready to be used for the preparation of food, the mill-stone and the hand-grinder were brought into action to make flour.

Underground stores

That part of the grain which was not immediately put to use was stored in earthenware jars and stone vats kept in people's homes or in underground plastered communal storage bins. Large underground silos of this type have been uncovered by archaeologists at Beth Shemesh, dating from around 900 BC and containing the remains of harvests long past.

With their large agricultural vocabulary describing a wide variety of field types, agricultural products and seasonal pursuits, it can be seen that the ancient Israelites viewed life very much in terms of farming. Their agricultural implements, while primitive from our standpoint, were designed systematically to provide as much food as possible to meet the community's needs. Since many of the steps in this food production process required group effort, it also drew people together into tightly-knit families working together for the common good.

ARCHAEOLOGY
AND THE
NEW TESTAMENT

What did Jesus Look Like?

We cannot know what Jesus, Mary, the apostles or any other major New Testament figure actually looked like. Christian art, as a distinct form, developed long after anyone could remember the actual appearance of the people of the New Testament. When Christian artists did begin to depict New Testament events they borrowed the approach common in the pagan religious art of their time.

Obviously no one had ever *seen* the pagan deities. Gods and goddesses were recognizable in pagan art because the artists developed conventional symbols to represent them. For example, the public knew that a statue or painting represented Apollo because the artist placed nearby two symbols associated with this deity: a tripod and a snake. The god Pan could be identified by his legs and feet (those of a goat), or because he was holding a shepherd's flute. Hercules might be recognized by the lion's skin thrown over his arm, or by the club in his hand.

Christian symbols
When Christian art began to develop, artists used a similar system. Luke the Evangelist might have an ox nearby, Mark a lion, Jesus a lamb, and so on. This made it possible to identify the people the artist intended to represent, but unfortunately it tells us nothing about their actual appearance.

Usually the only contemporary portraits of people from New Testament times are those of the mighty, especially the ruling or important families of the period. The surviving busts or full statues of such people are often remarkably realistic and for this reason the features of the Roman emperors of the New Testament period are well-known. Augustus, Tiberius, Nero, Vespasian, Titus and others were depicted so often and so accurately that, should a bust of any of these be uncovered today in an archaeological excavation, the excavators could immediately identify it.

Above: Tiberius Caesar.
Left: Caesar Augustus.

Coin portraits

The most common and accessible source of ancient portraits is the coins of the time. The features of the emperors and their families were made familiar to their subjects through the currency. Ancient coins have survived in great numbers, and are found in almost every archaeological excavation. Such discoveries allow us to know quite accurately what Mark Antony and his famous consort Cleopatra looked like. Similarly, Nero, the executioner of the apostles Paul and Peter, can be easily recognized, as can Titus, who destroyed Jerusalem in AD 70.

While we have no portraits of the key figures in the New Tes-

Coin portrait of the infamous Emperor Nero.

tament, we do have some of people much closer to the heart of the story than the imperial families of Rome. Unfortunately, no portrait of King Herod the Great, the slaughterer of the children in Bethlehem (Matthew 2) has survived. In his efforts to make peace with the Jewish population of Israel, Herod carefully avoided depicting himself on coins. This was because at that time the Jewish religious leaders took a very strong stand against picturing people or animals in any way, arguing that such a practice violated the commandment forbidding graven images. However Herod obviously followed this prohibition more in the letter than the spirit. While his coins feature no human images, they are filled with symbols normally associated with pagan deities. Nevertheless, this compromise seems to have satisfied the Jews, who could use the coins without overtly violating the commandment as it was then interpreted. So while Herod's name is common on coins, his picture never appears on any of them.

The Herod family
Some members of Herod's family, however, for one reason or another, felt freer to place their own portraits on coins, and this has provided us with some remarkable information. At Herod's death, three sons succeeded him, each inheriting part of his kingdom. Herod Philip II, for example (4 BC – AD 34), was given the primarily gentile areas of Gaulanitis, Batanaea, Aurani-

Coin of Herod Philip II.

and Trachonitis. He was apparently the first Herodian ruler to depict himself on a coin[1]. The large cheeks, deep-set eyes and small forehead seem to be family characteristics. (This is not the Philip whose wife Herodias was stolen by Herod Antipas, another of the heirs of Herod the Great (Matthew 14:3; Mark 5:17; Luke 3:19) but rather the *other* Philip, mentioned in Luke 3:1. The family tree of the Herodians is notoriously complicated!)

Portraits do exist, however, of two of the other figures in the scandalous story of the illicit relationship between Herod Antipas and Herodias, wife of his half-brother, a relationship roundly denounced by John the Baptist. John was beheaded after a dance by Salome, the daughter of Herodias by a previous marriage. Salome's name is not given in the Gospels, but is well known to history. She eventually became the wife of Herod Philip II, and then of yet another Herodian king, Aristobulus of Chalcis (AD 57–92). Aristobulus put Salome's portrait on a coin of his realm, giving us some idea of the appearance of this famous New Testament character[2].

In order to marry Herodias, Herod Antipas had first divorced his wife of twenty years, a Nabatean princess, the daughter of the Arab King Aretas IV (9 BC – AD 40). Although we do not even know the princess' name, we have several good coin portraits of her father. King Aretas is himself mentioned in the New Testament in the story of the apostle Paul's escape from Damascus, following his conversion to Christianity. 'In Damascus,' Paul says, 'the governor under King Aretas had the city of the Damascenes guarded in order to arrest me. But I was lowered in a basket from a window in the wall and slipped through his hands' (2 Corinthians 11:32–3). Aretas is usually depicted alongside his queen, sporting a long, wild head of hair quite in keeping with his image as a fearsome desert sheik.

Coin portrait of Aretas IV, father of Herod Antipas' first wife.

Portrait of Agrippa

The best preserved and most dramatic of all the coin portraits of New Testament characters is that of Herod Agrippa I (AD 37–44). This king, the grandson of Herod the Great, is the villain of Acts 12 – persecuting the church, killing James the apostle and imprisoning Peter. Though the author of Acts brings out the dark side of Agrippa's reign, and records his horrible death as a case of divine retribution for his crimes, the Jewish population of first century Palestine regarded him as something of a hero. His grandmother had been a member of the Jewish royal family, the Hasmoneans. He enjoyed, therefore, an aura of legitimacy never achieved by his grandfather, Herod. The Jewish establishment had great hopes for Herod Agrippa, because he seemed to offer a chance for self-government, or at least for less Roman interference; and he could be expected to understand, and to be more sympathetic with, Jewish religious feelings than could the Roman governors such as Pontius Pilate, who had ruled Judea since AD 10.

Agrippa's demise

From the Christian point of view Agrippa's reign was a disaster. In order to curry favour with the Jewish religious establishment, he lashed out against the new messianic movement centred around Jesus, the teacher of Nazareth, and especially against its leaders. His plan to put Peter on public trial demonstrates his political motivation (Acts 12:4). He had come to power through subtle political manoeuvring in Rome as a young

man. By befriending the mad emperor Caligula, Agrippa gained for himself the territories which had belonged to his uncles Philip and Antipas. By supporting Caligula's successor, Claudius, at just the right moment, he received the rest of Herod the Great's kingdom in AD 41.

Coin of Herod Agrippa I, whose death is recorded in Acts 12.

It was a self-assured Agrippa who addressed the crowd in the Roman port of Caesarea one day in AD 44. Dazzled by him, the crowd cried out, 'This is the voice of a god, not of a man' (Acts 12:22). Such praise, common among pagans, was considered blasphemous for a Jewish king. The author of Acts comments, 'Immediately, because Herod did not give praise to God, an angel of the Lord struck him down, and he was eaten by worms and died' (Acts 12:23). A similar, though somewhat different, version of Agrippa's death appears in the writings of the Jewish historian Josephus.

We have a wonderfully clear coin portrait of Agrippa I³, the finest example of which is now shown in the Israel Museum, Jerusalem. An inscription on this coin bears out the literary evidence about Agrippa's self-glorification and his dependence upon Rome. It reads: THE GREAT KING AGRIPPA, LOVER OF CAESAR. The portrait shows Agrippa with a protruding lower forehead, prominent chin and long nose. It is interesting that the coins of this type bear dates of either AD 43 or AD 44, and thus were minted within months – even weeks – of the death of Agrippa.

Another rare coin, minted earlier in Agrippa's reign, also gives us his portrait, and on its reverse the last of the New Testament characters to have been portrayed during their own lifetime: Agrippa's son, Herod Agrippa II. Unfortunately the portrait of Agrippa II, who is pictured as a young bcy on horseback, is far too small to draw conclusions about his features. Another coin, minted by Agrippa himself, gives us a better idea of his appearance.

Paul and Agrippa II

Still, it is interesting to have a contemporary picture of a person who figures so prominently in the New Testament story of the hearing of Paul (Acts 25:13–26:32). At his father's death, the Romans considered Agrippa II too young to take power. Instead, they once more placed Judea under Roman governors, who ruled from Caesarea rather than Jerusalem. Arrested in the Holy City, Paul was transported to the coast for his own safety. There he was held until he appealed his case to Caesar.

Before sending him off, the governor, Felix, who happened to be married to the sister of Agrippa II and Berenice, asked his royal visitors to examine Paul. The dramatic confrontation, described with great skill in Acts, seems to have touched the young prince. He promised to talk with Paul again about the new faith (though apparently he never did so) and assured his brother-in-law Felix that Paul had done nothing to deserve death or imprisonment (Acts 26:28, 32).

The list of New Testament portraits is admittedly short, but still extremely interesting. And who knows but that one day, in some excavation, another coin will turn up which pictures the face of another royal figure mentioned in the New Testament?

Where are the Lake Cities of Galilee?

Sometimes the ruins of ancient cities lie beneath modern urban centres. The streets, twentieth century buildings and bustle of traffic obscure the ancient landscape, making it difficult even to imagine the view which met the traveller in Roman times. The modern cities of Rome and Athens, for example, have swallowed up the sites of antiquity. Protruding here and there among the accretions of the centuries, the delicate columns, pediments and inscriptions seem almost to be gasping for breath as they crumble beneath the onslaught of smog and exhaust fumes.

The modern resort of Tiberias lies a short distance north of the ancient city.

But the experience of the modern visitor to the ancient sites around the Sea of Galilee is totally different. Here, strangely, it is the serenity of the quiet green hills and the deep blue water which hinders the imagination. The tranquillity contrasts with the ancient situation; in Jesus' day the lake supported a flourishing string of sophisticated cities. The steel blue water was filled with commercial boats. Major highways carried heavy traffic from the east towards the Mediterranean. Palaces and villas vied for space in the densely populated towns, full of merchants, craftsmen, fishermen and entrepreneurs.

Tiberias survives
Only one of the ancient lakeside cities has survived the centuries, the modern resort town of Tiberias. Fortunately, even this city has gradually shifted northwards in the course of time, so that the medieval and modern buildings do not stand over the Roman ones. In fact, it is archaeologists' good fortune that Roman Tiberias lies beneath the modern city refuse-tip, where excavation is not difficult.

Apart from Tiberias, the busy cities of the lake are gone, victims of war, conquest, earthquake, economic disaster and neglect. Eighteenth and nineteenth century travellers found even

Lake Cities of Galilee

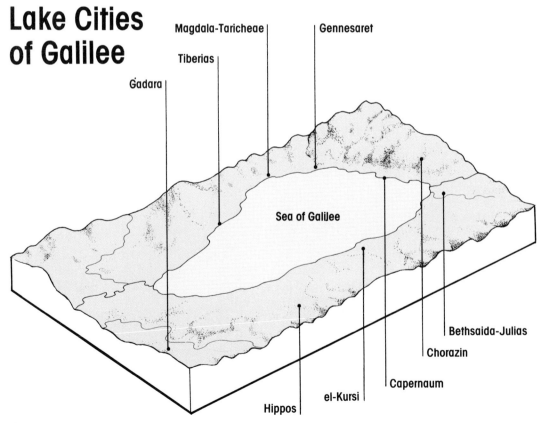

Magdala-Taricheae

Gennesaret

Tiberias

Gadara

Sea of Galilee

Bethsaida-Julias

Chorazin

Capernaum

el-Kursi

Hippos

Tiberias to be a dirty little village of no consequence. Their accounts, combined with the common impression that Jesus'
Galilean ministry took place in a quiet, rural countryside populated by simple Jewish farmers and fisherfolk, have often led to
the false assumption that Jesus gathered his first disciples and
proclaimed his message in the backwaters of the Empire.

The site of ancient
Tiberias is today the
town refuse-tip.

Town and country

Nothing could be further from the truth. Josephus, who commanded the Jewish rebel army in Galilee during the First Revolt
against Roman rule in AD 66–70, has left detailed accounts of
life around the lake. He makes it clear that large, sophisticated
cities crowded the lakeside, one almost meeting the next, like
the successive suburbs of a modern conurbation. These lake
cities boasted large public buildings, amphitheatres, fountains,
elaborate baths, palaces and columned market-places. Most of
them went on to yet greater glory during the late Roman and
Byzantine period, minting their own coins, and competing with
each other in their attempts to build the most magnificent public structures. Their ruins remain, mostly unexcavated, sometimes scattered over the hillsides, often buried only a few centimetres beneath the cultivated fields which surround the Sea of
Galilee today.

Modern Migdal stands near the site of biblical Magdala.

It is true that some of Jesus' greatest imagery is agricultural. Interestingly, in the midst of the urban complex described above lay one of the richest agricultural areas in the world, the famed Plain of Gennesaret. In fact, the plain gave the lake one of its several names (see Matthew 14:34; Mark 6:53; Luke 5:1). Stretching between Tiberias, Magdala-Taricheae and Capernaum, this fertile area was 'a region whose natural properties and beauty are very remarkable. There is not a plant which its fertile soil refuses to produce ... the air is so well-tempered that it suits the most opposite varieties. The walnut, a tree which delights in the most wintry climate, here grows luxuriantly, beside palm trees, which thrive on heat, and figs and olives, which require a milder atmosphere.' So said Josephus. It is as though, he continued, all the seasons were trying to claim the area at once!

The fishing industry

Jesus' major ministry occurred, apparently, in a trio of lake towns: Capernaum, which was his home-base, Chorazin and Bethsaida-Julias. Lying just to the south-west of these towns, the lush plain of Gennesaret was a perfect source for his parables about farming. The nearby lake itself provided further material for illustrations. The Sea of Galilee was, and still is, teeming with enough fish to support a significant commercial fishing industry. We must not think of Peter, James and John as poor fishermen eking out a living in quaint seaside villages. James and John were partners in the prosperous firm of 'Zebedee and Sons' which employed hired men (Mark 1:19–20). They fished in the most productive part of the lake, along the north shore from Gennesaret to Bethsaida-Julias, the area which the fishing industry of Tiberias exploits with great success to this day.

Magdala-Taricheae

The names of some of the lakeside towns indicate the importance of this industry. Most scholars believe that Magdala, best known to Bible students as the home of Jesus' friend Mary (the 'Magdalene'), is to be identified with the major lakeside town which Josephus calls 'Taricheae'. The Greek work for 'salted fish' is *tarichos* and it seems likely that, as the city was the source of this delicacy, Taricheae naturally became the name used by its Greek-speaking customers. The town was twice blessed, by the fish off its shores, and by its proximity to the fields of Gennesaret, which were undoubtedly worked mostly by Magdalenes.

The name 'Magdala' is related to the Hebrew word for tower, *Migdal*, and probably lies behind the names 'Magadan' (Matthew 15:39) and 'Dalmanutha' (Mark 8:10), used of the place where Jesus went just after performing the miracle of the loaves and fishes.

Before the building of Tiberias by Herod Antipas, Magdala-Taricheae was the most important city on the lake. Josephus notes that it had a hippodrome (horse-racing stadium) and a wall 'where not bounded by the lake'. He was very familiar with the city, using it as a base during his days as a rebel general.

Small fishing boats still ply Galilee today.

79

Archaeologists have not undertaken any substantial excavations at Magdala-Taricheae.

Josephus' references imply that it had a large, sophisticated population which was somewhat influenced by Greek culture – or 'hellenized'.

A wrecked ship

Very little excavation has been done at Magdala-Taricheae, but three interesting discoveries have been made. In 1961, a group of marine archaeologists, called the 'Link Expedition', reported a find off the lake-shore at Magdala. About twenty-seven metres (seventy-five feet) off the present shoreline, in five metres (fifteen feet) of water, divers found a strip of paving ten metres (thirty feet) wide and ninety metres (300 feet) long, parallel to the shore. This strip apparently represents the line of the ancient shore (several facts indicate that the lake was somewhat smaller in Roman times) and would have served the fishermen as a place to lay out their nets to repair or dry them (see Matthew 4:21; Mark 1:19; Luke 5:2).

Further off-shore, the divers found twenty-nine cooking pots exactly like those often found in first-century tombs, together with juglets, dishes and two oval stone anchors. Although no sign remained of a boat, it was clear that these objects were the contents of a vessel which sank while transporting a load of ceramic ware across the lake. The archaeologists suggested that 'the ship may have foundered in one of the sudden storms which sweep down so frequently from the surrounding hills and turn the placid lake into a boiling cauldron within a few minutes'.[1]

This unfortunate ship went down very close to the site of the similar sudden storm, described in Luke 8:22–24: 'One day Jesus said to his disciples, "Let's go over to the other side of the lake." So they got into a boat and set out. As they sailed, he fell asleep. A squall came down on the lake, so that the boat was being swamped, and they were in great danger. The disciples went and woke him, saying, "Master, Master, we're going to drown!" He got up and rebuked the wind and the raging waters; the storm subsided, and all was calm.'

An early synagogue

On land, the limited excavations so far carried out at the site of Magdala-Taricheae have revealed a building which the archaeologists believe to be a first-century synagogue. It is quite small – they call it a 'mini-synagogue' – only some eight metres by nine (twenty-four by twenty-six feet), but has a floor-plan commonly found in very early synagogues. Standing only sixteen kilometres (ten miles) or so from Capernaum, this building may be one of those Jesus used to introduce his message to his fellow Galilean Jews, when he 'went through all the towns and villages, teaching in their synagogues ...' (Matthew 9:35; 4:23; Mark 1:39).

A fishing boat nears the ruined city of Capernaum.

Bethsaida-Julias

At the north-east corner of the lake, just east of where the river Jordan flowed into it, stood the city of Bethsaida-Julias. The name 'Bethsaida' means 'house of the fisherman'. John's Gospel identifies the place as the home-town of the apostles Philip, Andrew and Peter (John 1:44; 12:21) though Matthew, Mark and Luke suggest that the brothers Andrew and Peter lived in Capernaum at the time of Jesus' ministry there (Mark 1:21; verse 29). Actually the two towns are situated quite close together – less than six kilometres (four miles) apart – and, though separated by a territorial boundary, a major highway connected them. We may therefore suppose that their inhabitants were constantly in close contact.

Bethsaida is mentioned in the New Testament in connection with the feeding of the five thousand and the miracles of walking on water (Mark 6:45), the healing of a blind man (Mark 8:22) and as a stop on the disciples' boating itinerary (Luke 9:10). Josephus says that Herod Philip built 'Julias in lower Gaulanitis'[2] and that he died and was buried there[3]. The boundary between Philip's territories and those of Herod Antipas seems to have been the river Jordan itself. Thus, when going from Bethsaida-Julias to Capernaum, the traveller crossed a border. As we shall see, this explains several matters about the town of Capernaum as described in the Gospels.

The site of biblical Bethsaida, the ruin-strewn hill of Et-Tell.

The archaeologist Bargil Pixner has shown that a ruin-strewn hill called Et-Tell, two kilometres (one mile) from the present seashore, is the site of ancient Bethsaida. Three facts point to this conclusion: firstly, Et-Tell fits the description of the place given by Josephus, who fought a battle there in AD 66 during the Revolt[4]; secondly, recent construction work by Israeli engineers has shown that the Jordan has silted up the ancient shoreline, which accounts for the two kilometre (one mile) distance between the site and the present shore; thirdly, Syrian army trenches, dug into the hill between 1948 and 1967, revealed pottery from the early Roman period[5].

No archaeological excavations have as yet been done at this site, though visitors to the hill, now part of a park, can easily see portions of ancient walls, dressed stones and other remains. The splendid tomb of Herod Philip, where he was buried at the end of his long reign, has yet to be discovered[6].

Chorazin has been explored by archaeologists, and a number of its buildings reconstructed to give the modern visitor an idea of their appearance in ancient times.

Jesus' curse

The most famous biblical reference to this city is the fearful curse pronounced upon it and its neighbours by Jesus: 'Woe to you, Chorazin! Woe to you Bethsaida! For if the mighty works done in you had been done in Tyre and Sidon, they would have repented long ago in sackcloth and ashes' (Matthew 11:20–24; Luke 10:13–15).

The third city Jesus condemned was 'his own city' Capernaum (Matthew 4:13; 9:1): 'And you, Capernaum, will you be lifted up to the skies? No, you will go down to the depths. If the miracles that were performed in you had been performed in Sodom, it would have remained to this day. But I tell you that it will be more bearable for Sodom on the day of judgment than for you' (Matthew 11:23–4).

These three cities – Bethsaida, Chorazin and Capernaum – were, according to Matthew 11:20, 'the cities in which most of his miracles had been performed', and thus the centre of his Galilean ministry. The last two places have now been extensively excavated.

Chorazin

Opposite: The entrance to the synagogue, Chorazin. These remains date from later than the time of Christ.

Chorazin is located only four kilometres (two and a half miles) from Capernaum. It is situated along a valley some distance from, but in full view of, the lake. Excavations there have thrown up some interesting results. An impressive basalt synagogue has been excavated, in which was found a stone 'chair of Moses', the seat where the authorized teacher of the synagogue sat during services. Jesus condemned those Pharisees, who 'love to sit in Moses' seat' (Matthew 23:2). A number of public buildings were also uncovered. All these date from later than the time of Jesus, however. So far the first-century city has eluded the archaeologists.

Below: The synagogue at Chorazin, built of black basalt, has been partially reconstructed.

The restored walls of a house at Chorazin.

Capernaum

Capernaum is another matter. Extensive excavations have been carried out at this site for many years. The city was one of the largest of the thirty fishing towns surrounding the lake, standing some five kilometres (three miles) from the estuary of the Jordan to the south-west. It stretched along the shore-line for a considerable distance, between the lake itself and the main highway which came from the Decapolis and Syria and headed south towards Egypt or west towards important Mediterranean ports such as Caesarea, Ptolemais and Tyre.

The recent discovery of a Roman milestone at Capernaum proves that a Roman road ran by the city and helps explain the presence of a Roman centurion in a primarily Jewish town (Matthew 8:5–13; Luke 7:1–10). As a port of entry for caravans from the rich East, it is also logical that Capernaum should house an important customs house, whose officer became a disciple of Jesus (Luke 5:27–8; Matthew 9:9).

These facts alone point to a significant city, suited by its location to be the centre of Jesus' ministry. He selected a place that was far from being a mere backwater; he consciously chose to enter the mainstream of Roman provincial life.

Jesus' home town

Capernaum is the site, or the implied site, of so many events in the Gospels that space does not permit a complete listing. Some examples include: the call of Matthew-Levi (Matthew 9:9; Mark 2:14; Luke 5:27–9), the location of the house of Peter and Andrew (Mark 1:29), the miracle in the synagogue (Mark 3:1–5), the raising of Jairus' daughter (Mark 5:22–41), the stilling of the storm (Matthew 14:25–33; Mark 4: 37–40; Luke 8:23–

4), walking on the water (Matthew 14:25–33; Mark 6:48–51), the coin in the fish's mouth (Matthew 17:27), various healings (Mark 1:23–8; 30–1; 32–4; 40–5; 2:3–12; 5:25–34; Luke 7:1–10; see also Matthew 8:5–13), and others. Matthew 4:13 notes that 'leaving Nazareth, he went and lived in Capernaum'.

Capernaum is also prominent outside the Synoptic tradition (that is, the sources which lie behind Matthew, Mark and Luke). The events of John 6 centre there, for example. The town was obviously Jesus' adult home and the hub from which his Galilean ministry expanded throughout northern Palestine.

The name 'Capernaum' is a Greek spelling of the Hebrew 'Kephar Nahum' (town of Nahum), the official modern name of the site. No city exists there today. Jesus' dire prophecy ran 'And you, Capernaum, will you be lifted up to the skies? No, you will go down to the depths' (Matthew 11:23). In order to find the Capernaum of Jesus' day, the archaeologist must literally 'go down to the depths', because the Roman town lies several feet below the present surface. Above the Roman levels are those of succeeding cultures; the city did not fade away suddenly. It survived as a place of considerable importance until the eighth century AD, and as a smaller village for several centuries longer. The site is now covered by the ruins of primitive stone fishermen's huts from the Middle Ages, which must be laboriously removed in order to excavate for the ancient city.

A view from the site of Capernaum, looking towards biblical Magdala.

Excavations at
Capernaum during the
summer of 1984.

Nineteenth-century explorers were drawn to the desolate spot because the ruins of an elaborate white limestone synagogue could be seen scattered over the area. The land on which this synagogue stood was purchased in 1894 by the Franciscan order of the Roman Catholic church, and the land immediately east of it was purchased by the Greek Orthodox Patriarchate of Jerusalem. Today a large modern stone wall separates the two parcels of land; extensive excavations have taken place on both sides.

The Capernaum synagogue

Most discoveries so far date from after Jesus' residency in the town. The white limestone synagogue has been partially restored from the scattered ruins (though unfortunately not with complete historical accuracy) and is a major tourist attraction. The date of this impressive building is a matter of controversy, but it is certainly not from the days of Jesus. The original hope of the excavators, that they were uncovering the very building in which so many of the famous miracles of Jesus occurred, has been dashed. The building dates from at least the late second or third century, and more probably from the fifth.

However, the Franciscan archaeologists Stanislao Loffreda and Virgilio Corbo, who have been working at the site since

The white limestone synagogue at Capernaum has been partially restored, though unfortunately with less than complete historical accuracy.

1968, have discovered that the white limestone synagogue is built on top of another impressive building, constructed from the native black basalt. The walls of the white limestone building rest on one metre (four foot) thick walls of well-worked but mortarless basalt stones. The excavators probed beneath the white limestone floor, and discovered an extensive cobbled stone floor of black basalt, which they date to the first century. On this floor they found impressive column drums and fragments of elegant cornice moulding. All this has led them to the conclusion that they have found the original synagogue of Jesus' day, built, according to Luke 7:1–5, by a Roman military officer who lived in the town. While it cannot be said that this conclusion is proved, or even that the basalt building was without

The remains of the building at Capernaum traditionally held to be Peter's house.

question a synagogue, the possibility is strong enough to receive serious consideration.

Around the synagogue, Loffredo and Corbo have found a neighbourhood consisting of quite simple stone houses, which they also date to the first century. These houses seem to have had roofs constructed of wooden beams and perhaps straw or tree branches mixed with mud (see Mark 2:4, where the paralytic is let down through a hole 'dug' in the roof of a Capernaum house). Fish-hooks were found on the floors of some of the houses, clearly indicating the presence of a fishing industry in the town.

Peter's house?

Among these houses, one had clearly received special attention from very ancient times. It had been transformed into a place of worship, perhaps as early as the second century, though this has not yet been proved. In the fourth century this house was enlarged and surrounding houses were pulled down, to establish a courtyard with plastered walls. These walls were covered with graffiti by Christian pilgrims who obviously considered it to be a holy site. In the mid-fifth century, the Byzantines built a fine octagonal church on the site, its floor decorated with a beautiful peacock.

Opposite: The walls of a bath-house discovered at Capernaum.

Opposite: Beth Shan, another member of the Decapolis, was known as Scythopolis in Roman times. The theatre seated huge audiences for its spectacles.

Whether this was actually Peter's house, the house where Jesus lived in Capernaum, as the Byzantine pilgrims apparently believed, or simply the house used by the early followers of Jesus as a meeting-place (a custom we know was common in the earliest days of Christianity, see Acts 1:13–4; 12:12; Romans 16:5 etc.), its discovery is very important. More than once the ancient traditions of the rabbis mention the presence of heretics or 'minim' in Capernaum; they may well refer to the group of Jews who followed Jesus and who met in this very house.

On the other side of the modern dividing wall, excavations have been conducted for several years under the direction of Vassilios Tsaferis. The Greek Orthodox site has thrown vital light on the later history of Capernaum, particularly the time of the invasion and conquest of Palestine by the Moslem armies (the seventh and eighth centuries AD). A gold treasure, the largest ever found in Israel, consisting of gold coins minted in Damascus by the Moslem Khalif, was uncovered on this site. Alongside the lake, the excavators discovered a Roman-style bathhouse dating from the early Roman period, first or second century AD, further evidence that Capernaum was a town of some size and sophistication at that time.

Jerash, biblical Gerasa, boasts very fine Graeco-Roman remains. The city belonged to the Decapolis confederation.

The site of Hippos can be seen on the distant hills in this view from Capernaum.

Cities of the Decapolis

Further proof that Jesus' ministry took place in a culturally diverse situation comes from the continuing archaeological discoveries at the sites of the cities of the Decapolis. From the time of the conquest of the East by Alexander the Great, some thirty Greek-style cities had been established in Palestine and the surrounding area. Jesus' ministry often took him into these cities or the areas around them, and their inhabitants are specifically mentioned in the Gospels as hearing and responding to his message (Matthew 4:25; Mark 7:31, for example).

These cities had been colonized by Greeks and Macedonians who mixed with the local Syrians, though most of them also had Jewish inhabitants. The result was a sort of hybrid culture which had the visible trappings of Greek civilization but centred around a basically oriental world-view. Pompey, the Roman general who took control of Palestine for the Romans, removed these cities from Jewish control and some of them were organized into a confederation called the Decapolis (Greek for 'ten cities') under Gabinius, the governor of Syria.

These cities boasted all the trappings of Greek urban life: stadiums for holding athletic games, theatres, public baths, colonnaded streets, forums, temples and the rest. So many of these features have survived the centuries that the sites of the Decapolis cities offer rich opportunities for archaeological excavation. The best preserved Decapolis city is Gerasa (Jerash in modern Jordan). Major excavations have occurred, or are occurring, in other Decapolis cities such as Scythopolis (Beth Shan), Pella and Abila.

Hippos

Two Decapolis cities are closely associated with the lake of Galilee: Hippos and Gadara. 'Hippos' means horse in Greek; the Aramaic name for the city was Susita, which also means horse. The horse was the city's symbol, and appears on its coins.

The ruins of Hippos lie scattered on top of a majestic mesa, or flattened mountain, which protrudes as a dramatic backdrop to the modern kibbutz of Ein Gev on the south-east shore of the lake. Directly across the lake from Tiberias, its major rival in Roman times, Hippos' gleaming monuments could be clearly seen from Capernaum in Jesus' day. The modern visitor, making the difficult climb up to the location, is rewarded by the sight of massive red columns, capitals, decorated pilasters, and the remains of mosaic floors, cisterns, streets and public buildings. A huge public fountain or 'Nymphaeum', a theatre, and several churches can be clearly distinguished among the ruins.

Some of the ruined columns which mark the site of the Decapolis city of Hippos.

At Hammat Gadara, south-west of the Sea of Galilee, impressive remains of hot baths have been uncovered.

The city of Hippos was built according to the typical Roman plan, and the main street or *cardo* can still be used as a path to walk through the ruins. Most of what can be seen dates from later than the first century, though excavations in the 1950s uncovered an impressive round tower and gate made of basalt, which dates from the Herodian period. A road paved with basalt stones leads up to the gate, towers guard it, and a stone water-conduit, made of collared sections which fit into each other, runs under it. This seems to be the east gate of the city, and may well have been used by Jesus during his trips through the Decapolis. The road leading up to the gate is lined with tombs and monuments to the dead, as was typical of the time.

Gadara
A short distance south-west of Hippos are the ruins of the Decapolis city of Gadara and its wonderful warm-spring resort, Hammat Gadara. The four springs, believed by ancient and modern inhabitants to possess great medicinal powers, poured into the river Yarmuk from its north bank. The city itself stood on the south bank of the river, less than three kilometres (two miles) from the springs and about eight kilometres (five miles) south-west of the Sea of Galilee. Gadara was a place noted for a high level of Greek culture and, while it had been given to Herod the Great by the Emperor Augustus, it disliked his rule and much preferred to consider itself a part of Syria than of Palestine.

Today the ruins of the city lie within the state of Jordan, while the remains of the baths (Hammat Gader) are in territory controlled by the state of Israel. Since 1979, extensive excavations have gradually uncovered the magnificent baths clustered around the ancient hot mineral spring (52°C, 126°F) called Ain Makleh ('Frying Pool') in Arabic and Ma'ayan Hagehinom ('Hell's Pool') in Hebrew. The incredible bath-complex emerging from the earth seems to date from the late second to early third centuries AD. It was used continually for many hundreds of years, until as late as the ninth century AD. We know that the hot springs were used even before the time of Jesus; the Greek traveller Strabo, writing in the first century BC, mentions them.

The bath complex at Hammat Gader probably dates from the late second or early third century AD.

Gadarenes or Gergesenes?

Josephus says that the territory of Gadara extended all the way to the lake itself.[7] This probably explains the appearance of ships on some of the coins of the city. It may also have some bearing on one of the continuing mysteries in the Gospels, the location of the strange miracle of the two thousand pigs (Matthew 8:28; Mark 5:1–20; Luke 8:26–39). The manuscripts of the Gospels differ over the name of the place where Jesus cast the demons into the herd of swine, which then 'rushed down the steep bank into the lake'. It is called the country of the Gadarenes in some ancient New Testament manuscripts, implying the lakeside territory of the city of Gadara, though the city itself was several miles from the lake. Other manuscripts

A large Byzantine church and monastery have recently been excavated at el-Kursi, on the east shore of Galilee.

have 'the country of the Gerasenes', but Gerasa (now called Jerash) is a wonderfully well-preserved Decapolis city almost thirty miles from the lake – hardly a good candidate.

Still other manuscripts read 'the country of the Gergesenes', implying another site altogether. The Byzantines apparently believed the place to be several miles north of Hippos, at a spot called el-Kursi where the steep hillside drops to the lake. Vassilios Tsaferis excavated a very large monastery and church at the place in the early 1970s. In 1980, during the preservation and restoration of the ancient church, a tower was found on the slope behind the monastery, enclosing a large boulder, and behind the tower a small chapel. The excavators believe that the boulder was somehow linked to the miracle of the swine in the minds of the Byzantines, who made it a place of pilgrimage. On the shore below the monastery are the remains of an artificial harbour which seems to date from Roman times, so at least the geography of the spot fits the Gospel accounts, even if absolute proof is still lacking that this was indeed the 'country of the Gergesenes'.

Baths and health

Opposite: Part of the impressive remains of the Byzantine church at el-Kursi, possible location for the miracle of the two thousand pigs.

Even if the hot baths at Hammat Gader do not figure in the story of the swine, they do shed some light on another aspect of Jesus' ministry. We cannot help being struck by the almost constant presence of sick and disabled people around Jesus. His fame in Galilee seemed much more tied to his ability to heal than to his role as a teacher or prophet. The state of public health in a Roman province such as Syria-Palestine was undoubedly abysmal; any town would have included many people who were crippled and ill. Still, the emphasis on the great numbers of people coming to Jesus for healing is remarkable.

Hot-water springs at Hammat Tiberias.

The presence of a great centre for medicinal hot baths may help explain this phenomenon. In fact, among the rooms in the baths at Hammat Gader is one known as the 'Leper's Pool'. This pool was described by Antonius Plakentia, a sixth-century traveller: 'Next to the hot pool is a large bath which, after being filled, all of the doors are closed and the lepers are brought in through the entrance with candles and incense, and in this bath they sit all night. When they fall asleep the ones to be healed see visions ...' Among the artifacts found during the excavation of this room were a number of ceramic candle-holders! Even today thousands of people visit the hot springs hoping that the waters will cure various ailments.

Hammat Tiberias
The same is true of the other major medicinal springs on the lake, located at Hammat Tiberias. These springs flow out of the hillside quite close to the lake, just south of the city of Tiberias. In fact, the presence of the springs probably helped influence Herod Antipas' decision to build himself a beautiful new capital city on the lake. The springs still accommodate some 2,500 bathers every day, seeking relief from such complaints as rheumatism in their 60°C (140°F) waters. Moshe Dothan excavated the area in the early 1960s, uncovering a synagogue from

Coin depicting the goddess Hygeia, symbol of the hot springs, from Tiberias.

Part of a Roman-style bath-house has been reconstructed at the museum at Hammat Tiberias.

the first half of the third century AD which boasts some of the most beautiful mosaic floors in Palestine. But Dothan also found remains of the baths from Herodian times and, in fact, signs of large public buildings dating from the first century BC and earlier.

Hammat Gader and Hammat Tiberias could, between them, easily provide the multitudes who crowded around Jesus' door (Matthew 8:16–17; Mark 1:32–34; Luke 4:40–41), causing Matthew to exclaim, 'This was to fulfil what was spoken by the prophet Isaiah, "He took our infirmities and bore our diseases."' In fact, these two places must have been included in

Remains of the synagogue at Hammat Tiberias, dating from several centuries after the time of Christ.

Matthew's list when he said, 'So his fame spread throughout all Syria, and they brought him all the sick, those afflicted with various diseases and pains, demoniacs, epileptics, and paralytics, and he healed them. And great crowds followed him from Galilee and the Decapolis and Jerusalem and Judea and from beyond the Jordan' (Matthew 4:23–25; see also Mark 3:10,7,8; Luke 6:18–19).

Herod's Tiberias

We finish our tour of the buried cities by the Lake of Galilee with a word about Tiberias itself, the only surviving lakeside city and the most magnificent of all in Jesus' day. Herod Antipas founded the city as his capital, partly to provide a place where Jewish and Hellenistic cultures could mix, and partly to have a capital free from the more conservative Jewish cultural and religious scruples. A whole series of coins was issued here, some depicting the goddess Hygieia (symbol of the hot springs),

Above: Mosaic depiction of a menorah, from the floor of the synagogue, Hammat Tiberias.

An eighteenth-century engraving of the ruins of Tiberias.

some with Antipas' name on them, carefully avoiding any pagan symbolism.

In Jesus' day the city was gleaming and new – about ten years old. High on the hill above the city itself stood Herod's magnificent palace which, according to Josephus, who had been inside, had a golden roof and pictures of animals painted on the walls – something which the strictest Jewish sects would have forbidden. The site of this palace has not yet been excavated. Josephus also mentions a stadium by the sea shore, and a huge prayer house or synagogue which could accommodate a large crowd; no sign of these buildings remains today.

As we saw earlier, the ancient city was located between Hammat Tiberias and the present city, an area now shared by a cemetery and the city refuse-tip. Fragments of ancient pottery, or sherds, are scattered in profusion on the ground. In 1973–74 excavators found the southern gate of the city which, they concluded, apparently stood by itself some distance from the southern edge of the city. Its purpose seems to have been ceremonial, marking the beginning of a street running from the hot springs to the city. The latest sherds found under the street date from the first century BC, so this gate and street may well have been part of Herod Antipas' original construction, and thus have been standing in Jesus' time.

The Gospels never mention any visit by Jesus to this magnificent city, though it was only about twenty-four kilometres (fifteen miles) from Capernaum. Some scholars have suggested that this was because the city was considered unclean by the most orthodox Jews of the day, having been built over a cemetery. However, Jesus, as is well known, was not scrupulous about Pharisaic restrictions. Perhaps he did not visit Tiberias because he needed to avoid Antipas, who from time to time threatened him (Luke 13:31). Perhaps he visited the city, but the Gospels simply do not mention it.

Tombs and Bone-boxes

Surrounding the Holy City of Jerusalem on the east, north and west is a huge burial ground consisting of thousands of graves, many of them dating from New Testament times. A large number of these tombs were disturbed in ancient times, but fortunately some escaped this fate. From time to time additional tombs are discovered, sometimes in planned excavations, but more often during construction work, since these areas of Jerusalem have been subject to rapid urban development in recent years.

Although this graveyard (or necropolis) was used for many centuries, and indeed is still in use today, tombs dating from the first century are relatively easy to identify. Certain types of pottery, cooking pots, perfume jars, glassware and lamps, all of which were used only during that period, are almost always found in the tombs. These items were apparently used during the ceremonies which accompanied the burials. Sometimes excavators even find dated coins in the tombs.

Bone-boxes

In addition, first-century tombs can often be identified by the presence of boxes made of soft stone, called ossuaries. When found undisturbed, an ossuary contains the bones of one or more persons, stacked carefully inside. The size of these boxes is determined by the length and width of the largest bones in the human skeleton. Ossuaries first appeared in the Jerusalem necropolis at about the time of Herod the Great (37 BC – AD 4) and continued to be used until early in the third century. Their use appears to have started in Jerusalem and spread to Jericho and other Jewish centres. In Jericho, the excavations of the archaeologist Rachel Hachili have revealed a huge necropolis rivalling that of Jerusalem and over eleven kilometres (seven miles) long! Here the ossuary burials may be even more closely dated – they began in 10 BC and ended in AD 70.

Ossuaries were often decorated with rosette designs, and sometimes with incised drawings of the *outside* of tombs, the facades or monuments commonly fronting the burial places of

Jerusalem is surrounded on three sides by thousands of graves.

The Tomb of Bene Hezir in the Kidron Valley.

the wealthy, and with lilies and date trees, plants often planted in the graveyards. These decorations were put on the ossuaries in the workshops where they were produced. Presumably people would purchase an ossuary as elaborate as the family budget allowed.

When the ossuary was put into use, other marks were often made on the box, quite without regard for the existing decorations. Sometimes these were merely symbols designed to indicate the proper way to put on the lid. In other cases there were words in Hebrew, Aramaic and Greek – the three most common languages in contemporary Palestine. These words, often hur-

riedly and almost carelessly inscribed, sometimes give exciting insights, as they seem to draw us very close to the world of the New Testament.

City of tombs

But before examining these graffiti-like inscriptions, let us take a closer look at the necropolis itself. In the Kidron Valley, east of the Temple Mount in Jerusalem, three or four tombs from the first century have somehow survived all the vicissitudes of history. They appear today very much as they would have appeared to Jesus and the apostles when they approached the city from Jericho or Bethany. The elaborate facades and monuments cut from the living rock along the side of the valley give us some idea of what the necropolis must have looked like when literally hundreds of such tombs were visible around the edges of the city on the slopes of Mount Scopus, the Mount of Olives and other rock faces in the area.

But what we see are only monuments drawing attention to the tombs; the tombs themselves are cut into the rock. Entering through a small passageway, so low that you must stoop to get in, you step down into quite a large room with a stone bench around the sides. This is the place for the first burial; for two burials took place, the second after the body had decomposed and the skeleton could be dismembered and placed in the ossuary.

A number of rock-cut tombs stand out impressively in the Kidron Valley. Several would have been standing in Christ's day.

107

The body perishes

Why would such a strange practice have arisen? The answer may be found in the beliefs of the Pharisees. The Pharisees differed from their main rivals, the Sadducees, on many points, but perhaps the most famous disagreement concerned the resurrection of the body, a doctrine held strongly by the Pharisees, but denied by the Sadducees. Both Jesus and Paul, despite their own conflicts with the Pharisees, agreed with them on this point (see Mark 12:18–27 and Acts 23:6–8). To this belief was added another, that the sins of the flesh adhered to the fleshly part of the body, and only disappeared totally when the flesh which carried them had decayed. Thus, an ancient collection of teachings of the rabbis, the *Babylonian Talmud*, says: 'The decay of the flesh too is necessary (for forgiveness)'.

In order to understand the practice of secondary burial, we need to remember one other Pharisaic belief, best expressed in this exchange between a rabbi and a Min (heretic) in the *Talmud*: 'A certain Min said to Rabbi Abahu, "You say that the souls of the righteous are stored up under the Throne of Glory. How did the necromancer call up Samuel by witchcraft?" [I Samuel 28:12]. He said to him, "That happened within twelve months [from death]. For it is tradition, that *during twelve months a man's body remains*, and his soul goes up and comes down; *after twelve months the body perishes*, and his soul goes

The rich could afford an elaborate tomb with an underground chamber. A stone slab was placed across the doorway to guard the entrance.

Underground Tomb

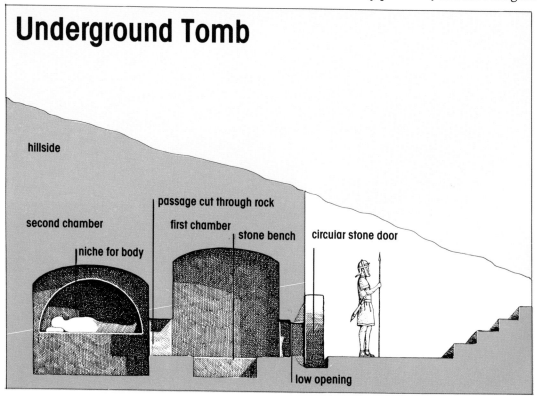

hillside

second chamber

niche for body

passage cut through rock

first chamber

stone bench

circular stone door

low opening

up and does not come down again'"[2] (present writer's italics).

It is interesting to recall the apostle Paul's use of the word 'flesh', remembering that he lived and studied in Jerusalem at precisely the time of burial customs described here: 'I know that good does not dwell in me, that is, in my *flesh*' (Romans 7:18); 'In my *flesh* I serve the law of sin ...' (Romans 7:25); '*Flesh and blood* cannot inherit the kingdom of God, nor does the perishable inherit the imperishable' (I Corinthians 15:50); 'The one who sows in his *flesh* will harvest decay, but the one who sows in the spirit will harvest eternal life' (Galatians 6:8) and so on (present writer's italics).

Entrance steps and rolling-stone door to Tomb of the Kings.

The burial process

The archaeological and literary evidence can now be brought together in order to reconstruct a picture of the burial process among those first-century Palestinian Jews who believed in the resurrection. After death, the deceased was brought to the family's rock-hewn tomb outside the city (if the family's wealth allowed the ownership of such a tomb). The body was placed on one of the stone benches which surrounded the first, or entrance, room inside the tomb. Ceremonies were held, and various ointments, perfumes and spices were placed on the body. Then the tomb was sealed by rolling a circular stone over the small entrance-way. Such rolling stones have been found intact

The stone benches can be clearly seen in this photograph taken inside the first chamber of the Tomb of the Kings, Jerusalem.

109

This rolling stone guards the entrance to the so-called Tomb of Herod's Family, Jerusalem.

and in place in several tomb excavations, and may be seen today at the tomb of Queen Helena, north of the city, and the so-called tomb of Herod's Family, to the west of the city.

After a period of about one year, the family returned to the tomb, removed the sealing stone and gathered the bones of the deceased into an ossuary, following a carefully-prescribed ritual. At this time the family sometimes scratched words on the box with a nail or a piece of charcoal – perhaps the name of the deceased, or some comment about his or her life or death. Then the box was placed in one of the smaller niches, called *kokhim* or *loculi*, which had been cut into the sides of the main room, there to await the resurrection.

Hundreds of ossuaries have been recovered; many have inscriptions which from time to time open fascinating windows into the world of the New Testament.

Simon the temple-builder

Two ossuaries, for example, relate directly to the magnificent Temple built by Herod the Great and admired by Jesus' disciples (Mark 13:1). The first came from a tomb brought to light during construction activities at Giv'at Hamivtar, in north-eastern Jerusalem. Carved twice on the sides of the ossuary are the words 'Simon the temple-builder' in the Aramaic language. The excavator of this tomb, Vassilios Tsaferis, points out that

the quite modest nature of the tomb probably indicates that this Simon was not *the* temple-builder, that is, the chief of construction; he was more likely one of the workmen whose family was proud enough of his participation in erecting this, one of the world's most impressive buildings, to scratch this description on the box holding his bones.

The ossuary of Simon 'the temple-builder' was found in the early 1970s. In 1902 a monumental cave-tomb was found on Mount Scopus, not far away from Giv'at Hamivtar, with an ossuary mentioning 'Nicanor of Alexandria who made the gates'. This tomb obviously belonged to the wealthy and famous family known for the fact that one of its members had donated a magnificent set of gates to the temple. The gift is mentioned in the *Talmud* and in the writings of Josephus, who describes the gates as being made of fine Corinthian bronze. They may very well be the gates which furnish the backdrop for the story of a healing by the apostle Peter: 'One day Peter and John were going up to the temple at the time of prayer – at three in the afternoon. Now a man crippled from birth was being carried to the temple gate called Beautiful, where he was put every day to beg from those going into the temple courts ...' (Acts 3:1–2).

Many of the names found on ossuaries are identical with those of people mentioned in the New Testament. Of course these names were quite common in the first century and it

An ossuary inscribed 'Simon the temple-builder', discovered in the 1970s.

would be wrong to conclude immediately that such inscriptions refer to the biblical characters. Nevertheless, the occurrence of names such as Mary, Martha and Lazarus (all found in the same tomb!), Sapphira, Joseph, Jesus and others, shows that the people buried in the Jerusalem necropolis moved in the same culture and language group as people who are named in the New Testament.

The tomb of Simeon Barsaba

Sometimes the similarities are so great that we may speculate that the ossuaries actually contained the bones of biblical characters – or at least of members of their families. For example, in 1945 a tomb was accidentally found near Talpioth, a suburb of Jerusalem, containing an ossuary inscribed in Hebrew 'Simeon Barsaba'. The name Barsaba is not a common one, and

This ossuary bears the inscription: 'Bones of the family of Nicanor the Alexandrian who made the gates'.

is in fact known only in the New Testament, where it occurs twice. One of the two men nominated to replace Judas in the Twelve is called Joseph Barsabas (Acts 1:23); and one of the two disciples who accompanied Paul and Barnabas from Jerusalem to Antioch is named Judas Barsabas (Acts 15:22). Thus we may have found in Talpioth the tomb of a family who had members in the very earliest Christian community in Jerusalem, companions of the apostles.

Another intriguing possibility arises with the discovery of a tomb found south of the village of Silwan, which clings to the eastern slope of the Kidron Valley, within sight of the Temple Mount. The tomb was discovered, untouched by grave robbers, in the year 1941, though news of the discovery was not published until many years later. The Israeli scholar Nahman Avigad studied the names inscribed on the eleven ossuaries found in the tomb and concluded that all had some connection with the North African province of Cyrenaica. Thus, he said, we may conclude that the tomb was that of a family whose members 'apparently belonged to the community of Cyrenian Jews which is known to have existed in Jerusalem in the time of the Second Temple'[3].

Son of Simon of Cyrene?

This would be quite interesting in itself, since Acts 6 notes that the beginning of the opposition to the early Christian leader Stephen, which resulted eventually in his martyrdom, came from 'members of the Synagogue of the Freedmen (as it was called) – *Jews of Cyrene* and Alexandria as well as the provinces of Cilicia and Asia' (Acts 6:9, present writer's italics).

But the discovery is all the more striking because on the side of one of the ossuaries we read 'Alexander (son) of Simon', and on its lid 'Alexander' (in Greek) and 'Alexander QRNYT' (in Hebrew). If, as some scholars have maintained, 'QRNYT' is an Aramaic spelling of the word 'Cyrene', then we have the undisturbed bones of someone called 'Alexander of Cyrene, son of Simon'. Dare we suggest that these are the very bones of the son of the man who carried the cross for Jesus? Or is it only coincidence that Mark notes 'A certain man *from Cyrene, Simon, the father of Alexander* and Rufus, was passing by on his way in from the country, and they forced him to carry the cross'? (Mark 15:21, present writer's italics). Of course there is no way to know for sure.

The discoveries in the Jerusalem necropolis are especially helpful in throwing light on the accounts in the Gospels of the death and burial of Jesus, which we discuss later ('Where was Jesus buried?'). Only one example will be given here. In one of the Giv'at Hamivtar tombs there is an inscription, written in old fashioned, or Palaeo, Hebrew script. It reads:

I, Abba, son of priest Eleazar, son of Aaron the high (priest), I Abba, the oppressed and the persecuted, who was born in Jerusalem, and went into exile in Babylonia and brought (back [to Jerusalem]) Mattathiah son of Juda(h), and I buried him in the cave, which I acquired by the writ.

This is a curious and rather mysterious inscription. We do not know who Abba was, why he was persecuted and forced into exile, or why he felt called upon to list his troubles on the walls of another man's tomb. He obviously wanted to be remembered as the one who returned the bones of Mattathiah (whose identity is likewise unknown) to Jerusalem and purchased a tomb in which to place them.

A rich man's tomb

It is the parallel with the story of Joseph of Arimathea and the body of Jesus which makes this inscription particularly interesting. The Gospels describe Joseph as a rich man, a disciple of Jesus, who was sufficiently close to the Roman governor Pilate to convince him personally to hand over Jesus' body. He then 'placed it in his own new tomb that he had cut out of the rock. He rolled a big stone in front of the entrance to the tomb and went away' (Matthew 27:60). We can now picture the situation quite vividly, having surveyed the nature of such monumental cave-tombs above (see also Luke 23:53 and John 19:41). According to the rabbis, a tomb could be bought, provided no-one had yet been buried in it, that is, it was a new tomb, 'one in which no one had yet been laid' (Luke 23:53). Says the *Talmud* 'a new tomb ... may be sold, an old one ... may not'.[4]

Thus, both Jesus and Mattathiah were placed in tombs which were the property of others, and both in 'new tombs' not yet used by their owners. Both cases fit perfectly with the rabbis' rule that no stranger could be laid in an 'old tomb', that is, one in which members of the family of the owner were already buried. Incidentally, we can see the great sacrifice made by Joseph of Arimathea when we realize how enormously expensive the monumental cave-tombs must have been. By placing Jesus in his unused tomb, he probably forfeited the right to use it for his own family – a generous gesture indeed!

The Jerusalem Temple

The Jerusalem Temple plays a central role in the New Testament story. The first building in which the God of the Jews 'caused His Name to dwell' had been built by King Solomon a thousand years before the beginning of the Christian movement. Destroyed by the Babylonians in the sixth century before Christ, the building had been reconstructed in a poor way by the Jews who returned from Exile. When Herod the Great took the throne, he rebuilt the Temple, partly in an attempt to gain favour with the Jewish religious establishment and partly, no doubt, because he wished to build a magnificent structure in his capital city to bring glory to himself.

The Temple figures prominently in the stories about the infancy of Jesus found in the Gospel of Luke. The father of John the Baptist had his famous vision while serving as a priest within the Temple sanctuary (Luke 1:1–25), and the infant Jesus was blessed by an old man and woman, Simeon and Anna, within the Temple courts (Luke 2:46,49). At the age of twelve, Jesus was found in the Temple asking questions of the theologians there (Luke 4:9; Matthew 4:5). In the most dramatic act of his public ministry, Jesus drove the money changers from the Temple courts (Matthew 21:12; Mark 11:15–16; Luke 19:45; John 2:14–15).

Jesus and the Temple
In the Gospels, the Temple is often the backdrop for important teaching by Jesus. He proclaims himself to be 'greater than the temple' (Matthew 12:5–6). He mentions the custom of swearing by the Temple (Matthew 23:16–17, 21), and predicts 'destroy this temple and I will raise it up in three days' (Matthew 26:6; Mark 14:58; Matthew 27:40; Mark 15:29; John 2:19–20). The setting for the parable of the Pharisee and the Tax Collector is the Temple court (Luke 18:10), and Jesus' teaching on the Last Things is initiated by a discussion on the Temple's destruction (Matthew 24:1; Luke 21:5; Mark 13:1–2).

During the climactic last days of his ministry, Jesus 'occupied' the Temple in order to confront its guardians and establish his sovereignty over it (Matthew 21:33; Mark 11:27; Luke

20:1; Luke 19:47; Matthew 26:55; Mark 14:49; Luke 22:53). After the arrest of Jesus, Judas threw the blood money he had received for his betrayal 'into the Temple' (Matthew 27:5) and at Jesus' death the curtain within the sanctuary was torn (Matthew 27:51; Mark 15:38; Luke 23:45).

The prominence of the Temple continues into the early days of the church, as portrayed in the book of Acts. During the interim between Jesus' ascension and the coming of the Holy Spirit, his disciples spent their time in the Temple (Luke 24:53) and the church established at Pentecost had its mass meetings in its courts (Acts 2:46). Peter and John healed a lame man there (Acts 3:1–11) and Peter was arrested for preaching publicly there (Acts 5:20–21, 26). Important events in the life of Paul also occur in the Temple, including his arrest and the beginning of his long imprisonment (Acts 21:26–30; 22:17; 24:6,12,18; 25:8).

Josephus describes the Temple

The New Testament writers assume that their readers are familiar with the general layout of the Temple and its courts, but fortunately we have quite a complete description of them from those who had actually seen them. Josephus, who had seen the Temple many times, describes it in detail, and gives a vivid ac-

Herod's Temple stands in the foreground of this carefully-researched model of Jerusalem.

count of its destruction by Roman troops in the year AD 70[1]. The Mishnah Tractate *Middoth*, a collection of the traditions of the Jewish rabbis, dates from around AD 150, but preserves the memories of earlier rabbis, providing valuable additional information for us.

To these literary sources we may add the considerable number of archaeological discoveries relating directly to the Temple as it existed during the ministry of Jesus and the time of the earliest church. Before looking in detail at some of the most interesting of these discoveries, we will give a general description, making use of both the literary and the archaeological sources.

Herod's architects constructed a massive platform on the ancient hill where the earlier temples had stood. Such platforms were typical as massive pedestals for Herodian temples. (Herod constructed a number of *pagan* temples at places such as Caesarea and Sebaste, as well as the Jerusalem Temple. Some of these have been excavated.) A similar platform can be seen intact at Hebron, where the structure built by Herod to cover the 'Tombs of the Patriarchs' has somehow survived all the vicissitudes of history and can still be visited today.

Herodian remains

At several points the Herodian platform in Jerusalem too is still visible, most notably at the so-called 'Western Wall' – a place of Jewish pilgrimage for centuries. Herod's stone-masons cut the face of their building stones in a distinctive way, helping us to determine which parts of the walls existing today date from New Testament times. More such stones can be seen at the south-east corner of the ancient platform (incorrectly known by tradition as the 'pinnacle of the Temple'). This corner is actually an artificial extension of the Temple Mount, which in its natural form was too small for Herod's grandiose design, and is constructed of a series of stone arches called 'Solomon's Stables', which have survived until the present day.

From the south, the Temple enclosure could be reached through two sets of double gates which led to tunnels emerging inside the inner courts. These entrances, called the 'Huldah Gates', are also partially visible today, as is the stairway which led up to them (see below). To the east, the Temple platform ran along the edge of a deep valley which cut through the centre of the city and was called the Tyropoean Valley or 'Valley of the Cheesemakers'. To leave or enter the Temple from this side you could cross a bridge (portions of which were discovered by the Englishman, Colonel Wilson, in the nineteenth century – and is hence called 'Wilson's Arch'), or descend into the valley itself by means of a monumental staircase. The plan of this staircase

The 'Huldah Gates' to the Temple, from the model of Jerusalem at the Holyland Hotel, Jerusalem.

Inset: The remains of the steps leading up to the Huldah Gates as they may be seen today.

was discovered during the Temple Mount excavations led by Benjamin Mazar after 1967. Mazar found that the 'Robinson Arch' named after the nineteenth-century American explorer who first noticed it, was not the arch of another bridge, as had been thought, but the beginning of this monumental staircase.

The money-changers' site

On top of the platform were several buildings in addition to the sanctuary. Across the southern end was the magnificent 'Royal Stoa', a huge colonnaded structure used for public meetings. Other porticos surrounded the enclosure, one of which, 'Solomon's Porch', was the meeting place of the earliest Jerusalem church (Acts 5:12). We may also assume that in these porticos the scholars and theologians taught (and the boy Jesus questioned them) and merchants and money-changers set up shop, angering the young Messiah.

Around the sanctuary itself was a series of courtyards, each more exclusive than the last. A three cubit high fence – the 'middle wall of partition' between Jew and Gentile (Ephesians 2:14) – marked the limit to which any non-Jew might go and featured inscriptions with dire warnings for those who did.

Climbing fourteen steps, the Jewish worshipper entered first the Court of the Women. Passing through a gate (probably the

Nicanor Gate, see 'Tombs and Bone-boxes', male Jews could enter the Court of the Israelites. Only priests could proceed into the Court of the Priests, where stood the altar, the laver and the place for the slaughtering of sacrificial animals. In front of the sanctuary stood two beautiful columns, one on each side of a magnificent doorway, and covered with a vine made of gold given by the faithful. The sight of the white marble and massive golden vine, the impressive colonnades and the gigantic platform overwhelmed the visitor; Josephus could hardly find enough superlatives to describe the sight.

The sanctuary

The interior of the sanctuary was divided into two rooms, the Holy Place, into which priests chosen by lot went to perform service (Luke 1:8–9), and the Most Holy Place, where only the High Priest might go, only once a year, on the solemn Day of Atonement.

The sanctuary and the associated buildings were destroyed by the Roman Tenth Legion during August, AD 70. The destruction was systematic and thorough, designed to break the spirit of the Jewish rebels, and it is amazing that any remnants of the original Temple enclosure have survived at all.

We cannot expect, of course, to find more than a fragment here or there. The archaeologist B. Mazar's excavations uncovered a narrow street and a broad plaza at the southern approach to the Temple Mount. The plaza was probably designed for gatherings during festivals. In addition the steps which led up to the Huldah Gates were found. A large building was discovered between the two sets of gates, perhaps a ritual bath for the use of worshippers coming up to the Temple. Tunnels found beneath this building may have led to the Temple treasury. A building found to the east of the eastern-most set of gates was probably the *Beth Din*, the Jewish religious court[2]. This building may well have been the scene of Peter and John's hearing before the Jewish Council, and also perhaps of Paul's hearing later on, both described in the book of Acts.

An impressive curbed street twelve metres (forty feet) wide was found running alongside the platform on the west. This street forks just north of the south-west corner, the right fork going to the Fortress of Antonia and the left to the upper market and the gate now known as the 'Damascus Gate'. Beneath this street excavators found a large aqueduct.

At the south-west corner of the enclosure, the western and the southern streets met. Mazar found many shops there, some with their roofs still in place, some nestled under the piers holding up the monumental staircase. Here, he concluded, was 'the focal point of daily life in the city'. High above the street, the

This remarkable inscription reads: 'To the place of trumpeting to [declare]…'.

south-west corner of the Temple enclosure commanded a view of the entire city.

The place of trumpeting

A dramatic archaeological discovery has shown this to be the spot where the trumpet was sounded officially to begin and end the Sabbath. Lying on the street immediately below the corner was a large stone with a niche for a person to stand in, with an inscription reading 'TO THE PLACE OF TRUMPETING TO (DECLARE)…' (the beginning and end of the Sabbath). Thrown from its place during the destruction of the Temple, the stone lay on the buried pavement for almost two thousand years, a witness both to the faith of those who entered the Temple to worship, and to the tragedy which befell the place.

As noted above, in several places the huge stones from which Herod's builders constructed the Temple platform may be seen today. Stones like these could well have prompted the comment of one of Jesus' disciples as he was leaving the Temple, 'Look, Teacher! What massive stones! What magnificent buildings!' Their tremendous bulk must have made them seem indestructible, and Jesus' prediction incomprehensible: '"Do you see all these great buildings?" replied Jesus. "Not one stone here will be left on another; every one will be thrown down,"' (Mark 13:1–2).

Jesus' prediction was quite literally fulfilled as far as the buildings were concerned. Here and there a few courses of the platform itself have survived, enough to demonstrate the immensity of the project. But the size of the stones still pales

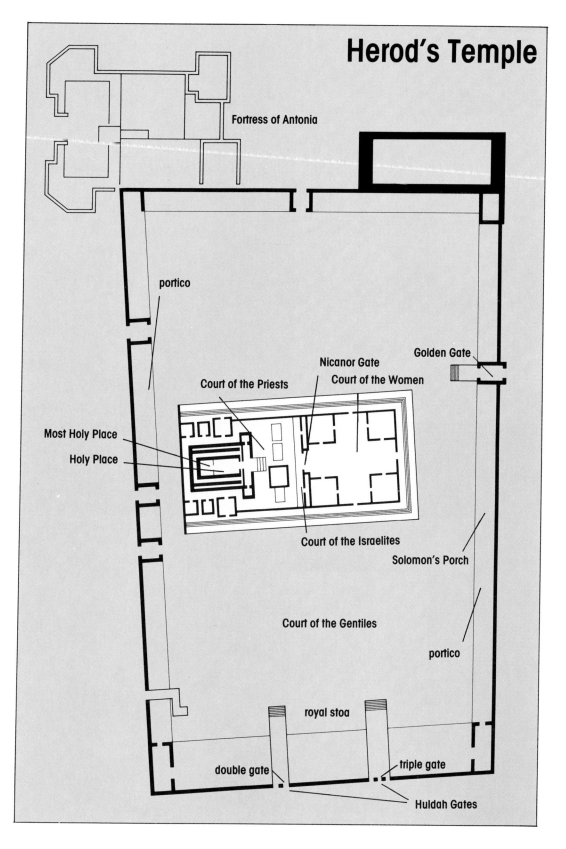

Herod's Temple

Fortress of Antonia

portico

Golden Gate

Nicanor Gate

Court of the Priests

Court of the Women

Most Holy Place

Holy Place

Court of the Israelites

Solomon's Porch

Court of the Gentiles

portico

royal stoa

double gate

triple gate

Huldah Gates

visibly in comparison with those found during the digging of the so-called 'Rabbinic Tunnel' which runs for some 180 metres (600 feet) along the western wall of the enclosure, beneath the Arab houses and shops on the site today. The tunnel, dug to allow worshippers to pray somewhat nearer the supposed site of the Holy of Holies, is entered by passing under Wilson's Arch. This arch was found in 1864 under the modern Gate of the Chain leading into the sacred enclosure, and it was here that the English excavator Sir Charles Warren found a series of vaulted rooms, a corridor and a large hall between 1867–70.

The rabbis' tunnel

The modern rabbis have extended the tunnel along the wall past some incredibly large building stones. One of these stones measures seventeen metres (forty-six feet) long, three metres (ten feet) tall, and three metres (ten feet) deep. It weighs 450 tons! According to Josephus, even this monster is dwarfed by another which he says was twenty-two metres (seventy-five feet) long. By comparison, the largest stone at Stonehenge weighs a mere forty tons.

Naturally, the question arises how such stones could have been put in place without the use of modern machinery. The stones are not cut from the bedrock on the site, but can be traced to a quarry about one kilometre (half a mile) north, just outside the present Damascus Gate. How were they transported? One theory is that they were quarried as cylinders and rolled down the twelve-metre (forty foot) street, between the curbs. When in place, one side was cut flat and the stone rolled over, the sides trimmed (the pieces trimmed off in this way might weigh up to sixty tons!) and finally the top was cut flat, ready for the next course. This theory gains some credence, because a large stone cylinder which had broken, and was thus rejected, has actually been found in the quarry area, and a five metre (sixteen foot) long D-shaped stone (a 'trimming') has been found in the the rabbinic tunnel.

The Golden Gate

On the other side of the enclosure, the east, there stands today a gate blocked by stones and known as the Golden Gate. This gate dates to relatively modern times, but in 1969 a young man named James Fleming was examining the gate, when something curious happened. The ground gave way beneath his feet and he found himself inside a Moslem tomb, looking at *another* gate beneath the modern one. On either side of this second gate were stones which scholars believe to be even older than the Herodian ones. It is even possible that this gate is much older than the Herodian Temple and is perhaps a remnant of the en-

closure of Solomon's Temple. Perhaps this gate, already a thousand years old in Jesus' day, was incorporated into the plan of Herod's Temple. Situated to the east, this would have been the gate used by pilgrims coming from the direction of Bethany, and thus quite possibly the gate used by Jesus during his triumphal entry into the city (Mark 11:1–11; Luke 19:41–5).

Inside the present Golden Gate, at its south-west corner, there is the head of a pillar or capital, which has been assembled from two older ones. The style and craftsmanship of these older capitals has led scholars to date them to the Herodian Temple; they may originally have formed part of the older gate, now buried beneath the ground, as it was remodelled by Herod the Great's builders.

Within the sacred enclosure, no excavation is possible today. This area is not only sacred to the Moslems, but is also very sensitive politically. In 1972 a plumbing ditch was dug in the enclosure which showed no signs of accumulated debris. This may mean that, should excavation be permitted, parts of the structures connected with the Temple could still be found directly beneath the present buildings. We know that some early Christian writers suggest that such remains could still be seen on the Temple Mount after the destruction of AD 70. One scholar has studied the pillars in the present buildings in the south-west corner of the enclosure, called the Moslem Museum and the

The city walls and Golden Gate, Jerusalem.

123

Women's Mosque. He concluded that these buildings stand right over the columns which once held up the Royal Stoa of Herod, suggesting that the foundations of the Stoa may still exist beneath the floors of the present structures.

Inside the sanctuary

According to eyewitness accounts, the sanctuary and its accompanying buildings were highly decorated. These decorations showed great skill, but conformed strictly to the rabbinical prohibitions against showing any representations of people or animals (one striking exception is discussed below). While excavating along the southern enclosure wall, Mazar's workers found many fragments of these decorations featuring geometric and floral designs. In fact, just inside the double gate are two domes on which the original Herodian plaster designs have almost miraculously survived *in situ*.

Bits and pieces of the Temple complex may be seen re-used in the ruins of later buildings uncovered on the site. For example, columns which probably once belonged to the Royal Stoa are found in the walls of Arab palaces built later at the foot of the southern wall.

Among the shops beneath and around the monumental staircase, the excavators found weights inscribed 'YEAR 5 OF KING AGRIPPA, LOYAL TO CAESAR. MINA.' A 'Mina' is a measure of weight, and the fifth year of Herod Agrippa, the grandson of Herod the Great, is AD 41/42. These weights, therefore, were in use by merchants serving pilgrims coming to the Temple during the first decade of the existence of the Jerusalem church.

The seven-branched candlestick

During excavations conducted in the nearby section of Jerusalem called the Jewish Quarter, archaeologists found a seven-branched candlestick, or menorah, inscribed on plaster which had once decorated a house in the area. Since the house may date from before AD 70, this menorah is especially important because it was drawn by someone who had actually seen the seven-branched candlestick in the Herodian Temple – indeed, the house was itself in sight of the Temple enclosure. Although the drawing is simple and schematic, it is carefully done, and more likely to represent the actual first-century menorah than the famous representation on the Arch of Titus in Rome, a representation which probably came from the artistic imagination of a Roman sculptor.

One object found in the Temple Mount excavations seems to flout the prohibition against depicting persons or animals. Scratched rather crudely on a stone vessel are depictions of two pigeons or doves; alongside the pictures is the word KRBN, 'corban' – a word meaning 'a sacrifice dedicated to God'. It is the term which, according to Jesus, the Pharisaic legalists used to try to avoid fulfilling their responsibilities to their parents (Mark 7:9–13).

The 'corban'

This simple vessel carries us dramatically into the New Testament world, for it is clear that it is inscribed to indicate to anyone who saw it its specific use: 'When the time of their purification according to the Law of Moses had been completed, Joseph and Mary took him to Jerusalem to present him to the Lord (as it is written in the Law of the Lord, "Every firstborn male is to be consecrated to the Lord"), and *to offer a sacrifice in keeping with what is said in the Law of the Lord: "A pair of doves or two young pigeons"'* (present writer's italics). It must have been into a bowl like this that the sacrifice which consecrated the infant Jesus was placed. The word 'Corban' was thus a warning to any who might see the slaughtered birds that they were not for secular use, but were holy to the Lord.

Other inscriptions have been uncovered which take us back to Herod's Temple. Two ossuary inscriptions marking the burials of 'Simon, the Temple Builder' and 'Nicanor of Alexandria who made the Gates' are described elsewhere, in the chapter 'Tombs and Bone-boxes'. Perhaps the most striking of all has been the recovery of two of the actual stone inscriptions warning Gentiles not to pass beyond the 'middle wall of partition' between the outer court and the Court of the Women. Josephus says that these warnings were inscribed in the Greek, Hebrew and Latin languages.

Two inscriptions

The two inscriptions which have been recovered are both in Greek. The first was found in 1871 by the French archaeologist C. Clermont-Ganneau. A second example came to light in 1938, having been found near St Stephen's gate, a modern gate in the north-east section of the eastern wall of the Temple enclosure. The inscription is chilling. It reads: 'No foreigner is to enter within the balustrade and enclosure around the temple area. Whoever is caught will have himself to blame for his death, which will follow.'

The totally uncompromising tone of this inscription helps us to understand the reaction of the crowd described in a story about the apostle Paul recorded in Acts 21. Some of Paul's enemies from Asia saw him in the Temple. Having previously seen him in the company of a Greek named Trophimus, the Ephesian, they concluded that he had taken a Gentile beyond the forbidden fence. They then seized him and shouted 'Men of

Israel, help us! This is the man who teaches all men everywhere against our people and our law and this place. And besides, he has brought Greeks into the temple area and defiled this holy place' (Acts 21:28). The whole city was aroused and a mob seized Paul, dragged him from the Temple 'and immediately the gates were shut' (21:30). The inscriptions help us to see just how serious was Paul's supposed crime in the eyes of a first-century Jewish crowd, and how flagrant his alleged act of ignoring such a stern warning.

Souvenir bottles

Curiously, one artifact linked directly to the Temple of Jesus' day may be found in the New York Metropolitan Museum of Art, resting unobtrusively in a case with other examples of ancient glasswork. This small six-sided bottle attracted little attention until a similar one was found during excavations in the Jewish Quarter in Jerusalem in 1976. Both bottles have the signature of their maker, Ennion, a famous first-century glassmaker from Sidon, a city on the Mediterranean coast of southern Lebanon. Each of the remaining five panels has a representation of some aspect of the Jewish Feast of Sukkoth (the Feast of Tabernacles). On each day of the seven-day festival, water was brought from the Pool of Siloam and poured out at the altar on the Temple Mount in an attempt to ensure that enough rain would fall to water the flocks and produce the crops for the following year.

One panel on the bottle pictures the tall jug used to bring the ceremonial water; another depicts the reed-flutes used by the musicians; a third shows keys, the symbol for the autumn and spring rains, and of rain and resurrection. A vine and grape cluster are the common symbols for Israel, and possibly the vine design around the jar echoes the golden vine decorating the facade of the sanctuary.

These beautiful little bottles seem to have been 'souvenirs' produced in Sidon, but sold in the market-places around the Temple to pilgrims who had come to the Holy City for this important feast. The example in New York was found in Cyprus, no doubt carried there by a faithful Jew, who may even have filled it with precious water from the Pool of Siloam during his pilgrimage, just as modern pilgrims sometimes take home water from the river Jordan or the Sea of Galilee.

Again, by means of these humble souvenirs, the New Testament world is brought very near, for the seventh chapter of John's Gospel records Jesus' own experience during the Feast of Sukkoth. We may easily imagine the scene: Jesus was teaching in the Temple court (John 7:28) when the priests entered with the sacred water from the pool of Siloam, carried with great ceremony up into the holy enclosure: 'On the last and greatest day of the Feast, Jesus stood and said in a loud voice, '"If any man is thirsty, let him come to me and drink. Whoever believes in me, as the Scripture has said, streams of living water will flow from within him"' (John 7:37–38).

Holy of Holies

As we have seen, the sanctuary itself has been completely lost. It would certainly have borne the brunt of the general destruction by the Romans in AD 70. We are not even certain as to precisely where it stood. One author has suggested that the Holy of Holies stood where the little Moslem dome called the 'Dome of the Spirits' now stands. He points out that the ancient Golden Gate leads direct to this site, and believes that bits of the actual foundations of the sanctuary may be seen in the north-west corner of the present enclosure. His theory has been much criticized, however; proof of the precise location of the sanctuary, one of the world's most beautiful buildings, still eludes us.

This coin, dating from the time of the Second Revolt, depicts Herod's Temple, with a stylized version of the Ark of the Covenant inside.

We do, in all likelihood, have a picture of the sanctuary. Like other first-century illustrations, this one is found on a coin. A large silver coin issued by a Jewish government almost certainly depicts the sanctuary. The scholar Alice Muehsam has argued that some of these coins were actually minted during the First Revolt, in the years AD 66–68, and thus were designed while the Temple still stood. Most experts, however, believe the coins date from the Second Revolt of the Jews against the Romans, which occurred in AD 132–35, and was led by the enigmatic leader called Bar Kokhba. If so, it is quite possible that some people who had seen Herod's Temple were still living, though they would have been quite old by that time. They could presumably have provided the information used in designing the coin.

At any rate, the coin's depiction of the Temple façade with its two columns, framed below with a colonnade (most likely 'Solomon's Porch') may be confidently taken as an accurate representation of the appearance of this famous building. Within the doors, instead of the cult statue which normally appears on ancient coins depicting temples, there is an object in the shape of a chest – the Ark of the Covenant. The actual Ark had been lost to the Babylonians centuries before, but the stylized box shown on the coin was as close as any pious first-century Jew might be expected to come to depicting the presence of God in the Holy of Holies.

Where was Jesus Buried?

According to the Gospels, the trial of Jesus took place in a praetorium or a fortress, which is also called a palace (Mark 15:16). The Roman military governor, Pontius Pilate, pronounced the sentence from 'The judge's seat at a place known as The Stone Pavement, which is in Aramaic Gabbatha' (John 19:13). After being mocked by soldiers inside the praetorium, Jesus was then taken to 'the place called Golgotha (which means The Place of the Skull)' (Mark 15:22; see also Matthew 27:33; Luke 23:33; John 19:17), for execution.

For many generations it has been customary for Christian pilgrims in Jerusalem to follow a street leading from St Stephen's Gate, in the northern part of the eastern wall of the city, winding its way to the venerable old Church of the Holy Sepulchre. This, they have believed, was the *Via Dolorosa*, the Way of Sorrows, down which Jesus passed on his way to death and burial. On the right of the street, a few paces west of the gate, they have seen an arch (called the *Ecce Homo* arch, 'Here is the man', John 19:5), and perhaps even visited the excavations inside the convent of the Sisters of Zion, where an ancient stone pavement has seemed to them to be Gabbatha itself.

The garden tomb
Other pilgrims, from a different tradition, have visited a quiet garden just outside the walls north of the Damascus Gate, and gazed respectfully at a tomb cut into the rock there, close to a small rocky bluff which seemed to look like a skull, confident they were visiting the tomb of Jesus. Having visited the Church of the Holy Sepulchre, with its dark maze of chapels, its ornate altars, its smell of incense and sound of strange chants in strange languages, they have been convinced that such a place cannot possibly be the location of Golgotha and the tomb. They have preferred to accept the opinion of the British general 'Chinese' Gordon who, noting that the Church of the Holy Sepulchre was inside the walls of the city, and reading that Jesus was killed outside the walls (Hebrews 13:12: 'Jesus also suffered outside the city gate'), found the quiet garden a more likely spot.

Modern archaeological investigation has thrown considerable light on the old controversies regarding the place of Jesus' trial, crucifixion and burial. While we cannot consider the question of locations definitely proved one way or the other, we can draw tentative conclusions with some confidence.

Gordon's Calvary

First, modern archaeologists almost unanimously discount the validity of 'Gordon's Calvary'. Gordon did not know what is now known, namely, that the walls of Jerusalem follow a different course today than in the days of Jesus. His rejection of the Church of the Holy Sepulchre as the place of crucifixion and burial, because the church is inside the walls, no longer holds. We know now that in Jesus' time the area where the church stands was in fact *outside* the walls. Further, anyone who has studied Gordon's reasoning for locating the tomb in the garden north of present walls will see that some of his arguments border on the bizarre, and cannot be taken seriously.

On the other hand, the traditional route of the *Via Dolorosa* may now be seriously questioned, too. Archaeological discoveries, and the careful study of the ancient records, make it much more likely that Jesus carried his cross through an entirely different part of the city. This conclusion is based on the growing belief among historians and archaeologists that the praetorium mentioned in the Gospels was not the 'Fortress of Antonia', the imposing military building standing at the northwest corner of the Temple enclosure. Josephus describes this fortress in detail in his account of the ferocious battle that took

Modern pilgrims follow the *Via Dolorosa* through the narrow streets of the Old City of Jerusalem.

Above: 'Gordon's Calvary': a rock-face with a supposedly skull-like configuration, held by General Gordon to be Golgotha.

place there during the First Revolt against Rome[1]. Herod the Great's predecessors built the fortress; Herod enlarged and improved it, using it as his headquarters in Jerusalem from 35 to 32 BC. At this point, he built himself a huge new palace on the western hill of the city[2].

The Antonia Fortress

The fortress stood, as we have said, at the north-west corner of the Temple terrace, separated by a deep trench sixty-four metres (seventy yards) wide and 180 metres (200 yards) long, from the 'hill of Bezetha', a new suburb outside the walls of the city and to the north. The fortress was built on a base of solid rock running 111 metres (123 yards) west to east. This rock has since been mostly cut away; what is left forms the foundation for a Moslem girls' school which stands today on the site of a nineteenth-century Turkish barracks. Portions of the rock can still be seen from inside the Temple enclosure. Herod had the rock covered with marble slabs, and built two large stairways leading down to the Temple terrace. At the north-west entrance was a double pool called Strouthion ('the Swallow') which served as a protective moat. During the First Revolt, the Roman general Titus put an earth dam across this moat to force an entrance to the fortress[3].

Although the trial of Jesus probably took place elsewhere, the Fortress of Antonia does play a prominent role in one biblical story – the arrest of the apostle Paul (Acts 21:27–22:29). Seized in the Temple enclosure, Paul was dragged out and a riot began. The Romans kept a contingent of soldiers in the Antonia precisely because riots occurred so often in and around the Temple. From their high vantage point, the soldiers could react quickly to such upheavals. Paul was 'rescued' by the Roman soldiers and taken to the Antonia. He stopped on the steps (Acts 21:35,40) and, standing there, delivered a speech to the crowd. After this, he was taken into the barracks to be flogged (22:24).

Hadrian's city

Excavations during the last hundred years have gradually revealed the history of this corner of ancient Jerusalem. We now know that the Emperor Hadrian reconstructed the area in the early second century, building a monumental gateway to the city from the east, with a large paved courtyard just inside. Two arches of the gateway remain, one the so-called 'Ecce Homo' arch, the other inside the chapel of the convent of the Sisters of Zion. Parts of the pavement have been found under a nearby Franciscan monastery, under the convent, and under a Greek Orthodox building. This pavement extended over a large area some thirty-two metres by forty eight metres (2270 square yards) and covered over the Strouthion Pools, converting them into cisterns *under* the pavement. So this pavement cannot possibly be the 'Pavement' of John 19:13, since it was constructed one hundred years after Jesus' trial.

Besides, the name given to the pavement in the Gospels, Gabbatha, means 'height'. It would seem more natural to seek for it in the Upper City, that is, the area where Herod built his new palace. For this, and other reasons mentioned below, the trial of Jesus seems much more likely to have occurred there.

Herod's palace is also described in detail by Josephus[4], particularly because it was also the site of a battle during the First Revolt. Although sumptuous in its appointments, this complex also served as a fortress, surrounded by its own set of walls. Herod, ever cautious, had constructed it so that he could protect himself from any future uprisings among his unwilling Jewish subjects.

The Roman garrison was quartered in the Antonia Fortress in Jerusalem, seen here as reconstructed in the scale model at the Holyland Hotel.

Herod's towers Phasael, Hippicus and Mariamne, from the model of Jerusalem.

Opposite: The citadel, Jerusalem, probable site of Herod's Palace.

Herod's towers

To the north of his lodgings, Herod built three impressive towers: Phasael, Hippicus and Mariamne. Almost a hundred years old when the city was destroyed, Titus left the towers intact as an offering, says Josephus, 'to his own luck, which had proved his ally and enabled him to overcome impregnable defences'[5]. The archaeologist C.N. Johns, excavating between 1934 and 1948, showed that Herod had inserted the towers in an older wall, just as Josephus had said. One tower has survived to a height of several courses until the present day; it is usually thought to be Phasael (though Hippicus has also been suggested) and is one of the most substantial remains from Jesus' day still standing above ground in modern Jerusalem.

The Israeli archaeologists Ruth Amiran and A. Eitan, excavating in 1968–69 inside the 'Citadel' (the Turkish fortress just south of the modern Jaffa Gate), found the remains of the massive platform on which Herod's palace complex had been constructed. More of the same platform was found in excavations in the Armenian garden some distance south of the Citadel. The platform was thus found to measure over 300 metres (325 yards) north to south and some 60–130 metres (65–140 yards) east to west.

On the platform in the Citadel were found the foundations of two buildings, many fragments of coloured plaster (used to decorate the wealthy homes of the time), many pieces of bowls in

'*terra sigillata*' style (a type of red pottery typical of Herodian times), Herodian lamps and many coins dating from before AD 70. There was also evidence of the fire which destroyed the palace in AD 70. No structures were found on the platform in the Armenian garden, probably because a thousand years later the Crusaders had cleared everything away in order to build their own palace on the platform, so destroying whatever remained of Herod's palace. The excavators of the Armenian garden, D. Bahar and M. Broshi, believe that the area between the towers and the main palace was filled with storerooms, workshops, quarters for servants and barracks for soldiers.

The site of Jesus' trial

The Gospel of John makes it clear that the trial of Jesus took place at the residence of the Roman military governor, Pontius Pilate – more precisely, a good deal of the activity took place *outside* the residence: 'Then they led Jesus from the house of Caiaphas to the praetorium ... they themselves did not enter the praetorium, so that they might not be defiled ... So Pilate went out to them ... Pilate entered the praetorium again and called Jesus ... he went out to the Jews again ...' (John 18:28–38). Notice especially John 19:13: 'He brought Jesus out and sat down on the judgment seat at a place called The Pavement [literally "the paved place"], and in Hebrew, '*Gabbatha*' [literally "the raised place"].'

The description here suggests an outdoor *bema* – a podium with a large paved square, where large numbers of people could see and hear a speaker. In fact, Josephus describes a scene at this precise location some years later, when the procurator, or Roman governor, was Florus. 'Florus slept in the palace, and the next day had a dais erected outside and took his seat'[6] from which he addressed the people. Compare this with Matthew 27:19: 'While Pilate was sitting on the judgment seat, his wife sent word to him ...' We may presume that the large gathering of the chief priests, the rulers and the people described in Luke 23:13 took place at Gabbatha as well.

Following Jesus' trial, 'the soldiers led him away inside the palace (that is, the praetorium); and they called together the whole battalion ...' to mock him (Mark 15:16; see also Matthew 27:27). This battalion would be the regular palace guard of the procurator. Finally, they 'led him out' (of the palace), seized a passer-by, Simon of Cyrene, 'who was coming in from the country' (and thus was near a city *gate*) and forced him to carry the cross. The true *Via Dolorosa*, then, most probably began somewhere just to the east of the present Armenian garden, and moved north, past a large reservoir called Hezekiah's Pool, and out through the wall to the place of execution.

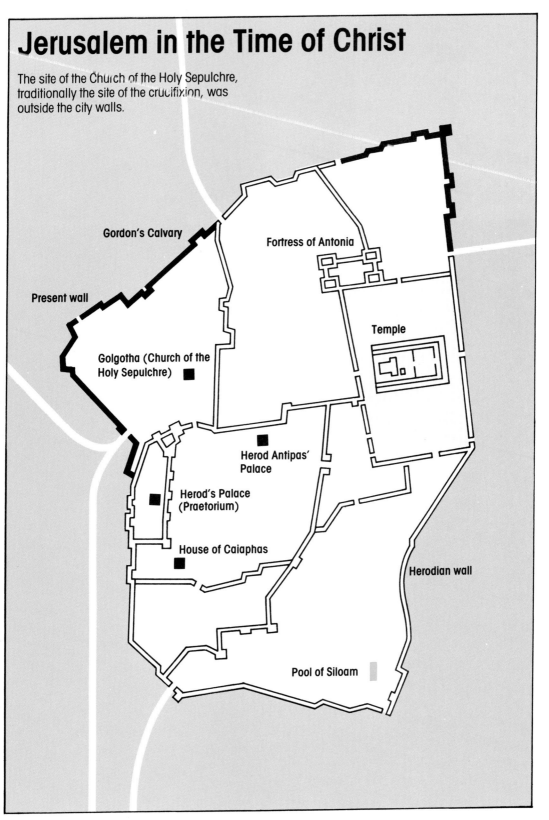

Jerusalem in the Time of Christ

The site of the Church of the Holy Sepulchre, traditionally the site of the crucifixion, was outside the city walls.

Gordon's Calvary

Fortress of Antonia

Present wall

Temple

Golgotha (Church of the Holy Sepulchre) ■

Herod Antipas' Palace ■

Herod's Palace (Praetorium) ■

House of Caiaphas ■

Herodian wall

Pool of Siloam

Above: The Church of the Holy Sepulchre.

Below: A first-century tomb at the Church of the Holy Sepulchre.

The site of Golgotha

Before attempting to locate Golgotha, let us gather together some additional biblical evidence which bears on the location of the site. It was, as we have seen, 'outside the wall' (not simply on the basis of the theological statement in Hebrews 13:12, but because by custom executions and burials were carried out only outside city walls). Nevertheless, the site was 'near the city' (John 19:20). A multitude followed, implying a procession through the streets (Luke 23:27). The site was near a roadway, since 'passers-by mocked him' (Mark 15:29; Matthew 27:39). It was not on a high hill, since these passers-by could read the inscription placed above Jesus' head (John 19:20). It was in a 'garden' (John 19:41; 20:15) which included not only a place of execution, but also a tomb (John 19:41).

The overall effect of recent archaeology is to make more and more plausible the traditional site of the crucifixion – the area now covered by the Church of the Holy Sepulchre. It cannot be said that this tie is *proved* to be correct, but at least the evidence does not make such an identification impossible, and in fact builds up to make it a strong possibility.

The Temple of Venus

A key to positive identification lies in what we make of a story told by the ancient church historian Eusebius in his *Life of Con-*

stantine. About AD 340, the Emperor Constantine, intent on building a monument to the burial place of Jesus, asked the local residents of Jerusalem where the site was to be found. They pointed him to the ruined Temple of Venus, constructed by the Emperor Hadrian when he rebuilt the city of Jerusalem some two centuries before, renaming it Aelia Capitolina. The spot was well within the walls of the fourth-century city. There was no way that mid-fourth century Jerusalemites could know first-hand what lay beneath the Hadrian's immense temple, yet they convinced Constantine that he should go to great effort and expense to remove this building. Constantine was no fool, and we can only presume that the local conviction was so tied to a long tradition that he felt confident enough to undertake the project.

To this day, the results are there for all to see. Under Hadrian's temple, in the area which formed the very centre of Aelia Capitolina (for the palace and forum were next to it), Constantine's 'excavators' found a tomb! In fact, more than one tomb existed at the spot – a small cemetery, as the casual visitor to today's Church of the Holy Sepulchre may discover by walking behind the monument called the sepulchre and viewing the openings cut into the rock.

In 1885 yet another tomb was found, in the Coptic monastery near the church. These tombs are *kokhim*-type tombs; in one of them was found an ossuary or bone-box. There is thus no doubt that they are first-century tombs (see 'Tombs and Bone-boxes').

If any Christian tradition were to survive the early centuries in Jerusalem, the tradition of the location of the tomb of Jesus would seem the likeliest candidate. The Christians of Constantine's day would hardly have simply made a lucky guess, and indeed the site they pointed out was so improbable that only the strongest of traditions would have held out against the improbability.

The Place of the Skull

Nearby, Constantine's workmen uncovered a rock outcrop, apparently already cut away to around five or six cubic metres size, but obviously once considerably larger. It will be remembered that the Gospels call the place of crucifixion Golgotha (John 19:17) or *Kraniou* (compare the English 'cranium'; Luke 23:33), or 'The Place of The Skull' (Mark 15:22; Matthew 28:33). General Gordon, and others since, have thought this meant 'looking like a skull', that is, having depressions resembling the eye-sockets of a skull. We know, however, that to this day the Arabs call a small rocky hillock a *ras* ('head'), and it is likely that the term 'skull' in the Gospels means no more than that the crucifixion took place on such an outcrop.

Further, V. Corbo's excavation below the so-called 'Adam's Chapel' inside the church of the Holy Sepulchre revealed an extensive quarry-bed west of the Golgotha rock, out of which the rock seems to have jutted. To this we should add the discovery by the famous British archaeologist Dame Kathleen Kenyon, in the nearby area called the Muristan, that no-one inhabited the area between the seventh century BC and the second century AD (the time of Hadrian). Several feet of fill lay beneath the present surface, containing pottery from those two periods *only*, with no pottery from the period between. Then, beneath the fill, she found evidence of quarrying, which not only showed that the quarry was extensive but also that the area was *outside the walls* between the seventh century BC and the second century AD. (No-one would build a quarry *inside* the city!)

The 'garden' gate

In fact, Josephus describes not only a city wall running from Herod's western palace to the Temple Mount but also a 'second wall' which, he says, 'started from a gate in the first wall called Gennath Gate. It enclosed only the district on the north and extended as far as Antonia'[7]. Why did this wall not enclose the area north of the palace? We may presume it was because this area was covered by an old quarry, which made it difficult to build on. The name of the gate leading from the city into this area is very significant: Gennath means 'garden'!

The archaeologist B. Pixner's reconstruction of the situation seems entirely reasonable: An ancient quarry dating from before the Exile covered the area now called the Muristan quarter. Herod converted the unusable land between the first and second walls into a sort of park or garden, so that visitors going in and out of Jerusalem by the Gennath Gate would have pleasant surroundings. However, at the north end of the garden, an outcrop of rock (perhaps not suitable for quarrying) was gradually covered by the accretions of time and became a hillock or 'skull-hill'. This hillock, conspicuous to all who entered or left the city, became an ideal spot for public executions. During the same period another part of the quarry, north of the hill, became a private garden in which a number of wealthy people had tombs built for themselves. One of these people was Joseph of Arimathea, and one of the tombs, tended by a gardener, became the tomb of Jesus. The resurrected Jesus was mistakenly identified by the woman as the gardener (John 20:15).

Agrippa's wall

King Herod Agrippa, the grandson of Herod the Great, started to build a third wall for Jerusalem, which would have circled the city from the Hippicus tower, around the new suburb which

The nail-pierced bone of a young man who had been crucified, discovered in 1968 by the archaeologist Vasilios Tsaferis.

had grown up north of the city (called Bethesda, 'New City' in Aramaic), and ending at the north-east corner of the Temple enclosure. The British archaeologist Hennessy, during his excavations at the Damascus Gate in the present northern wall of the city between 1964–66, found that Agrippa apparently did not finish this project.

Some eighty-five years later Hadrian incorporated Agrippa's work into his own extensive rebuilding project. Recent excavations make it possible to walk through one side of the ancient gate and stand inside the massive guard rooms built by Hadrian at that time. Since the quarry area was now inside the walls, we must assume that the garden tombs had to be abandoned. Undaunted by the difficulty of the task, Hadrian filled in the quarry in order to build a large civic complex, complete with a temple to Venus, on the site. In so doing, he covered both the tomb of Jesus and Golgotha, hiding and preserving them until the time of Constantine.

In addition to the excavations of Corbo, mentioned above, it should be noted that in 1975–76, the archaeologist D. Katsimibinis was able to uncover for the first time the whole eastern slope of what remains of Golgotha. He found that the rock rises from the quarry floor to a height of thirteen metres (thirty feet). At several places in the Church of the Holy Sepulchre we can now see portions of the white rock exposed to view.

The crucified man
Until recently archaeology has not helped us understand the nature of the act of crucifixion itself. The written records of Roman times document thousands of executions by crucifixion, but among the hundreds of excavated burials from the period no actual case of crucifixion was found until 1968. Most probably victims of crucifixion, which was designed to be the most

Artist's impression of the position of the body during crucifixion, based on the skeleton discovered at Giv'at Hamivtar.

degrading of deaths, were simply torn from their crosses and thrown into the rubbish tip, where they eventually disappeared without a trace.

In 1968, Vasilias Tsaferis found a number of first-century burials in a tomb at Giv'at Hamivtar in Jerusalem, among them an ossuary with the bones of a baby and a young man in his twenties. An inscription on the box reads: 'Yehohanan, son of the one hanged with his knees apart'. An eight-inch nail has been driven through the anklebones of the young man, and scratches on the bones of the forearm tell the story – that he met his death by crucifixion.

We do not know whether he was killed during the mass crucifixions carried out in 7 BC, during the First Revolt, when the Romans crucified thousands, or whether this was simply an individual execution. Experts have analyzed the bones and concluded that the knees had been semi-flexed during the crucifixion and the nail driven through the side of the foot, causing the man to hang in an unnatural, twisted position. Nails were also hammered into the forearm just above the wrist, where the scratches betray the agonized writhing of the victim. The feet did not bear the weight of the body (the nail had been bent over after it passed through the legs), so perhaps the man was placed on a sort of seat on the cross, his trunk contorted and his arms stretched out. The quite clean break in the leg bones suggests that he was either cut down from the cross, or had his legs broken (see John 19:31–33). Like Jesus, this young man, having suffered this horrible form of execution, was taken by loved ones and given a respectable burial in a family tomb.

The Gospels claim, of course, that Jesus' body did not decay, but that he was raised from death long before the customary second burial in an ossuary could be performed. This may be why they speak of his being placed in the *mnemeion* (literally 'monument') rather than a *taiphos* ('grave'). We have noted elsewhere the burial practices and the nature of the rock-hewn tombs which form the backdrop for the account of Jesus' burial. The Gospels seem to suggest that the body of Jesus was laid in the entrance room of a tomb complex, perhaps on one of the stone benches surrounding this first room. From that place, they maintain, he rose and came forth.

References

The Bible and Archaeology

1. *Life of Constantine* 3.42–27
2. Hist. Sac. 2.33
3. Hist. Eccl. 1.7–8
4. Hist. Eccl. 1.17
5. Hist. Eccl. 2.1.2
6. Hist. Eccl. 1.17

What Did Jesus Look Like?

1. Kindler, *Israel Exploration Journal* I (1950) p.176 Pl 32:2
2. Reif 71; Hendin 78 (p.42)
3. Madden p.106–7; Meshorer Pl XIII: 92; Kindler 55

Where are the Lake Cities of Galilee?

1. Ben Dor, 'Link Expedition', BA 24 (1961), 58
2. *War* II:168
3. *Ant.* XVIII:V:6
4. *Vita*: 71–4
5. *Christian News from Israel* XXVII:4

6. Josephus, *Ant.* XVIII:4:6
7. *Vita* 9

Tombs and Bone-boxes

1. Sanhedrin 47b
2. b.Shabb.152b
3. *Israel Exploration Journal* 12:1962, p.1–12
4. Massekhet Semahot 14:3

The Jerusalem Temple

1. *War* V:184–247; VI:220–87
2. Mishnah *Sanhedrin* II:1

Where was Jesus Buried?

1. *War* 5:192, 238–45, 467–71
2. Josephus, *Ant.* 15:292
3. Josephus, *War* 5:467–71
4. *War*, Book 5
5. *War*, 4:402
6. *War*, 2:175, 301, 308
7. *War*, 5.4.2 (146)

Index

Photograph acknowledgments

British Museum   8, 9 (bottom),
22, 23, 24 (both), 39, 43, 44
(bottom), 45, 63 (bottom), 69
(both), 70, 101 (margin), 112,
127.
Tim Dowley   10, 18 (bottom),
21, 26, 30 (top), 36, 40 (top), 48,
60, 75, 81, 84, 85, 86, 89, 90, 93,
98, 102, 105, 108 (top), 110, 116,
123, 131, 133.
Sonia Halliday Photographs   64,
65.
Illustrated London News   13.
John McRay   19, 20, 25, 92, 118
(inset).
Radio Times Hulton Picture
Library   9 (top), 103 (bottom).
Zev Radovan, Jerusalem   30
(bottom), 32, 33 (top), 35, 40
(bottom), 46, 47, 51, 52, 53
(both), 57 (inset), 58 (both), 61,
71, 72, 73, 111, 120.
John Wilson   17, 18 (top), 77,
80, 82, 87, 88, 91, 94, 95, 96, 97,
118, 136 (bottom), 139.
Peter Wyart   6, 7, 29 (both), 44
(top), 59, 63 (top), 78, 79, 83, 99,
100, 101, 103 (margin), 106, 107,
108 (bottom), 129, 130, 132, 136
(top).

All maps, diagrams and
illustrations by James Macdonald

cooked for myself. I was a student, I didn't have much money, and I basically lived on pasta for three years. Oh, and chips. And pitta bread and hummus. And then, of course, there was alcohol – rivers of it. We drank all the time, as though it was perfectly normal, which maybe for students it is. It is also unbelievably fattening, at least if your mixer of choice is lemonade, as mine was, and your favourite drink is (or was) Southern Comfort. At this point, needless to say, the daily walks and the compulsory lacrosse had gone out the window, though I did bicycle everywhere. I left university a size fourteen to sixteen on top and a twelve below. I was well upholstered, shall we say, more curvaceous than was entirely fashionable, but I looked pretty good, in a 1950s kind of way. I certainly had no 'issues' with my weight. Indeed I never weighed myself: I didn't own a pair of scales until the summer of 2005.

Life went on. I worked in a series of newspaper offices, which are seldom what you'd call dry zones. Pub at lunchtime. Quick drink or three after work. More sandwiches, grabbed on the hoof. Crisps. Sausage rolls. Chocolate bars and biscuits and cups of sugary tea. Egg McMuffins. No more bicycling, exercise down to zero, unless you count walking to and from the Tube. I was a sixteen all over, and it had just started to bother me slightly – I was reconciled to the tits, but the size sixteen waist wasn't part of the plan. I'd got to the stage where I vaguely thought I probably ought to do something about it. Then I got pregnant.

Chances are you've been there. It's so bloody hard to shift, isn't it? And it hardly seemed to be a priority; I was too busy being delighted with my baby to worry too much about my waistline, or the lack of it. But it was at this point, aged around twenty-seven, that I started having minor difficulties with clothes shopping. I could no longer buy anything very fitted or tailored; it just really didn't look good. But I put it to the back of my mind and lived, as many young mothers do, in leggings and baggy jumpers. When I needed to dress up, I wore forgiving, stretchy things with a high Lycra content. I took comfort in the knowledge that I still had good legs; if I felt fat, I'd wear slightly shorter skirts and a bit of a heel. It didn't occur to me at the time that I was storing all my weight on my upper half, or that I was heading for egg balanced on pipe cleaners territory. I still didn't own a set of scales.

I got pregnant again a few years later, and had a second Caesarean section. By this stage my stomach – never my best feature – was a disaster area. I avoided looking at it in the bath and made sure my then husband never got a look at it. I was so successful at concealing it from him that one year he bought me some Agent Provocateur lingerie for Christmas, complete with tiny, sexy little knickers which, had I worn them, would have sat right on my C-section scar, with my excess of stomach muffining attractively over the top.

The stomach wasn't the only thing muffining. At home all day with two small children, I seemed to be eating constantly. I'd make the boys breakfast, and hoover up their leftovers. We'd have a snack at about eleven. I drank cups and cups of tea, with one big sugar per cup. I'd have my lunch, then pick at theirs. Then I'd pick at their tea. Then I'd make dinner, and eat it with my (irritatingly whip-thin) husband. We'd usually have some wine, and then blob out on the sofa, perhaps with a bag of crisps. I used food as punctuation to my day: when the boys had a nap, I'd have a biscuit. When I'd dropped the eldest off at nursery, I'd have more tea and toast.

I got fatter and fatter – incrementally, not dramatically. What is really weird about this period is that, while I could obviously tell that I was getting bigger, I was oddly reluctant to do anything about it (and this reluctance continued, unbelievably to me now, for *well over a decade*). There are several reasons for this, and I think they're worth examining.

1. Arrogance. There isn't a likeable way of putting this,
so I won't bother trying. I thought I was still pretty good-
looking. Okay, maybe not first thing in the morning, puffy
from lack of sleep and with baby sick on my dressing gown.
But I scrubbed up well. You perfect all kinds of tricks when
you're unhappy with your weight, and one of mine was
makeup. With a face full of artfully applied slap, a pair of
control-top knickers, some cleavage on show and a good
haircut, I thought I looked all right. More than all right,
actually. I'd always been popular; I'd never in my life been
short of boyfriends. My husband clearly found me attractive;
my trusty bathroom mirror (head and shoulders only)
was flatteringly lit; I'd learned never to look down past
my bosom; and I could be extremely charming when I felt
like it. I behaved like a confident person – indeed I was
a confident person, about everything except my weight.
My weight bothered me. But not enough to do anything
concrete about it. I was pretty cocky. And very complacent.

Oh, and another thing: I'd always had (and still have)
a real horror of the kind of women who obsess about their
weight. It seemed to me to be deeply uncool. I hated people
who called chocolate cake 'sinful', just as I hated those very
thin women who push a salad leaf around their plate and
call it lunch. If the choice was between being like them
and being on the Rubenesque side, there was no contest.
It didn't occur to me that there was a middle way.

2. A weird, skewed acceptance of fate. There was a part of
me which thought that my youth was over (in my twenties!)
and that being slightly overweight was the price you paid for
being a married woman with children. I didn't have many
friends in the same boat – most of the women I knew who
had children were older than me, and had 'let themselves
go', as I saw it. I thought this was what you did. I sort of
carried my extra weight as a badge of honour: 'I'm no longer
the flibbertigibbet you once knew. I am a woman of

substance (literally). I have better things to do than faff about with a step machine.' I'd had a pretty good innings, I thought, being young and attractive, and if I carried a bit too much heft, well, hey, there were worse things.

3. Bloody-mindedness. Like the smoker who smokes an extra packet on National Non-Smoking Day, I ate an extra helping every time someone mentioned weight. That someone was pretty much without fail my mother, who only had to mention the phrase 'losing a few pounds' for me to unleash a giant tirade about how she was un-feminist and retrograde, and how women didn't have a wretched duty to be attractive at all times, especially when they were knackered from running around after two small children and at home all day long. 'It's not the 1950s,' I'd mutter crossly, before helping myself to a Danish pastry.

4. Dawn French, I'm sorry to say, and other vocal self-proclaimed Happy Fatties. They were quite persuasive there, for a while. They made a very good job of equating fatness with sensuality, appetite for food with appetite for life, the inability to resist thirds with largeness of spirit. Fat women, they seemed to be saying, loved life, and lived it in a joyous, celebratory way that thin people didn't. I believed this, or more accurately made myself believe it for convenience's sake. I even bought an outfit by French & Teague, which made me look like a beached whale. And then there was all the stuff about men loving curves, much of it written by Vanessa Feltz shortly before her husband dumped her.

This thing about men is just delusional, I'm afraid. Men like a nice rack. Men don't like a flappy pouch of skin overhanging the stomach, or droopy upper arms, or more than one chin. But nobody said this (it would have been 'fattist'), and women all over the place decided it was easier to believe this guff than to go on a diet. I was one of them. And when I thought of myself, it was as Anita Ekberg in

La Dolce Vita, not – more realistically – as Brutus from *Popeye*. Another thing about Dawn French: she is very, very pretty. Unusually so. She is perhaps marginally less pretty as a size twenty-six than she would be as a size fourteen, but not much. That's why she looks good: not because she's fat, but *despite* it. This is not a trick many people can pull off. Besides, having a pretty fat face doesn't magically exclude you from the horrendous health risks of being obese. And your body still looks like a doughnut.

5. Laziness, which overlaps with arrogance. This one is self-explanatory. I had no energy – partly because of haring around after the children, but partly (though I didn't know it at the time) because I ate enormous quantities of stupor-inducing food, which totally sapped me of strength. I was permanently exhausted. I felt like a nap within a couple of hours of waking up. So I'd sit at the kitchen table and nibble things instead.

6. (This is a weird one) Deliberately bulking up. Done subconsciously, but over the years I've spoken to dozens of women who say they've done the same thing.

We're now five years on from all of the above. As my marriage started falling apart, I did the very opposite of what you'd expect someone in that situation to do (pine away): I ate more. I didn't, as far as I am aware, do this consciously. But having thought about it, and compared notes with friends, it seems to be true that, in moments of stress, some women bump up the portions to make themselves bigger. Bigger equals stronger, braver, harder to squash, harder to hurt, harder to ignore or dismiss. It's as though the fat becomes a carapace, a sort of protective outer shell which will shield you from harm. Illness, divorce, stress, the death of a parent: if you're the 'coper' in your family (and I always have been), chances are you'll realize at some stressful point that you can't actually cope at all.

You don't want to create more stress by admitting this, so you coddle and 'reward' yourself with food, which has the supplementary benefit of making you 'bigger' in all respects – 'My shoulders are broad' – not all of them bad in coping terms. There is certainly an apparent comfort (it's another delusion, but never mind) in feeling you are big enough to take anything life throws at you: it's a 'Come and have a go, if you think you're hard enough,' thing. Easier to say, or feel, this when you're not a scrawny little shrimp. Some women start doing this in childhood.

7. I should probably also mention that a close relative had an eating disorder from the age of fourteen. In my head, weight issues were her department. Some members of my immediate family had a peculiar-seeming relationship with food: irrational hatreds of some random things, an odd take on vegetarianism, a devotion to health food shops, a compulsion to order off-menu. Sometimes they were on the plump side, sometimes they were rakes. My mother either ate a lot or didn't eat at all. I thought of myself as the sensible one when it came to food: I didn't make a fuss and I ate everything. Literally.

I don't want to oversell this by making myself sound like I hit a size thirty-two during this period. I was a size eighteen – sometimes the eighteen was looseish, sometimes it was skin-tight. And then, in the late spring of 2005, my size eighteen clothes suddenly stopped fitting. And that, dear reader, was when I finally decided I'd had enough. It was 15 July at around 2pm. I was in the fat people's department of Selfridges (they don't call it that, of course – they call it something absurd like 'relaxed clothing') and suddenly I felt like bursting into tears. I also felt a great rush of anger – rage, really – at what I'd done to myself. It was a moment of revelation. A light went on in my head, and I thought, 'For fuck's sake. ENOUGH!' 'Scuse my French, but that's what I thought, verbatim.

Unlike Neris, who as we shall see is a champion dieter of many years' standing, I'd never got to this point before. I had, as I've mentioned, a little panoply of tricks – magic knickers, makeup, décolletage, self-deprecating jokes, blah blah blah. I remember feeling murderous at a party some years ago, when a woman – then rather admired for her sartorial style – came up to me and complimented me on mine. 'You're so well dressed,' she said. 'I love the way you're so comfortable with your size.' She wasn't being a bitch (I don't think), but I wanted to stab her. But encounters like this were the exception rather than the norm. And in my head, until 15 July 2005, I wasn't a carb-guzzling blimp. I was 'slightly overweight'. That was all.

But as the clouds parted and the dazzling light shone down to expose the truth, I realized that that wasn't all at all. I WAS A SIZE TWENTY. I was a woman in my prime, frankly, with an okay face and a well-proportioned body, and for some crazy reason known only to myself, I was entering my fortieth year weighing nearly sixteen stone – the same as two skinny people welded together. It wasn't okay. It didn't look nice, or even a little bit nice. It was utterly grotesque. A few times in the previous couple of months, I'd decided at the last minute not to attend a party that I'd really been looking forward to. I told my boyfriend it was because I was tired. I wasn't tired at all. I was too fat. I had, for the first time ever, become embarrassed to be seen in public, is the truth of it. I had nothing to wear. I was Giant bloody Haystacks.

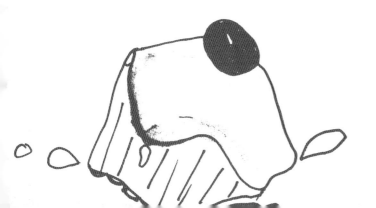

I told myself so many lies. Here are some of them:

I am curvy, not fat.
As we have seen, this is pure delusion. Curvy people aren't egg-shaped.

Okay. Then I'm Rubenesque. Junoesque. You know, voluptuous.
Those are synonyms of 'fat'. And you're in denial.

I have a bubbly personality.
I don't at all, actually. I developed a personality to match my weight – I turned myself into a jolly fat person because it seemed appropriate. I am much grumpier now I'm thinner, and it suits me just fine. And dropping the self-deprecating fat jokes – 'I'll just insult myself, shall I, before you insult me' – has been heaven.

I am still rather marvellously physically attractive.
Really? To whom – weirdo chubby-chasers? And (horrified gulp) do I want my boyfriend/husband to have people think that he's one of them?

I'm awfully unphotogenic.
No, just really fat. The camera doesn't lie. Not 100 per cent of the time, anyway.

How glad I am not to be a self-obsessed clothes-horse!
Well, it's hard to be, when normal clothes don't fit you.

These knickers are so comfy. Silly little scraps of lace are for sissies, or the sexually desperate.
And how I wish with all my heart that I could buy them.

Why don't M&S do bras in my size? The fools.
Because there's a limit, and 40H is probably about it.

There must be something wrong with my thyroid.
There wasn't.

I look good naked. I must feel quite nice.
Then why be scared of full-length mirrors? Why be shy of
walking around naked? Why come out of the shower and make
a point of never, ever looking down?

I have very wide feet.
No, just fat feet (and I've gone down a shoe size since starting
the diet).

I can't see my feet because I have such big tits.
True. Also, such a big stomach.

I have big hands.
No, just fat fingers (and my rings have had to be adjusted since
I lost weight).

I'm a fun person. I like to eat, drink and be merry.
Well, I certainly ate and drank. But it made me about as merry
as a six-mile tailback. And there's nothing 'fun' about seconds
of mash. You don't dole yourself out another scoop, clapping
your hands with delight while thinking, 'Wahoo! This is great
fun!' Or if you do, you need to get out more.

Ooh, I just love life. I devour it, me.
People who love life don't turn themselves into blimps, risk
their health, impair their sex lives, or make it impossible for
themselves to ever walk around in their underwear. People who
love shopping (and I do, so much so that I wrote a whole book
about it) don't exclude themselves from ninety-nine per cent
of clothes shops because there's nothing in their size.

At least I'm not some ghastly, neurotic, brittle, anorexic-looking
obsessive. Take me out to lunch, and I eat.
True. But the choice isn't between looking like Victoria Beckham
or Johnny Vegas. There is a middle way.

And so on. There were dozens of these lies, as you'll see – they're scattered throughout the book. Our mission is to demolish them one by one.

But back to 15 July. There I was, boiling with rage, surrounded by hideous plus-size (waaah) clothes for outsize matrons. I put down whatever elasticated-waist horror I'd been examining and marched down to the basement, to the books department, where I bought all the diet books I'd ever heard of. I started reading them that night. The ones that made most sense were Atkins, South Beach, the Zone, Protein Power and the GI Diet. South Beach and Atkins have an identical Phase 1, lasting a fortnight. What you are holding in your hands right now is our take on the above diets: we cherry-picked, and then made up our own version. I went to the supermarket the next day, and started dieting – for the first time in my life – on 17 July.

Neris

I've done Slimfast, liver detox and fasting. I've had kinesiology. I've had my blood examined for allergies only to discover I'm allergic to haddock and I don't like haddock anyway. I've had the Zone Diet delivered to my door every day for two months, only to eat the perfectly proportioned food as snacks between meals. I've done colonic irrigation, Fit for Life and food combining. I've been to a hypnotist and taken away a tape that I still use to help me sleep. But none of it helped me lose weight.

I went to famous (and not-so-famous) dieticians and nutritionists. I did the Oprah boot camp (which is seriously hardcore), but couldn't stick to it for more than a week. I bought Gillian McKeith. I went up to Carol Vorderman at a do and just said simply, 'Thank you for your detox, Carol, I feel great,' before tucking into pudding. I joined a nutrition home study course and only got to lesson one and couldn't be bothered with the rest of it. I have been a member of a gym on and off for seven years and – although it pains me to say it – if I am really honest I've only been twenty times. It looks like a hobby, when you see all the diets I've done. I'm a bloody expert. I've spent thousands and thousands of pounds and felt so much heartache and so much pain and so much numbness and so much not really understanding what is going on …And I've spent so much time thinking about and trying to work out why, when I am pretty successful in the rest of my life, I couldn't do this one thing. Why wouldn't it happen for me? Couldn't I buy the thing that would make the weight go? Couldn't I wake up and fit into a Jigsaw dress?

I had a happy childhood. I had a bit more flesh on me than most children at school but actually, looking at the pictures now, I was just a happy girl who was an average size. Healthy looking. I didn't think a bit about my size until the 'puppy fat' was noticed by other children (and adults who should have known better). I ate good food. My mum had a thing about tins, and insisted on cooking food from fresh – but we were allowed the occasional treat.

I remember eating pie and chips in front of *Happy Days*. My sister and I would cut our pies into four. She would eat her largest bit first. She reckoned she would be full by the time she got to the smallest bit, and didn't want to leave more than was strictly necessary. How boring was she? I would leave the biggest bit until the end. When everyone else was finished, I would look at my pie with pride. Pie was power. My grandfather used to say, 'Always leave the table while you've got space for more,' but I can't remember doing it. Ever.

I remember one particular ballet class. I'd been with the same school since I was six or seven and I did enjoy it but the Gaston Payne School of Dance wasn't called the Ghastly Pain school of dance for nothing. One day when I was ten, I was busily doing my bit of dancing in a class when Sara, the owner's daughter, walked up and down the row of us girls by the bar and said to me in front of everyone, 'Neris

Thomas, do you eat lots of cakes? Because it looks like you do. If you don't stop you are going to look like the back of a bus.'

I didn't say anything. All I could think was, 'I don't actually eat many cakes so why is she saying that?', and I kept trying to work out what she meant by 'the back of a bus'. There were a few girls sniggering by my side, but I didn't even really register them at the time. My lovely friend Alison Evans was there to give me a reassuring little word at the end of the class and make me feel better. I seemed to attract these kinds of comments throughout my childhood. I assumed everyone did.

I remember the boys at the back of the bus on the way home from school who would shout and sing, 'Nelly the Elephant packed her trunk' whenever I walked on, brilliantly changing 'Nelly' to 'Neris'. I just smiled at them and sat down. It didn't really bother me that much. I just thought they were a bit mean. I was happy as I was, and luckily I had my parents at home telling me to 'rise above it'. But it must have registered. To this day it's not a song I encourage my daughter to sing.

Puberty changed everything. I became aware of my body in a new way. I remember seeing a girl called Caroline P.W. in her swimming costume at the age of eleven, and wondering why I didn't look like that – not an inch of fat on her. I do remember my darling friend at secondary school getting more and more anorexic in front of my eyes and not being able to help her. I didn't understand the fuss back then.

And I remember the school lunches. I just ate the white rolls and butter every day – every single day. Thank goodness I was going home to eat normal food because lunch just consisted of warm white rolls. I still remember them being lovely. I certainly didn't think about nutrition.

I didn't cook myself. I don't think my all-girls' school did domestic science. The school was too busy investing in the new science block.

I avoided PE as much as possible. I remember queuing patiently for the trampoline at an Open Day for the local secondary school. I felt a bit nervous in my tights and leotard, only to step on to the trampoline, and to hear the gym teacher say, 'Now everyone, step back – you might feel the vibrations from this little lady.' What a bastard. But I got through it. It wasn't the worst thing in the world and I was always told how lovely and pretty I was by my mum and dad and sister and I just swallowed the feelings. I was never cross.

By the time school finished, I was still what could be described as an average size: not skinny-mini, but not too big either. It wasn't until university that things changed. In the first year away from home I gained a lot of weight. Not cooking meant my food was a bit limited. I relied on easy things to make. I remember eating a lot of bread. Toast in the morning followed by sandwiches for lunch and pasta for tea. Carbohydrates kept me going for three years. I started to eat chocolate, and the bars just seemed to be getting bigger and bigger. And, of course, so did I.

At university, I had really lovely male friends, who remained just friends. I couldn't quite work out why. I was determined that one day the right boy would like me for who and what I was. I saw no reason to change, and I carried on dreaming that one day my prince would come. By the end of the first year at university I was weighing in at fourteen and a half stone. I glossed over it. Besides, I found girls who obsessed about food and what they looked like really infuriating and boring.

I wasn't desperate to change but I think I was becoming a bit more aware of what I looked like. I started eating low-calorie ready-meals for ease – it seemed like at least I would be sticking to some kind of regime. I even took myself off to the local branch of a weight-loss club but found it just too difficult. I do remember really liking the women in the group, but I was so disorganized. I was always losing my diet plans and found the recipes hugely complicated.

I watched Oprah Winfrey every day and got so excited when I saw her get slim and fit. It just hit a raw nerve. I would cry during every programme. Something was stirring in me. By the time I graduated I was still around that fourteen-stone mark. I went back home just to regroup, but I decided that, finally, at twenty-one, I wanted to lose the weight. I had been ensconced in a highly unsuccessful relationship throughout my third year at university which was so on and off, and I wanted it to be on so badly that I was on a mission.

For three months I was hardcore. Weight Watchers. Brilliant. I had three months to go before I would see any of my university friends. I had a date in September (my close friend's leaving party as she was off to Australia for a bit) and I knew my old flame would be there. I wanted to wow him. Back at home, I was in control. I even started doing exercise classes. I felt safe – and the weight just dropped off. Even though it was fifteen years ago, I remember it so clearly – knocking on Jules' front door, three months on and four stone lighter, and her opening it and literally not believing what she saw. I was wearing a little red jacket and jeans. I looked good. 'Wow,' she shrieked, and all my friends were amazed. The boy I liked couldn't believe it either ... but he was later found snogging my friend upstairs.

And at that point I remember consciously deciding to eat the cake at the party. There was no point in depriving myself. And there, at that moment, something changed. Despite being thrilled by my transformation, all my hard work went out the window and was quickly overshadowed by my emotions. That pattern of emotional eating has continued on and off, *EastEnders*-style, ever since.

I moved to London and started work in the film industry. It was all so exciting – film sets, late nights and gorgeous actors. But the set catering, lunches out, parties and expense-account dinners weren't ideal for the waistline. The weight crept back on and I didn't get my act together

to try to lose it for a few more years when I got fed up with
not being able to wear all the clothes I wanted to, and it
started to feel uncomfortable. So I dieted.

Again, by being really low calorie I went right down
to ten and a half stone (my lowest adult weight). I went
on holiday to Bali with my friends and loved it. I felt I had
really got it this time. I was in the swing and couldn't believe
I would ever go back to my old self. Why would I, when
I looked and felt so much better? I was by the pool and
looking good. I wasn't even wearing a T-shirt over my
swimming costume. Back home, the men seemed to like
me more. They started coming out of the woodwork saying,
actually, they'd always liked me or that they *would* like me
once I lost those pounds . . .

Then, at twenty-eight, I met the man of my dreams,
a man that thought then – and still does now – that I'm the
most beautiful girl in the world. He really thinks that. By
week two I'd practically moved in and we were seriously into
our new life together. We were both eating more and more
and more. Huge plates of pasta. The three cheese varieties
were our favourite. Lots of late night takeaways in front of
satellite television. Blissfully in love, the weight came back.
But I was okay, now I had found my prince charming.

Over the years I've been with him, Richard has made
me feel amazing (sheesh . . . stop the love song on the record
player) but once, while I was moaning about my clothes not
fitting, he warned me that – at seventeen stone – even though
I was the love of his life and he loved me completely – if I put
on a lot more weight that he might stop finding me attractive.
He still thought I was the most beautiful girl, but he was just
being honest. Harsh words that made me so angry I wanted
to hit him – I thought he loved me! He still stands by what
he said to me that day and says that he is just telling the truth,
and saying out loud what every other man thinks. But I
thought love was blind. I was confused. And the bastard
who is now my husband had hit on a nerve. I was angry.

I wanted to prove everyone wrong – and lose the weight.
I started looking for the answer. The secret. And basically
I spent the next few years doing just that. I hired Fergie's
personal trainer for a day who was great but was way too
expensive for me, and I ended up looking a bit of a prat
running up and down the staircase in a house with my
landlady giggling at the noise from the next room.

I couldn't find a diet that worked for me. Some I
only stuck to for a few days, some I stuck to for longer.
Sometimes I just bought the book. Then I would feel great
relief when the introduction told me that I should read it
all the way through before preparing my kitchen and my
life for change. Hurrah! But by the time I got to the end
of the book I just couldn't be bothered with all the faff.

For my wedding I knew I had a target. I had to do it, so
I girded my loins and got down to twelve stone. I got into
exercise big time, for the first time ever. I met an amazing
woman called Sharon Saker who taught me to love, can you
believe it, jogging. I cut out wheat and I really went for it.
I had an aim – I had a dress to fit into. I did it, and felt like
I glowed for the whole day. I vowed again I wouldn't go
back to my old ways.

It lasted until our honeymoon and gradually, you've
guessed it, the weight came back.

For the last few years I've spent my time procrastinating,
trying to muster up the energy to change. 'If I lose two
pounds a week – no, maybe I could push it to three pounds
a week – every week for the next six weeks then by the time
it's so and so's wedding I'll look okay.' I kept on smiling and
procrastinating, and after a year of thinking I'd postpone
getting pregnant until I had lost all my weight I gave up
on the notion and got pregnant straight away.

We had our beautiful precious daughter. But our lives
were then taken over by her being extremely ill. We spent
a month living in Intensive Care and all I can remember
was going to the vending machine and eating chocolate.

My husband later told me he was going to the vending machine on the floor below. Eating was my only comfort.

Things thankfully, and incredibly, eventually got better, but when, weeks later, we emerged from the hospital, I weighed myself and I was topping the scales at just under eighteen stone.

I ate and ate, but we were home and that was all that mattered. I tried to carry on, but I think I had just lost my oomph. I'd felt frustrated and sad before, but I had never lost my spirit. By the time I had a one-year-old baby, my husband had an exciting new job. Having always been a very sociable person, I found myself making excuses to get out of meeting his new colleagues – for example, saying to him that his Christmas party clashed with my friends coming around – because my overwhelming feeling was that I was actually a bit embarrassing for him.

I wanted people to see him and think he was great and if they saw me they would think less of him. I thought that I would let him down. I had been overweight off and on and off and on for sixteen years but I think losing my oomph was the thing that made me really think. That hadn't happened before. I felt that I really had to do something about this and suddenly the years felt like they had passed really quickly and all the people I read about in *Slimming World* and the other weight-loss magazines seemed to be twenty-one when they reached their goal and I felt really jealous of them.

My force of nature, my all-or-nothing character, got me into this mess and it also kept me in it, because I wouldn't be told what I should be or what I should do. It has taken nearly twenty years to work out what I was doing wrong, and where I was going wrong. Finally the time had arrived to sort it out for once and for all. Who would have thought that India and me sitting in a café, chatting about everything, and then talking about how we both really had to do something about our weight would lead to me changing for ever. Never to go back. I promise.

2. Lessons We Have Learned

The million-dollar question is: what happened this time around that hadn't happened in the past (for Neris), or that suddenly spurred me (India) into action after so many years? I'd been overweight for well over a decade, and Neris, as we have just seen, had really struggled, on and off, for much longer. At this late stage, it might have been easier to give up, go with the flow, and live in tent dresses, finally reconciled to a life of lardiness. And yet here we are. How? What happened?

Well, we had each other. This is not to be underestimated: it was absolutely central to our weight loss, both in terms of kick-starting it and when it came to carrying on – and to getting back in the zone when one or the other of us had wandered off (because yes, we fully expect you to be human and go off-piste every now and then. We'll get to that later). The reason why diet programmes such as Weight Watchers work so well for some people is partly the strong social element. Nobody wants to feel lonely. Fat and lonely is even worse: the combination of being fat and feeling isolated in, and by, your fatness is simply fatal and resolution-sapping. There is something enormously comforting in knowing you're with people in the same boat, who have been where you've been, who know what you're talking about, who know what it's like.

We strongly recommend finding yourself a diet buddy. Be sensible: try not to pick your most competitive friend. A mild degree of competition is no bad thing, but you don't want a control-freak as a buddy, or someone who cheats like mad and starves themselves, or starts spending six hours a day in the gym so they lose faster than you. If there's no suitable candidate around, and even if there is, think of this book as that buddy. Seriously. Imagine it's a person. Ask it questions: use the Index. Really get to know it. This book doesn't just tell you what to do: it holds your hand at every stage of the way, gives you a nice hug when you've done well, and gives you an extra-big one when you're struggling.

(Maybe you want to know how Neris and I first met. We were always at the same parties wearing identical clothes. We were both expert at shopping for our size, but because the choice is so limited, we kept bumping into each other identically dressed, like Tweedledum and Tweedledee. We were quite well dressed, I have to say – because between us we had decades of experience and expertise. (There are tips on clothes, and on making the most of what you've got, whatever size you are now, on pages 102–4.)

Neris and I had both come to the stage where enough was enough. It is always being said of addicts of all kinds that they need to hit rock bottom before they can build themselves up again, and the same applied to us. I don't want to sound melodramatic, or to make light of people's addictions to narcotics or alcohol, but we were, after all, addicted to quantities of food, and in particular to carbohydrates. And we did hit rock bottom: me in Selfridges, Neris in the comfort of her own home. We had a moment of revelation, and the revelation was this: the thing about weight is that it doesn't have to be the boss of you. Even if it's been your boss for years, or decades. Even if you're in total despair because you have more than five stone to lose. Even if you think, ah, sod it, what's the point.

Have you had enough? You wouldn't have picked up this book if you hadn't.

▸ Do you want to feel fantastic, every day?
▸ Do you want to wear clothing of the kind you can't imagine owning, let alone fitting into, in a million years – and look great in it? Because you can, you know. It is a goal that is entirely possible to attain.
▸ Do you want to regain control over the one aspect of your life you think you have no control over?

Of course you do. Yes, yes, yes and yes, you're saying, like Meg Ryan in *When Harry Met Sally*.

Well, good. Because that's exactly what we're going to help you to do. And it's going to work for you, just like it worked for us.

Now, on to the trickier stuff. We came to understand why we ate, or overate, and before we get going properly you need to understand why you do it, too. It has absolutely nothing to do with hunger, needless to say. Your brain may interpret that empty, dissatisfied feeling as hunger pangs, but that's not what they are. And you're not going to get anywhere, frankly, until you've identified exactly why you overeat.

Why We Eat Too Much

Because we're unhappy. We can be massively depressed, or microscopically annoyed by something completely trivial, but if we associate food with comfort, we'll eat. We both ate if our children were unwell, and we both ate if the plumber had failed to turn up. We ate because it was raining. We ate because we'd had a titchy argument with our partners. We ate because we'd stubbed our toe, or because somebody was sick in hospital. The gravity or otherwise of the situation had nothing to do with it. We ate because, for whatever reason, we felt sad.

Because we're happy. For example, I (India) have always associated food with celebration. It's partly a cultural thing – I'm half Indian, and all the women in my family express their love through cooking, and through feeding you ('Eat, eat, I made it especially for you'). I don't know if white Anglo-Saxon Protestants do this too, but Jews certainly do, and Muslims, and the French, and the Italians, and pretty much everyone else I can think of. Food is a celebration of life and as such is central to certain cultures – not because they need to eat to live, but because food becomes a metaphor for everything good and loving and enjoyable about life. This is a lovely thing; I'm not knocking it. But it does create powerful associations that aren't especially helpful if you develop a problem with your weight. You start to believe that ALL food is about love. It isn't. Does food reinforce happiness? No.

Because it's a habit. Like smoking, or twirling your hair. Eating becomes a knee-jerk response. Got a spare ten minutes? Have a wee snack with your cup of tea. Watching telly? Have a biscuit. Out shopping? Don't forget to stop for coffee and sandwiches.

Because we're bored. Fatal, this one. Calamitous. Especially if you're at home all day, endlessly peering into the fridge or making toast to accompany your cup of tea. Some of us can't even read a magazine without having something to snack on. I've had many a bath with a bar of chocolate alongside me. When my children were small and I was up half the night, I'd sometimes eat in between their night feeds. And so it goes on.

Because we're already fat. The thin person's mindset says: 'Eat something else? Why would I want to do that? I just had dinner.' The fat person's mindset says, 'Okay. So, rationally, I know I'm not hungry. I ate a big dinner two hours ago. But I'm sitting here not quite knowing what to do with myself, so I might as well nip down to the kitchen and find something to pick at. I know it's not a good idea, because I don't need the calories and I'll get fat. But I'm already fat. So it's not going to make a huge amount of difference.' I thought this for years on end. My thought process went: 'Bloody hell, I've put on so much weight. It's really grim. I must do something about it. But not now, obviously, because who on earth starts a diet at eleven o'clock at night? No, I'll begin tomorrow. So I might as well have a cheese toastie.' Did the cheese toastie make me feel better? What do you think?

Because we have a weird empty feeling. We don't like the feeling, and what you do with an empty thing is fill it up. Here's a thing: the weird empty feeling has absolutely nothing to do with food. NOT A THING. It has to do with dissatisfaction or unhappiness or stress or worry, and possibly feelings of all four because of your appearance. But it does not have to do with appetite.

Because we believe the crap we're told. And why shouldn't we, when advertising is so sophisticated and psychologically astute? We believe that chocolate bars are a wonderful way to reward yourself. We believe life wouldn't be complete without balls of dough fried in oil and sprinkled with white sugar. We're told these foods are 'naughty' or 'sinful', and naturally that makes them even more attractive and desirable. You know how we laugh at how little children are mesmerized by TV ads for this or that must-have (supposedly) toy? We shouldn't laugh. We're exactly the same. We watch a lovingly, almost pornographically photographed shot of a milkshake (made with pig fat and sugar) and feel compelled to get in our car and drive to the nearest fast-food outlet.

Because we're greedy. And we've probably messed our bodies around so much that they're as confused as we are about what does and doesn't constitute feeling full. It's important to address greediness, and we will. Because the truth is, we're not 'big-boned' or 'well-built'. We weren't obese babies. We don't suffer from some bizarre biological malfunction that causes us to get fatter and fatter for no reason. Get it into your head: we're not *supposed* to look this way. We got fat. The totally brilliant thing is, we can get un-fat.

You may, of course, have some reasons of your own to add to the ones above, but they're broadly accurate, we think, for the majority of people. Now, don't just turn the page. Re-read the above. Nodding in agreement is one thing, but you

need to go further: you need to really understand (sorry
if we're sounding bossy. Bear with us. This is important).

Get this into your head.

If you're feeling sad, eating does not make you happy.
Eating does not make the bad thing go away. Sure, you feel
better for five or ten minutes. And then you feel much worse.
You're still sad about whatever you were sad about, and now
you're sad about having stuffed your face
as well. This is not a result.

    **If you're feeling happy, eating does not make you
happier.** Would you have enjoyed your wedding day more
if you'd been snacking on doughnuts as you walked down
the aisle? Do the mothers of new-born babies feel compelled
to eat pies as they gaze into their newborns' eyes? Would hot
sex be hotter if you had a tub of Pringles to hand? Please.

    Eating is not a habit. Nothing you do to yourself is
ever a habit. You *always* have a choice.

    Eating does not alleviate boredom. We think it often
causes it, because eating the wrong thing can make you feel
incredibly tired and listless.

    You don't need us to point out that eating because you're
already fat – the 'oh, sod it' factor – is not going to make you
thinner. Eating because you can't be bothered to do anything
about your weight is something we both understand really
well. It is born of despair. And there's no need to despair,
because even if you're really seriously overweight, you can
lose that weight. You can. We know. We did it.

    The weird empty feeling isn't about hunger. It is about
feeling dissatisfied, whether it's because you're having a bad
hair day or because you've just realized your marriage sucks.
Addressing the issue will lead to a resolution. Eating won't.
Really examine those ads. Think about that cultural
conditioning. The woman whose sugar-laden yogurt is so
good that she forgets to have sex with the dishy man waiting

for her? Yeah, right. Somebody's having a laugh, no? At your expense. Get wise to it.

Yes, we are greedy. Accept it. You're not going to starve on this diet. You can still be greedy. But in a good way, not an incontinent, out-of-control fat person's way.

Chances are that if you've ever forgotten to eat – and no, it's not something we've made a habit of, either – it was because you were too busy having a good time. Too busy full stop doesn't count, otherwise there would be no overweight office workers or stay-at-home mothers. You need to be busy *and* loving whatever it is you're doing to forget about food: for example, nobody has fantastic sex and pauses in the middle to reflect on how they're really starving, actually. You don't take to the floor on your wedding day thinking, 'I could murder a Cornish pasty.' You don't watch your child being Star Number Two in the school Christmas play and find your mind wandering to the question of jumbo bags of Twiglets. Or maybe you do – it's all subjective. Our point is that when you are fully, 100 per cent engaged with doing something you enjoy, whatever it is, appetite takes a back seat.

Even if this doesn't happen very often, chances are that it has at least happened occasionally. Focus on that time. What it tells you is this: the food you eat to excess is a crutch, and that crutch is not always necessary, since you don't need it when you're really enjoying yourself.

Here's a thought: you think you're eating to relieve your boredom, to ease your anxiety, to soothe your fevered brow, to calm yourself down or to rev yourself up. You're not. You are eating to punish yourself.

This is a bit of a head-fuck. You think you're being nice to yourself when you overeat. But you aren't. You're making yourself fat and unhealthy, and in the process you're making yourself feel terrible as soon as you've finished eating that pot of ice cream or that fried cheese sandwich. You are being horrible to yourself, is the truth of the matter. And the really mad thing about it is, you are punishing yourself for having no control over events (the thing, whatever it was, that drove you to the kitchen in the first place) by losing control of yourself. Do you see? It's a crazy lack-of-control double whammy.

Here's an example: it's after breakfast, which you've had, and you're feeling mighty pissed off. The children's rooms are like pigsties, and they're old enough to tidy after themselves. Then you trip over the dog and bang your shin. The phone rings: it's the friend you share the school run with, telling you that she's sorry, but she can't, in fact, collect the kids from school today because she has a sudden and unscheduled work appointment. You're by now feeling intensely irritated with the shape your day is taking, and it's only 10am. It starts raining, and you have to walk the dog. Lead in hand, you autopilot down to the kitchen, flick the kettle on and make a cup of tea. There's an open packet of the children's Jaffa Cakes calling your name from the shelf. You sit down and eat every single one. Better now?

No. Of course not. On top of your shin and the bedrooms and the stupid dog and the inept friend and having to go out in a Noah-worthy downpour, you've just eaten a gigantic amount of biscuits. How does that help? How is that being nice to yourself? What you've done is added to the general crapness of the day, because now on top of everything else you feel like a fat pig. Great. Fan-fucking-tastic.

It is really essential to grasp this point. You comfort eat. You think comfort eating is a way of showing yourself some love. It's not. It's the exact opposite. And just because you love food doesn't mean it loves you back. It's not saying, 'Ahh, kissy-kissy, I love you so much.' It's saying, 'Christ, there she goes again, shovelling me down. All right, Tubs? Shall we have seconds? Yeah, thought so. Any day now she's going to break this chair with the weight of her arse.'

No matter how much spin you put on it, no matter how hilarious you are when you talk about yourself and food, no matter how brilliant you've become at the self-deprecating

jokes, the truth is that overeating is a form of self-dislike, or, to put it less brutally, self-unease. You know the L'Oréal ad? You're the opposite. You don't really believe you're worth it. Even if – *especially* if – to everyone else, you're the acme of confidence and strength.

Here Are Some Good Ways of Showing Yourself Real Love

Go for a walk. Seriously. Whenever people suggested this to us, either in real life or in diet books, we wanted to laugh at how lame and prissy it sounded. What kind of a pussy suggestion is walking? This is what we thought of going for walks: marginally preferable to touching a poo with bare hands, but only just. Walk vs. Jaffa Cake: no contest, right? But bear with us. Give it a try. We're not talking a five-mile hike here: we're talking a quick walk to the shops, or to the park, if there's one nearby, or even a brisk trot around the block. Quite apart from its many health benefits, which we'll get to later, walking clears your head in a manner that sometimes seems miraculous. Nothing is as bad after a walk as it seemed before it (they're particularly brilliant in the middle of arguments). Obviously, there's a leap of faith involved here, but you'll have to trust us. Your head will feel a million times clearer, and your problems, whatever they were, will feel smaller or even, with luck, insignificant.

Have a cat-nap. Nothing is so important that it can't wait ten minutes. Lying down and closing your eyes not only energizes you but also has the most marvellously soothing effect on the mind. Take deep breaths. You'll feel better. Have a bath. Baths are bliss, especially if you're more used to having a shower. Buy some delicious things to put in the bath – scented oils or bubbles. Loofah your back. Lie there, soaking, sniffing the air appreciatively. Relax. If you have longer, read a book until you go all wrinkly and pruny.

Find your favourite song and dance around like a loony for three and a half minutes. Yes, it's an old women's magazine favourite. But it's also a guaranteed energizer, plus you feel all giggly for looking like a prat, and the giggliness lasts for some time. If you feel self-conscious, draw the curtains and do it in the dark.

Phone a friend – preferably the diet buddy we mentioned earlier. Have a gossip. Tell some jokes. Arrange to meet up later in the week.

Get as extravagant as your time or purse situation allows. Go shopping. Take yourself for coffee, and don't spoil the occasion by wolfing down a couple of cakes. You're taking care of yourself, not giving a spoiled toddler a treat. Sitting down with a cup of tea and the new issue of your favourite magazine is a lovely thing to do. Have a manicure. Get your hair blow-dried, or blow-dry it yourself (this makes us feel incredibly happy, for some reason – far happier than twenty minutes with a big brush and a hairdryer ought to warrant).

Watch an Inspiring Film
▸ *Rocky* – because it's brilliant . . . but only the first one
▸ *Forest Gump* – just to get you walking and running
▸ *When Harry Met Sally* – just to be like Meg Ryan was then
▸ *Billy Elliot* – we really do want to boogie
▸ *Strictly Ballroom* – you'll never be able to sit still again through 'Love Is In The Air'

Notice we're not suggesting re-decorating the children's rooms, or baking them a cake for a treat, or doing the ironing. All of these activities, and others like them, aren't about you. The point of this exercise is to be nice to yourself. It is exclusively about you. It doesn't mean you're a slattern,

or a selfish monster who doesn't love her family. It means you're learning to value yourself as highly as you value your loved ones. And there's nothing wrong with that – quite the opposite. If you'd like to read more about how, sometimes, selfishness is quite nice, turn to page 57.

While we're on the subject of love, here's a little more on one of the things we briefly touched on earlier, namely families that communicate through food. You'll either immediately know what we're talking about, or you won't have a clue, in which case you can probably skip this bit. Though we wouldn't, if we were you. The penny might drop.

Does this scenario sound at all familiar? You're overweight. You've been noticeably overweight for a while. You go and visit your mum.[2] She knew you were coming, so she's been cooking. She's pulled out all the stops. She's made you a feast. Isn't that nice? 'Eat, eat,' she says. 'I've been cooking all day/night.'

Aah, you think to yourself. That's so lovely! And you sit down, and you start eating. Your mother encourages you to have seconds. Thirds, even – 'Oh, just this tiny little slice won't hurt, I made it especially for you.' So you do. Nothing like your mum's cooking, is there?

Or it can go like this: she's made you the aforementioned feast. It's *quite* nice. Nice of her to spend the time and effort, but kind of odd to have baked three kinds of cheesecake, or samosas, or whatever, when you've explicitly told her you were trying to lose weight. And now she's urging you to eat it, and her face is going all sad and crumpled when you're saying you'll only have a small piece. Oh God, now you feel bad. You feel guilty. Whatever, you think. I'll eat the damnthing. I'll diet again tomorrow. As you swallow the first delicious mouthful, you ask yourself, 'Is my mum deaf, or something? Because she knows I'm watching my weight. Weird. Ah well.'

[2] We're not picking on mums, though they're more likely to do this than your dad. But insert whatever you need to here – mother, father, brother, sister, auntie, uncle, granny, grandpa or, more often than not, friend (so-called).

Or like this: same situation. The difference this time is that your mum absolutely knows you're overweight, and is always urging you to do something about it, much to your irritation. You go and visit. She's made a feast. The feast is lavish in your eyes – whether it's a three-course banquet or a jumbo portion of cod and chips – and one glance tells you it's super-fattening. You raise your eyebrows. 'Oh, I know,' she smiles. 'But once in a while won't hurt.' And you wonder to yourself why she has knowingly cooked you the food you both know you shouldn't be eating. 'Wow,' you think to yourself. 'There's something not quite right here.'

That third scenario is the worst, but actually none of them are great if you have a weight problem. As we were saying above, there are entire cultures – entire countries, in fact entire continents – that habitually behave in this way. It's not always a bad thing, though I have come to the conclusion that demonstrating one's love through food is only valid if it is demonstrated in other ways also. Put brutally, it's easy to cook (or to nip to the baker's to buy a cream cake). Pretty much anyone can do it. What's less easy is to say – for example – 'I'm still feeling quite cross with you over such-and-such, but I love you, whatever you do.' Food can be about love, of course, and in normal situations it usually is. But it can also be about avoiding the real issue – about replacing emotional sustenance with physical sustenance, i.e. food. And that, my dears, is often how and where emotional eating begins. And it can last a lifetime.

Let me explain. Say I was cross with my (not-fat) teenage son for having a messy room and coming home late on a school night. I could do two things. I could sit him down, explain that I was really pretty furious, listen to his side of the story, persuade him to listen to mine, and try to reach a happy resolution so we could both sleep easily in our beds that night. Or I could think, 'I can't be bothered with this

again. I'll just sulk for a bit, so he knows I'm cross with him.' By lunchtime the next day, I'd feel guilty and there would be a horrible atmosphere in the house. So I'd make him his favourite pudding, or pancakes for brunch, by way of an olive branch.

In families that don't have food issues, that might work perfectly well. In families that do, it would be a disaster, especially if I'd started this technique when my child was only a few years old, and especially if my child were overweight. We all do it, up to a point, with the doling out of sweeties or other sugar-laden 'treats', when we're feeling we haven't been as nice to our children as we might have been. But some families take it much further, and if you can't deal with it, then it's catastrophic.

What can you do about it? Well, that depends. We're not going to suggest you take your whole family and/or friends off for a spot of group therapy, because as suggestions go, that one's a bit too hardcore for most of us. No, all you really need to do is be aware of the situation. Knowledge is power. If you are able to calmly identify what's going on, and to think to yourself, 'I see. This is what's happening. It's part of a pattern that's been going on for years, and it is no longer a pattern I want to involve myself in,' then you're halfway there (give yourself a massive pat on the back, please). Be calm. Don't start frothing at the mouth and giving your loved ones a lecture about emotional eating. It's all about you, remember?

Don't give the people who encourage you to comfort eat any ammunition. If you feel that you're surrounded by them, ignore our admonition to do this diet in secret, and tell everyone you're on a diet, tell them what you can and can't eat, and explain that, come hell or high water, you will not go off-course, even for one meal. Don't apologize for yourself by prefixing any of this with 'I know it's a bore, but ...' What are you apologizing for? Getting in shape? Being good to yourself? The person you're talking to will probably say that they'll make something especially for you, something you can eat. Politely thank them, and explain that this won't be necessary. YOU are in control of what you put in your mouth. Nobody else.

You don't need special food, as you'll see when we get to the nuts and bolts of this diet. Unless you have friends or family who exist solely on carbohydrates, there will always be something you can eat. You don't need other people to create special menus for you – you're not an invalid. You don't even need to draw attention to your way of eating. If the worst comes to the worst, you'll go home feeling slightly peckish. So what, really? At home you'll have a fridge stocked with delicious food you can eat. Besides, we can all act, up to a point. Whatever you do, don't look miserable, even if you feel it at first (you won't feel it for long, we promise. Taking control is incredibly empowering, to use a horrible word). Eat what you can eat, cheerfully. Compliment the cook. For God's sake don't whinge about how you wish you could have the chips. Whinging, or looking glum, reinforces the negative and self-sabotaging message that you are somehow punishing yourself. Which is mad, because you are doing the exact opposite. You are celebrating how fantastic you're going to look and feel. Whinging also gives your host ammunition – they'll think, 'She'll never stick it out. I'm going to ignore everything she's saying.' Being confident and cheerful has the opposite effect. It makes your host think, 'Oh. She's serious.'

By doing this – explaining what the diet involves, and eating only what you are allowing yourself to eat – you are putting out the powerful message that from today onwards, when it comes to food, you are the boss. You are in control. You're no longer going to eat food that makes you fat out of politeness, or out of weariness, or because you want to show X or Y that you love them by eating their food. Take them a bunch of flowers instead. It's much easier on the waistline. Do you now understand how and why you overeat? It's okay if you don't, but if that's the case, please re-read this chapter. Understanding patterns of behaviour is essential if we are going to break them. If you're confident that you've got the basic idea, and if you recognize your overeating triggers, you're ready to turn the page. That means you're ready to embark on our diet. And *that* means you're about to take the first step to becoming thin/slim/healthy.

You'll see a real difference in two weeks. Keep hold of that thought.

3. Before You Set Off

It is an unfortunate fact of life that when you are trying to diet, obstacles sprout up like mushrooms – and we don't just mean your children's half-empty packet of Wotsits lying temptingly on the kitchen table (though there's always that, too). We think it's a good idea to identify possible pitfalls in advance of them occurring, and to develop some strategies to deal with them.

If you are worried about a specific upcoming event, turn to page 61 for a detailed index of how to cope in many given situations, such as parties, the pub, or Christmas dinner. What we have found far more troubling – and troublesome – than the odd stray sweetie, or the sudden overwhelming urge to think, 'Ah, bugger it, I'll just eat this sticky toffee pudding, and start again tomorrow,' are other people. As the writer and critic Mary McCarthy once said of someone who made a habit of always helpfully pointing out her bad reviews to her, 'There's always friends.'

Girlfriends, in particular, can be very peculiar about your dieting. They're pleased for you – up to a point. We've lost track of the number of times we've both been told, by well-meaning 'friends', that we didn't need to lose another pound and were utterly gorgeous just as we were (at fourteen and a half stone). Now, either these friends are so blinded with love that they can't see you as you really are, or, we're sorry to say, the idea of you controlling your biggest vice – your overeating – makes them distinctly uncomfortable.

Women are strange creatures. When I (India) got divorced, many of my girlfriends suddenly got very possessive of their husbands. I can honestly say that, to me, the majority of these husbands were monstrous gargoyles (I'm sure they spoke very highly of me, too). I wouldn't have touched them with a very long stick. They were my nice girlfriends' inexplicably dull, unattractive, or both, spouses, and over the years I'd learned to put up with them, and they with me. And yet, suddenly, their wives were behaving as though their fat, bald, braying, coma-inducingly boring husbands were Brad Pitt, and I was some sex-crazed, frenziedly lustful femme fatale, instead of a knackered single mother who'd really rather be asleep, but who'd come round for a drink because it seemed rude to say 'no' three times in a row. Weird, or what? But it happened with alarming frequency.

It's the same thing with weight. People don't like too much movement around the status quo. You're supposed to be fat, they think – it's just how you are. If you wanted to do something about it, surely you would have done it by now. No, you must be really comfortable in your skin, and happy with your lot. So you get pigeonholed: you sit in your little box, which says 'My fat friend', and you're not really allowed to jump out. People are threatened by change, and they are especially threatened by change in their close friends. This is particularly true of people who aren't especially happy, and for whom the smallest change can tip the balance in a negative way. For these people, the fact that you have done something and confronted an issue – your weight – head-on can seem threatening. But, do you know, that's their business. It's not yours.

So it shouldn't surprise you that the friend who's offered to cook you dinner 'forgets' about your eating plan, and puts a chocolate cake in front of you for pudding. You shouldn't be too shocked when, out for the evening, your friend urges you to eat something you're not supposed to, 'just this once'. And neither should you be surprised if the same friend – or another: this has happened to both of us with a variety of people – suddenly tells you that you're getting too thin, when you both know perfectly well that you've got another couple of stones to go before you're anywhere near a healthy weight for your height. It's not just your skinny friends: your overweight friends are more than likely to be incredibly dismissive of your dieting plans, because of course the act of you dieting reminds them that they could do with losing weight too; that you're doing something about your problem and they're not. We know this to be true because we've done it ourselves. As for colleagues: no one should have to put up with the nosy woman who sits opposite you and makes a point of investigating, and commenting on, your packed lunch every day.

This sabotaging *will* happen in one way or another, no matter how charming, lovely and supportive your friends are. And we suggest quite a radical solution to it. This is not to tell anyone that you're on a diet – excepting, of course, your designated diet buddy, if you have one.

Dieting is like giving up smoking: if you involve other people and make a great big song and dance about it, anything they say – from 'How boring of you' to 'Congratulations' – is potentially irritating and anxiety-causing. This is because you now feel that you're not just dieting for yourself, but for other people, and naturally their input matters to you. And by telling them about it, you're giving them licence to comment.

Do you really want their comments? Think about it. Probably not. If the person who originally said, 'Congratulations,' now says, 'Oh, go on, this little piece of bread won't hurt you,' a weird thing happens psychologically. You think, 'This person is on my side. And yet they're telling me to have the bread. That means it must be okay.' Conversely, the person who says, 'How boring,' is not on your side from the off, and is unlikely to be helpful. Why not simply avoid both scenarios by keeping quiet about the whole project? Life's too short.

You need to remember that you are doing this diet for you. You're in charge of yourself – nobody else is. Only you can influence what you eat – nobody else can. Losing weight is your responsibility, and no one else's. So we suggest you quietly get on with it. That way, nobody will be expecting you to succeed, and nobody will be expecting you to fail, which removes an enormous amount of stress and pressure. Nobody will stare at your plate and say, 'Doesn't look much

5. Neris and India's Idiot-Proof Diet

Put at its most basic, this is a high-protein, low-carb diet. Eating more protein and fewer carbs than we're used to results in the body using its own stores of fat for fuel. That means you're burning your own fat twenty-four hours a day, seven days a week. And *that* means you're doing some serious shrinking.

We said low-carb, not no-carb. You will be eating carbs, only they'll be good ones, which means GI-friendly ones. (See below for an explanation of how the Glycaemic Index works.)

As we've already said, all sorts of diets work. But we found that cutting back on carbohydrates was the most liveable-with of all the dieting options, and the least limiting in terms of losing weight while getting on with the rest of your life. When we started dieting, we followed the Atkins regime to the letter (most of the low-carb diets we have studied have a similar initial phase, where carbs are severely restricted for a minimum of a fortnight). A few weeks in, though, we started experimenting. What you are reading is the result of those experiments. We reintroduced foods in our own order. We made allowances for alcohol and chocolate. We fiddled about with existing diets and eventually, through the fiddling and through a process of trial and error, we came up with our own. We think it is more doable than many existing low-carb diets on the market – and we absolutely know, first hand, how well it works.

Here are some misconceptions about high-protein diets:

Bloody hell! My cholesterol levels are going to go through the roof!
You'll be amazed. Ours dropped quite dramatically.

What about my poor heart?
Your heart will thank you. Most high-protein diets were devised by cardiologists, and there's a reason for that: they're good for your heart. It was India's GP who encouraged her to follow a high-protein diet.

So I guzzle red meat and eggs three times a day, Atkins-style?
No. You can eat red meat, but you're going to be intelligent about it, and not wolf down insane quantities of it.

Will I have bad breath?
Yes, possibly, for a week or so. Not death-breath, or MO (for mouth odour), but a slightly weird metallic taste might appear.

Will I be horribly constipated?
Nope.

Will I feel all weak and strange? I've heard real horror stories about this way of eating.
You will feel peculiar for a maximum of five days. After that, you will feel more fantastic than you've felt in years, guaranteed. And we've all heard the horror stories. They happen because people hear about a diet like Atkins or South Beach, don't bother actually reading the book, and think they can drop all the weight they want by eating economy sausages fried in lard and triangles of processed cheese. Surprise! They can't. Double surprise: they feel like crap.

Will I eat fruit and vegetables?
Yes.

Eggs have long been demonised as being bad for the heart. Yet new research suggests that this is not only untrue, but that eggs could even be considered a 'superfood'.

Eggs could actually protect against heart disease, breast cancer and eye problems and even help you to lose weight.

For years people assumed eggs were bad for cholesterol levels. But a review just published in the British Nutrition Foundation's *Nutrition Bulletin* found they 'have no clinically significant impact' on heart disease or cholesterol levels.

Dr Bruce Griffin of the University of Surrey's school of biomedical and molecular science analysed 30 egg studies, among them one from Harvard University which showed people who consumed one or more eggs a day were at no more risk of suffering from cardiovascular disease than non-egg eaters.

Egg yolks contain cholesterol, but nutritionists now know it is the saturated fats in food, not dietary cholesterol, that raises blood cholesterol levels, a risk factor for heart attacks.

'To view eggs solely in terms of their dietary cholesterol content is to ignore the potential benefits of eggs on coronary risk factors, including obesity and diabetes,' Dr Griffin says.

Eggs are actually good for you. 'They are rich in nutrients,' says Joanne Lunn, nutrition scientist at the British Nutrition Foundation. One egg provides 13 essential nutrients, all in the yolk (egg whites contain albumen, an important source of protein, and no fat).

Lunn says eggs are an excellent source of B vitamins, which are needed for vital functions in the body, and also provide good quantities of vitamin A, essential for normal growth and development.'

Will I never be able to have a potato, or toast, or a plate
of pasta again?
Of course you will. Life's too short.

Can I drink alcohol?
Yes. Not for the first fortnight, but then yes.

What about tea and coffee?
Decaf at first, please. But then yes.

Can I have sugar?
**Not for a fortnight, and then only in moderation. You can use
sugar substitutes, though, if you are comfortable doing so.**

What about my Diet Coke? I'm addicted to Diet Coke.
**Funny, that. Everyone overweight we know – Neris included –
has or had this problem. No, you're not allowed your Diet Coke.
Not under any circumstances. Sorry. We'll explain later (see
page 179).**

But I can eat 'diet' everything else, right?
**No. You absolutely cannot eat 'diet' anything. The word 'diet'
means low-fat and high-carb. We don't fear (good) fat. We fear
(bad) carbs. And we don't fear calories either. If you've been
in the habit of counting them, forget about them right now.
They're over. They play no part in this way of eating.**

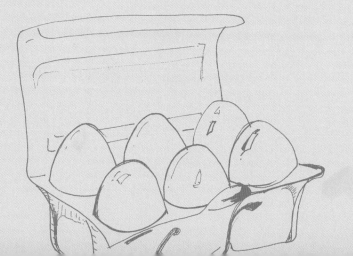

How It Works

All foods contain carbohydrates, whether you're talking about a glass of milk or about a loaf of bread. And all carbohydrates, wherever they come from, turn into sugar, or rather glucose (anything that ends in '-ose' basically means sugar – fructose from fruit, lactose from milk, etc. Bear it in mind when you're inspecting food labels). And the problem with having a lot of glucose in your system is a: that it impacts your blood-sugar levels (which is why so many of us have blood sugar 'spikes' throughout the day, when we're fine one minute and exhausted the next, until we have a bar of chocolate), and b: more crucially still, that once the sugar in your blood goes up, the pancreas kicks in and releases insulin, whose job it is to remove the sugar from your blood and get it into the cells, to be used as energy.

This is fine – unless you have so much glucose floating about that your body can't store any more. When this happens, the liver converts the glucose to fat. It doesn't tell your body to burn the fat; it tells it to store it. And hello, fat thighs.

Most of us eat too many simple carbohydrates – bread, rice, pasta, potatoes – and it thus follows that most of us have too much stored glucose, i.e. more glucose than our bodies know what to do with. This is why we're fat. In a number of cases, we may even be pre-diabetic without knowing it.

Still with us? On we go. Carbs come in two formats: complex and simple. Simple carbs are one, two or three units of sugar linked together in single molecules. Complex carbs consist of hundreds of thousands of sugar units, also linked together in single molecules. Simple sugars taste sugary, as you would expect them to. Complex carbs – potatoes, say – are not sweet. To complicate things further, complex carbs break down into two further groups: high fibre and low fibre. High-fibre carbs are difficult for us to digest, because we don't have the requisite enzyme (unlike,

say, cows, which do and thus can get calories out of grass).
The reason they're hard for us to digest is that they contain
cellulose. But being hard to digest simply means they hang
around inside our digestive tract for longer, and make our
bodies work harder. It's not that we shouldn't eat them.
The benefits of high-fibre foods such as broccoli or other
green leafy vegetables are well known, and eating them has
been associated with lowered incidences of hypertension,
cancer, arthritis and diabetes.

There are no comparable benefits to low-fibre carbs,
such as cereals, processed grains, pasta, potatoes or rice.
Furthermore, while we know about essential fatty acids
and essential amino acids, both of which are derived from
protein, there is no such thing as an essential carbohydrate –
i.e. it contains nothing you need that you can't get from
other, non-carb foods.

For most of us, our intake of carbs comes from cereal
and grain that has been processed and thus lost its fibre (just
squeezing a fruit to make juice does this – processing doesn't
necessarily have to involve industrial machinery. This is why,
on the Glycaemic Index – see below – a mashed potato has
a higher count than a whole, unpeeled boiled one).

So what we're basically doing is keeping a close and
watchful eye on the simple carbs, initially by dumping
them altogether. This will lighten the load both externally
and when it comes to your internal organs. If you don't
produce an excess of glucose, your body doesn't respond
by producing an excess of insulin (which can lead to
diabetes in the long term) and, crucially, your liver does
not convert the glucose to fat.

Furthermore, in the absence of carbohydrates – i.e. in the
absence of stored fat – your body has no choice but to start
burning its own fat stores for fuel and energy. That's *your*
fat, and this is why this diet works.

Eventually, you will go back to eating carbohydrates, but
you will shun the processed, simple kind – the ones that

made you fat in the first place. Instead, you will feast on complex carbs, which are full of fibre, vitamins, minerals and enzymes.

The first, kick-starting phase of the diet involves keeping all carbs to a minimum for a fortnight – longer if you have more than three stone to lose.

The second phase involves slowly reintroducing good carbohydrates while still losing weight.

The third phase of the diet teaches you how to maintain your weight loss and eat a healthy, nutritious, balanced – and delicious – diet for the rest of your life. And yes, you will be allowed the odd bowl of pasta. With garlic bread on the side.

The Glycaemic Index

The Glycaemic Index measures the speed at which you digest food and convert it to glucose. As we have just seen, if you don't produce an excess of glucose, your liver does not convert the glucose to fat, because you don't give it the chance to.

The faster the food breaks down and turns to glucose, the higher the GI index, which counts sugar at 100 and compares all foods against that number.

This is pretty much all you need to know for our purposes – if you've been following this technical bit, it will come as no surprise to find, for instance, that a piece of French bread registers very highly on the GI scale, whereas a chicken breast doesn't.

And that's the boring bit over.

6. Are You Ready?

Good. Here come your first instructions.

Go to your local health food shop and buy the following:
▸ One good multi-vitamin without iron. Solgar (call 01442 890 355 for stockists) do an excellent one. This is to keep you nutritionally healthy while your diet is relatively limited.
▸ Psyllium husks in capsule form. These are to save you from constipation. You must take them – two in the morning.
▸ A chromium supplement containing at least 200mg of chromium polynicotinate. Chromium builds muscle, decreases body fat and can lower cholesterol.
▸ A fish oils supplement. Because we all know they're good for you.
▸ 1000mg tablets of vitamin C if you smoke, to be taken once a day.
▸ A good vitamin B complex tablet, to be taken once a day.
▸ If you drink more than you should, you might want to give your liver a thirty-day cleanse by taking a capsule or two of Milk Thistle every day for a month.
▸ India has child-like faith in Coenzyme Q10, which boosts energy and is reputedly an anti-oxidant. I feel great when I take it (60mg daily) and less great when I don't.

Do not attempt to embark upon our diet without being armed with the above. Seriously. It won't feel good. Have a day-long carb party. Stuff your face. Have a chip butty. Have pasta and bread. Make pancakes. Eat biscuits. Eat crisps. You get the picture. Oh, and have some milk chocolate, too. Fizzy drinks, if you like them (they sure as hell don't like you, but never mind about that for the moment).

Now clear out your kitchen. Give away the following, or put them somewhere out of reach:

▸ All your biscuits and chocolate bars.

▸ Any cold drink that isn't water.

▸ Any hot drink that isn't decaf tea or coffee, or herbal tea.

▸ Anything containing sugar (check the label – the weirdest things contain sugar, like some jarred mayonnaise, and balsamic vinegar).

▸ All pasta.

▸ All potatoes and potato-based products, including those containing potato flour (which is in many ready-meals).

▸ Anything containing wheat (i.e. flour), whether it's sweet or savoury.

▸ Any oil that isn't olive or groundnut.

▸ Any fruit (yes, we know. Fruit's supposedly good for you. But it's also full of sugar. Bear with us, it's only for two weeks).

▸ Any legumes. That means lentils, chickpeas and the like.

The kitchen's probably looking a bit tragic. Time to go shopping for the following:

▸ Meat. Any kind you like, including roasts, ham, bacon, pastrami, salami, steak, chicken, sausages (posh ones only, please – the cheap ones are full of bready fillers, and also full of crap), pâté (the good stuff that comes in slices, not the weird stuff that's like paste-in-a-tube), and so on. Check that the bacon isn't cured with sugar, and try to avoid nitrates. We strongly urge you to buy organic meat, for any number of health reasons as well as for taste ones. Yes, it's more expensive. But it tastes incomparably better.

▸ Organic free-range eggs. They have to be organic, it's non-negotiable.

▸ Fish. Any kind you like, in whatever format, from fresh seabass (which is very nice stuffed with rosemary) to canned tuna (which is very nice mixed with mayo and spring onions).

▸ Speaking of which, make sure you have either the ingredients to make your own mayonnaise, or a big fat jar of your favourite brand (but make sure it's not loaded with sugar).

▸ Olive oil and groundnut oil, if you don't have them already. Hazelnut oil makes lovely salad dressings, too.

▸ Whatever kind of vinegar you like, apart from balsamic. We like tarragon and white wine. Buy a couple of different ones if you can, to add variety to your salad dressings.

▸ Organic, additive-free peanut butter, if you like it, crunchy or smooth, but with no added sugar.

▸ Double cream (yes – double cream!).

▸ Butter (yes – butter!).

▸ New herbs and spices – if you're anything like us, chances are yours have been sitting there for some time and taste musty rather than zingy.

▸ Sea salt.

▸ Black pepper.

▸ Nuts – any kind, provided they're au naturel and with no added sugar. Don't buy the nuts yet if you have the common problem of not being able to stop eating them once you've started.

▸ Any vegetables you like, excluding potatoes, carrots, corn and peas (which are too carby for us at this stage). The best vegetables, for this diet and in general, are green, leafy ones – any kind of salad greens, any kind of spring greens, spinach, cabbages, and so on. Eat onions in moderation, i.e. use them in recipes, but don't eat three huge baked onions a day.

▸ Avocadoes, which are technically a fruit.

▸ Lemons and limes, ditto. Oh, and tomatoes.

▸ All sorts of cheeses – buffalo mozzarella, blue cheese, cheddar, brie, whatever.

▸ Mineral water, if that's your preference. We drink filtered tap water. If you don't like the idea of tap water, stock up on bottles, because water is an essential part of the diet.

▸ Whey protein powder from the health food shop. Check the carb content – some are carbier than others. Buy the lowest-carb you can find. We like Solgar (stockists from 01442 890355).

DO NOT BUY ANY LOW-CARB PRODUCTS. No bars, no shakes, nothing. They may be low-carb, but they're filled with crap, which is not what we want. You are going to be eating pure, clean food – and that means unprocessed and not crammed with odd additives.

Hopefully the larder isn't looking quite as grim by now. One last thing: keep track of your progress.

Go to www.fitday.com and open a free account. This is a marvellous tool – it's going to count your carbs for you and keep track of your weight loss. Don't worry if you don't have access to a computer, but if you do, please check it out and try to log your food intake daily.

Or just buy a journal and write down what you eat and what you feel every day. We found this an invaluable thing to do.

Okay. You're now ready to go.

▸ Weigh yourself, naked, in the morning, after you've pooed (sorry, but it does make a difference).

▸ Measure yourself if you don't know your exact height. Now get a tape measure and take these measurements (keep the tape snug, but not tight):

▸ Neck circumference

▸ Wrist circumference

▸ Bust circumference – two measurements here: one under the bosoms, along the ribcage; one where they're biggest. Waist circumference. Measure your real waist, not your low-slung jeans waist

▸ Hip circumference. Measure at the widest part.

▸ Stomach circumference. This is the measurement that made us cry, you'll be glad to hear. And no wonder: we both looked pregnant.

Write them down in this box:

Today's date is _____

I am _____ feet/metres tall

I weigh _____ pounds/kilos

My neck measures _____ centimetres/inches

My wrists measure centimetres/inches _____

My bust measurements are _____ and _____

My waist measurement is _____ centimetres/inches

My hips measure _____ centimetres/inches

My stomach measures _____ centimetres/inches

All done? We're almost ready to go. One word of caution: you are about to embark on a life-changing way of eating. So think about when you're going to start. Don't start dieting if you have a wedding to go to next weekend, or if it's your birthday, or if you have a party coming up. Don't make feeble excuses to delay beginning, but if there's some massive social event on the horizon, delay starting the diet until it's been and gone. There is no point in making life unnecessarily difficult for yourself.

The first stage of the diet is the hardest. It is almost (but not quite) identical to the first stages of Atkins, the South Beach Diet, Protein Power and the Zone diet, among countless others. We make no apologies for this, because this shared initial approach demonstrably works.

It lasts a fortnight, during which you are cutting back carbs dramatically, to between twenty and thirty grams a day. The average-sized bowl of 'healthy' breakfast cereal contains roughly 120 grams of carbs, to give you an idea, so you're being quite hardcore here. There are two reasons for this. 1: it works and 2: you're taking control of your body, and of your eating, possibly for the first time in years. That means giving it a kick up the backside by breaking addictions to carbohydrates, primarily, but also to sugar, alcohol and caffeine.

You might feel a bit rough around the fifth day, by the way. We'd recommend timing this so that Days Five and Six are a weekend, or at least a time when you can have a little lie down. It feels a bit like coming down with the flu. We both got massive headaches on Day Five. Don't worry about it. It passes, and it doesn't come back. Much like your forthcoming weight loss, really.

The Diet, Made Simple

We're jumping the gun a bit by laying out the bare bones of the diet at this stage, but here they are. And when we say 'diet', we don't really mean 'diet'. This is more of an eating plan. For life.

Yup. We said for life.

It's okay! Don't run away! The reason it's for life is that this way of eating allows for every eventuality, *provided you stick to it in the long term.* If you do this, you can have the occasional chip butty or go on the occasional bender, and it won't affect your long-term weight loss, or weight maintenance (i.e. you won't put the pounds you've lost back on). If you stop following our method, though, the pounds *will* creep back on. This stands to reason: if you suddenly start adding two spoonfuls of sugar to every cup of tea, or scoffing half a pack of biscuits while watching telly, then you're going to get fat again. It's just a fact. A lot of diet books make all sorts of wild claims about keeping the weight off for ever. We tell it like it is. You will not put any weight back on provided you follow our plan. And if you don't, you will. Following our plan, as you will discover, is not a hardship. By the end of it, you can pretty much eat everything – though we won't lie to you and say you can go back to cereal, toast and jam at breakfast. Simple and

processed carbs are no good on a daily basis (they're no good ever, actually. We don't expect you to shun them for all eternity, but we do expect you to be intelligent about them). We'll explain more in the relevant chapters. For the moment, this is what you need to know:

You are following a high-protein, low-carb diet

The absence of bad carbohydrates will mean a stop to sugar cravings, weird periods of fatigue/energy dips in the middle of the afternoon, and that general sluggish feeling you get even though you're sleeping enough. On this diet, your energy levels will rise in a way that can seem nothing short of astonishing.

You will be eating meat, fish, eggs and seafood in unlimited quantities – and quite a lot of nuts, if you like them.

These will be accessorized by lavish helpings of (mostly) green leafy vegetables for the first two weeks. We're not going down the rabbit-food route, however: your vegetables can be served with the creamiest dressings imaginable, or with lovely melted herb butters.

After the initial two weeks, your veg intake will go up considerably – we always thought we ate reasonably healthily before we embarked on this diet, but we'd never eaten as many veggies as we do now.

Eventually – after you've lost ninety per cent of the weight you want to lose – you will be eating a totally balanced diet, which will include carbohydrates, but only good ones. So, for instance, you'll be able to have your poached eggs on delicious wholemeal bread, but not on white plastic bread. Not that unbearable, is it, as a lifestyle choice?

That's it, in a nutshell: you eat lots of protein and not very many carbs. Then you gradually up the carbs, fearlessly, knowing they are 'good' carbs, which give you energy, not 'bad' carbs, which sit on your hips and make you sluggish. You also eat fat – that's good fat, like butter and olive oil, not horrible

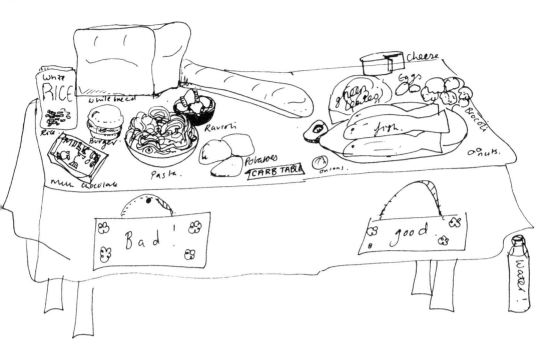

fat, like margarine (which is banned!) or 'vegetable oil'.

That's all you need to know at this stage. We'll lead you lovingly by the hand when we get to the next one.

One last thing, but it's an important one. We've said it already, but we'll just say it again. Try and eat organically wherever possible. There is no way of pretending that this doesn't make your weekly food bill more expensive, because it does. We believe the health benefits and peace of mind that come with avoiding processing, chemicals and additives are worth it. But if you are really, really hard up – we've all been there – and eating an exclusively organic diet just isn't possible, please at least try to buy organic meat. It tastes better, which is kind of crucial given how much of it you're going to consume, and it stands to reason that a battery chicken is nutritionally (to say nothing of ethically) so massively inferior to an organic one that there's really no contest. Also, when Atkins was supremely fashionable, a minority of people complained that eating the Atkins way made them feel unwell. My (India's) former neighbour was one of them, and hearing what she ate, I wasn't remotely surprised. Economy mince is not the same as ground steak. Battery chicken is not chicken. Ham made from artificially shaped 'mechanically recovered meat' is not ham. Cheap sausages made of minced snout and tail and filled with (high-carb) bread and fillers are not the same as proper butchers' sausages. And plastic cheese triangles are not the same as cheese from a proper cheese shop, or even the same as a lump of decent cheddar. Please bear all of this in mind: it can make all the difference to the diet, not only in weight-loss terms, not only in health terms, but also simply in how pleasurable you find it.

On the other hand, if this simply isn't feasible, then don't worry. But do, however you choose to shop, avoid buying items that have been obviously fiddled with in some way. You want to be buying and consuming foods that are as natural and unprocessed as possible. If all else fails, buy a large, shallow terracotta pot and grow your own salad and herbs – it's incredibly easy, super-cheap in the long term, and extremely satisfying.

The Golden Side-Rules of Our Diet

▸ **You must drink at least eight large glasses of water
a day.** This is a bare minimum. We try and aim for twelve,
and fifteen wouldn't hurt. It sounds odd, and like clichéd
women's-magazine stuff, but if you don't do this you will lose
weight at a far slower rate than if you do. You are also more
likely to be constipated, and your skin may mess up (a good
side effect of this diet: really great skin). So go for it: the more
water you drink, the faster you lose weight and the better you
feel. Have a 1.5 litre bottle of mineral water next to you at
work, and drink throughout the day. When it's gone, feel free
to start (if not finish) another one. NB: when we say water,
we mean water. Your minimum of eight glasses does not
include herbal tea, decaf coffee or any other liquid. And
that's still water, not fizzy. You can have a couple of glasses
of fizzy water a day, but no more.

▸ **You absolutely must have breakfast, lunch and dinner.**
On this diet, unlike on the usual calorie-controlled diets, not
eating actively counts against you, and slows weight loss down.
Skipping breakfast is forbidden. If your breakfast is normally
a cup of coffee, train yourself gradually to broaden it out.
Seriously: if you skip a meal, your weight loss will be
dramatically slower than if you eat three times a day. We
learned this the hard way, because it's so counter-intuitive
if you're used to the old *not eating = weight loss* equation that
may be familiar from low-calorie diets. You don't have to
learn the truth the hard way; just do as we tell you.

▸ **It is crucial to eat a combination of good fats and
protein at every meal** – so dress your salad, sauce your
steak, have your prawns dunked in (preferably home-made)
mayonnaise. The combination of fat and protein creates
weight loss with this way of eating.

▸ **Don't make the mistake of thinking that 'dieting' means
'low-fat'.** Not in our book, it doesn't. If you try to do your
own low-fat version of our diet, you won't lose the weight.
If you're having three meals a day and you still feel hungry,

butter dish

which is possible in the early stages of the diet before your appetite re-educates itself, then for heaven's sake EAT. Have a snack. Or two, or three. Don't graze all day, obviously. But don't go hungry either.

▸ **You must have a couple of handfuls of salad leaves or other leafy green veg every day.**

▸ **You need to get off your backside at least once a day**, in a very low-tech, low-effort kind of way. We suggest walking – it's easy, everyone able-bodied can do it, and it doesn't call for any expensive equipment or gym membership. How far and how often you walk initially is up to you – but you need to begin with ten minutes a day, and walk at a pace that leaves you slightly breathless (but not chronically puffed). We're going to step this up as we progress through the diet, so you might want to invest in a pair of comfortable shoes or trainers if you don't have them already.

▸ **We'll just say it again: you really, really need to take your supplements.**

▸ **Embrace fat.** Not your own, but good, friendly fats found in delicious butter and good oils. If you like crackling, eat it. Ditto streaky bacon, or mayo, or double cream drizzled (not poured) in vegetable soup. Once again, don't, whatever you do, try to do a low-fat version of this diet, thinking it'll speed things up. It won't. It'll stall you.

▸ **Weigh yourself once a week**, after your morning poo. As the diet progresses and the weight falls off, the temptation to jump on the scales five times a day is overwhelming. Try to resist it. Weight loss is not linear: your weight fluctuates fairly wildly even as you're losing it, and if you suddenly find yourself two pounds heavier today than you were yesterday, you'll get depressed – even though it all evens out in the end. So aim for once a week, and ignore the scales, or avoid them altogether, before and during your period.

▸ **Use a tape measure as well as the scales.** I (India) lost two inches off my waist before I lost a single pound. Mysterious. Again, don't measure yourself every day. Twice a week, tops.

The recipes given for the next fortnight are interchangeable.
If you don't fancy the suggestions on any given day, skip
forwards or backwards for other ideas – or ignore them
altogether and substitute your own favourites. And please bear
in mind that the recipes we're giving are for things we like to
eat. You don't have to make any of them if you don't want to!
They're here as guidance only. Any cookbook will contain recipes
for things you can eat, and if you're a keen cook, you can make
things up and adjust methods as you go along, substituting
parmesan for bread crumbs, for instance, or, in some cases
(and later on in the diet), ground almonds for flour.

If you need more recipes, or further ideas, or if the idea of
adjusting existing recipes makes you feel nervous, we strongly
recommend the two following cookbooks, which are specifically
low-carb, and which you can therefore cook from with impunity,
knowing you're not sneaking in any forbidden ingredients:

The Low-Carb Gourmet by Karen Barnaby. Published by Rodale
International Ltd, price £12.99, ISBN: 1405087935.

There are an awful lot of low-carb cookbooks around, but a
lot of them don't really float our boat. This one is wonderful, and
written with passion. We've not cooked a duff recipe from it yet.

The Low-Carb Cookbook by Fran McCullough, published in the
US by Hyperion, price $23.99 (you'll have to get your bookshop
to order this – we think it's worth it. The ISBN they'll need is
0786862734. Or order from amazon.com).

Extremely comprehensive, imaginative, glorious – a kitchen
bible, really.

Part Two
The Diet – Phase One

Phase One Day One

Oakey-pokey. Here we go: Good morning! And welcome to the first day of the new you.

Before you even get out of bed, realize this: you are NEVER AGAIN going to be as fat as you are today. Weight-wise, it's downhill all the way from here. Today, you are the fattest you're ever going to be.

So that's quite a nice thought, isn't it?

You can get up now, and go to the kitchen. If it's at all possible, feed your family before you feed yourself, or get up a bit earlier and feed yourself before you feed them. Or tell them to feed themselves, the lazy sods (unless they're infants, in which case, aaaah). You're only going to do this for a couple of days, while you get into the swing of things – afterwards, you'll all be eating at the same time. For now, though, ease yourself in.

Anyway, try and find the time for breakfast. Grabbing things on the hoof is not allowed. Sit down, please, in as calm an environment as possible, and use cutlery. Do not read the paper while you're eating. Do not put the telly on. Concentrate on what you're doing. If you are rushing out the door to the office on an empty stomach – STOP! Eat your breakfast first.

First Things First

Pour yourself a large glass of water, sip some, take your supplements, and drink up the rest. Have another glass of water if you can bear it. (Before you ask, yes, you are going to be peeing a lot for the first few days.)

This is why we're going to keep telling you to drink a great deal of water:

- ▸ Water suppresses the appetite.
- ▸ Water helps the body to metabolize fat.
- ▸ Your kidneys can't function properly if you're dehydrated –

and you're already dehydrated by the time you feel thirsty.

▸ If your kidneys can't cope, your liver helps out. This distracts it from one of its normal jobs, which is to metabolize stored fat to use as energy. If it can't do this, you don't lose weight.

▸ Water is the best antidote to fluid retention.

▸ Water helps maintain muscle tone by keeping muscles hydrated.

▸ Water helps to flush out waste.

▸ It regulates body temperature.

▸ It protects your organs and tissues.

So, when we say drink your water, we really, REALLY mean it. Not just because of anecdotal evidence, but because we know for ourselves that if you don't drink enough, you don't lose enough – plus you feel like crap. Just do it.

Breakfast

Today, it's bacon and eggs. If you don't fancy bacon and eggs, flip forward a day or two for other suggestions. But let's assume you find bacon and eggs delicious (who doesn't, really?).

2 eggs
4 rashers of bacon
freshly ground black pepper

Fry the whole lot up in a dash of groundnut oil. You can have a handful of mushrooms fried in butter on the side, and half a tomato, if you like.

You can drink decaffeinated tea or coffee, but with cream rather than milk. Or try any kind of unsweetened herbal tea. I (India) used to have a heaped teaspoon of sugar in my tea every morning (and on about twenty other occasions throughout the day). Going without it felt weird for a couple of days. Now, if I'm given sweet tea by accident, it tastes so nauseating I want to spit it out.

Useful Tip

Rooibos tea is wonderful. It's organic and caffeine-free, full of anti-oxidants, and incredibly good for you, plus it tastes yummy. The trick is to leave the bag in the water for at least four minutes (or more – it doesn't 'stew' like ordinary tea). It's good for everything from skin to sinuses, and more satisfying than ordinary herbal tea. Also, it makes you feel like a Number 1 Lady Detective. Ow!

Neris takes her decaf tea bags to work and keeps them in her desk drawer. She can't tell the difference between them and normal tea.

Have as many cups of decaf tea/coffee/herbal tea as you like during the course of today.

In a few days' time, you may find that post-breakfast is automatic pooing time. This is very good. Always weigh yourself after you poo, please – grotesquely enough, it does make a difference. Also, in time you'll notice that your poos stop being offensive. If you had any issues with wind (oh dear, what hideous nitty-gritty, and it's only Day One), they will disappear. If you had inconsistent bowel movements (varying from day to day), this too will, er, pass. You end up with incredibly efficient superpoos that just happen, are comparatively odourless, and require a mere couple of sheets of loo paper to deal with. Sorry if that's too much information, but this really isn't the place to be coy.

Find the time, between now and lunch, to go for a walk. We're talking ten minutes, but briskly. Get off the Tube one stop early and walk the rest of the way, or walk round your garden a few times, or round the block, or whatever. You want to break into a light sweat, but not be so puffed that you're practically jogging. Reward yourself with another large glass of water or two. If you're peckish, have any of the snacks allowed.

Lunch

Today, try one of these:

STEAK AU POIVRE

Easy way: have it in a restaurant, with a side salad. Marginally less easy way: make it yourself.

ONE STEAK	SALAD INGREDIENTS
peppercorns	avocado
butter	blue cheese dressing
double cream	(recipe on page 90)

Get a pestle and mortar or clean coffee grinder and crush a small handful of black peppercorns. Melt a knob of butter in a pan. Press the peppercorns into both sides of the steak so they stick. When the butter sizzles, add the steak and turn up the heat to medium.

Toss yourself a small salad while it's cooking. Put some avocado in it. Have blue cheese dressing if you wish.

Flip the steak over after a couple of minutes. It should be nice and crusty on one side. To test, poke the middle of the steak firmly with a finger. Springy – rare; less springy – medium; firm – well done.

Remove to a plate. Pour a glug of double cream into the buttery/steaky juice, let it bubble for a couple of seconds, then pour on to the waiting steak.

Eat. And don't forget to drink your water, too.

SALADE NICOISE

Ditto about the restaurant or café. Otherwise, mix together the following:

salad leaves of your choice	cut into four or six 'crescents'
half a tomato, chopped up small	flat leaf parsley
1 can of tuna in olive oil	sea salt and black pepper
a handful of cooked green beans	vinaigrette (recipe on page 00)
a couple of hard boiled eggs, each	

Jumble it all together.

Eat.

If you're still hungry, have more. If you're still hungry, have a plate of cheese.

Now carry on with your afternoon.

Supper

If you like olives or nuts, nibble on a handful while you're cooking. Have a glass of water while you're at it.

CAULIFLOWER FAUX-MASH

We used to HATE cauliflower. Now, to us, cauliflower rocks. Please try this – it's fantastic.

half a cauliflower	salt and pepper
butter	nutmeg, if you like
double cream	

Steam the cauliflower florets until very tender. Chuck into a blender. Blend with a generous knob of butter and a glug of cream. Season. Serve. (Use any leftovers for fried mash cakes for tomorrow's breakfast.)

Tip: faux-mash makes an excellent topping for this diet's version of shepherd's pie, or cottage pie (see recipe page 115), and works as a substitute wherever you would ordinarily use mash.

TARRAGON CHICKEN

1 organic chicken breast per person, more if you're starving	butter
	groundnut oil
1 bunch of fresh tarragon	half a lemon
1 small pot of double cream	

Cut the chicken into strips, or chunks if you prefer. Melt the butter in the pan on medium heat and add a tiny blob of groundnut oil. When it's sizzling, add the tarragon and chicken strips, and cook the strips until they go crispy and brown (if crispy and brown and a bit sticky is what you like. I know I do). Add enough cream to make a sauce – a third to half of the small tub should do it. Wait a minute for it all to meld and bubble. Add the juice from the lemon, taste, and season if you think it needs it. Eat with the mash. Drink your water.

That wasn't so hard, was it? And pretty delicious, if we say so ourselves. Give yourself a pat on the back, my friend – you've made it through Day One.

Thought for the Day

Obstacles are what you see if you take your eyes off the goal.

How We Felt on Day One

It doesn't feel much like a diet.

Here is more of what we thought when we were in your shoes, just starting out. We kept journals throughout our diet journey, and here are the relevant bits for today.

India: *I am just under sixteen stone. For God's sake.*

Not sure I'm doing this diet right – feel like I haven't stopped eating. Don't feel remotely hungry. Well, I did feel hungry every now and then, so I ate. Not sure about sugarless tea, but hey, there are worse things. What's different is that today I had that boring thing that nutritionists always talk about: Three Proper Meals. Usually I just graze constantly.

Must have had a lot of calories. Ah well. I have faith. Well, kind of … I can't get over how much I ate. Had salami for snacks, and olives. So much fat. Good fat, though – olive oil and butter.

Quite weird having nothing sweet at all. Don't have sweet tooth, so not too bad, but I'd be unhappy if I were a chocoholic.

Peed loads. Like being eight months pregnant.

Feel very gung-ho, though. Quite excited. My main thought so far is: this is painless. Actually, forget excited – am exhilarated by the possibilities.

Neris: *It's Day One and I weigh sixteen stone ten pounds.*

Have got to do this. This has to be the last diet I ever go on. I've got to try to stick to it.

If ever there was a sign that I should be doing this it must be the three people who stopped me yesterday:

10.00am: The bank manager said to me in the bank today,

'Mrs Johnson, obviously with the imminent arrival there will be a lot of changes for you so we should talk about some saving schemes!' Stunned. I'm afraid I went along with him. I could not be bothered to argue and just said, 'Yes it is going to be really busy. I won't be able to talk to you for a few months, until it has all settled down again.' What a cheek. Does it look that obvious?

Having never had a full-length mirror I have not had the time since my daughter was born (over two years ago!) to really think about the stark reality of what I actually look like. I know I have been a bit silly and kept wearing some of my stretchy maternity clothes. I know that is uncool and it is not something I am proud of.

Anyway, at 11.30 (this is not an exaggeration) I told the woman in the local clothes shop that I was about to go on a diet. She replied, 'Is that healthy when you are so far gone?' There followed a 3pm encounter with a woman I know (vaguely) who crossed the street to congratulate me on my bump. After these three incidents I thought it was all funny but I did feel slightly empty. I'm not joking but that really was all in one day.

So there you go. I've got to do this. I have spent years and years doing diets where I fixate about a date in the future, like a wedding, a birthday or a party, and I just go all out for that but then I lose my momentum. I need to change things long term now. I don't have the energy for anything else. So off I go.

Pm. I have a throbbing head. I feel like my shoulders weigh a ton. And I'm very, very bleary. But hurrah I've stuck to it.

I've had decaf tea, three eggs scrambled with two tablespoons of double cream and a blob of butter.

My lovely lunch left me strangely full: I got a salade nicoise from the sandwich bar around the corner from work. Hurrah. For dinner I made a huge effort making the Chicken Tarragon. I'm a rubbish cook but India assured me it was easy, and it was. And really nice to eat.

Felt really pleased with myself, like I'd achieved something.

I drank so much water and decaf tea. I'm on the toilet a lot which is a bit annoying but I feel quite good.

It's easy to stick to the food. I'm on a roll but don't expect me to be interesting. My head hurts too much.

I'm going to do it this time.

Staple recipes of the day

BLUE CHEESE DRESSING
Blend 1 cup mayo with 1 cup sour cream. Add enough olive oil to make it dressing consistency. Season. Add a good handful of crumbled blue cheese.

VINAIGRETTE
In a clean jam jar, put one third vinegar (not balsamic) to two–thirds olive oil. Add lemon juice or mustard to taste. Season. Put the lid on and give it a shake. That's it. Add garlic, herbs or both for variety.

Phase One Day Two

Good morning! We hope you're feeling good and full of optimism. You're also probably feeling slightly strange. This is absolutely normal. Work with it. Stick at it. It will pass. Not only are you losing weight, but you're also detoxing. Your body needs to catch up with itself, and when it does, it's going to be very, very happy, and reward you with some serious and dramatic shrinkage.

Before we start today, we'd like you to congratulate yourself on having made it through yesterday. The beginning of the diet is the hardest part, and you're on the way.

Like yesterday, and like every day in the future, yea, even until the end of time, start by taking your supplements and drinking a big glass of water, or two if you can manage it. You're allowed a slice of lemon or lime in there, if you like, for a bit of added zing.

Breakfast

Eventually, you're going to re-educate your taste buds so that certain foods that you don't traditionally think of as 'breakfasty' become part of your eating regime. For the moment, though, let's stick to the more traditional options. You're welcome to have bacon and eggs again, but let's say today you fancy sausages. Fry or grill them using butter or groundnut oil. Remember, if the former, to add a dot of oil to the butter to stop it from burning – this is always necessary when frying in butter, unless you deliberately want the nutty taste of 'burnt' butter. Accessorize with half a grilled tomato. Chuck in an egg if you fancy it, and/or a handful of mushrooms. If you have any cauliflower mash left over from yesterday, fry it up into cakes.

Eat sitting down, and with cutlery. Drink some water – before or after the meal, ideally, so that everything isn't sloshing about in your stomach like soup.

Do whatever you do in the morning (in our case, resist the fairly overwhelming urge to go back to bed, and try to get on with work instead). Mid-morning, if that's convenient, go for a little walk. Yesterday's was ten minutes. It would be good if today's was fifteen, if that's manageable. If not, then ten is fine. Remember: you want to be slightly out of breath, but not huffing and puffing.

Lunch

ROAST BUTTERNUT SQUASH SOUP WITH PARMESAN AND BACON
Piece of cake, this (well, not quite cake), and delicious.

one butternut squash
olive oil
vegetable or chicken stock (cubes
   are fine, Marigold is better)

Parmesan cheese, grated
crispy bacon

Cut the butternut squash in two lengthways. Brush it with olive oil and stick it in the oven, heated to 190°C, gas 5, for an hour or so, depending on its size – it's ready when soft. Scoop out the flesh and whizz it in a blender. Put it in a pan with enough vegetable or chicken stock to achieve a consistency that's pleasing to you. Gently heat through for twenty minutes or so. Serve with one big heaped tablespoon of Parmesan per bowl, and some crispy, crumbled bacon. Feel free to have seconds.

   If you want to gild the lily, you could add some rosemary leaves to the roasting squash, and/or drizzle the finished product with a little truffle oil.

If you're still hungry, have a side salad – not a gigantic, main-course size one, but a couple of handfuls of leaves, dressed however you like (excepting, of course, any sugary dressing). Good olive oil and lemon juice make a lovely, crisp dressing which is quite nice after the richness of the soup. Have a piece of cheese if you're still hungry.

This is all very lovely, but I work in an office. What do I eat?

You bring a packed lunch, or go out to your local sandwich bar.
A packed lunch isn't terribly glamorous, granted, but at least you
know exactly what's in it, which in the circumstances is extremely
helpful. The problem with ready-made stuff is that so much of it
contains hidden carbs, and also often hidden sugars. Most of the
recipes in this book can be slung into some Tupperware and
reheated, if your office should run to a microwave.

Failing that, though, what you're after – apart from lunch
on expenses, because as you'll already be able to see, this diet
is extremely restaurant-friendly – is an old-fashioned sandwich
shop, of the kind that has sandwich fillings laid out in boxes
behind a glass counter. If you should be lucky enough to be within
striking distance of such a gem, cherish it and make friends with
the staff. Have a recce, and then choose from any of the following
breadless options. Have generous dollops of any of the following:

- prawn mayonnaise
- egg mayonnaise
- tuna mayonnaise (there's a bit of a theme developing here)
- crispy bacon
- sliced tomato
- sliced cucumber
- sliced avocado
- sliced olives
- smoked salmon
- cream cheese
- any other kind of cheese – mozzarella is nice with
tomato and avocado
- roast beef (and you can have horseradish with it)[3]
- roast pork, lamb, etc.
- hams
- any fish

[3] Horseradish seems to speed up weight loss for some people. We don't know why. If you like roast
beef, try and have creamed horseradish on the side.

- salamis and other cold meats
- sausages
- pâté
- taramasalata, if it's not bulked out with bread (ask)

Ask for any of these ingredients in salad form, i.e. with lettuce and dressing (check for sugar), or have the salad on the side and use the lettuce to make wraps. It's not necessarily wildly exciting, but then neither is it significantly more boring than the usual lunchtime sarnie, frankly.

Get on with your afternoon, and remember – if you're hungry, eat. Have some nuts in your bag, like a squirrel. And please remember to keep drinking your water, along with any decaf tea/coffee you might fancy.

Supper

ROAST COD WITH HERBS AND TOMATOES; SIDE SALAD

1 cod fillet per person – two if
    you're starving
good olive oil
half a tomato per person, sliced

generous handful of any fresh herb,
    or mixture of fresh herbs, if you
    like – try thyme and rosemary

Brush each cod fillet – and it doesn't have to be cod, it could be any other robust and fresh-looking fish – with olive oil. Cover with sliced tomato. Crush the herbs a little so they release their fragrance, and stick them on top of the cod. Wrap the whole thing up neatly – or messily, if you must – in tin foil. Roast at 190°C, gas 5, for fifteen minutes. Serve. Don't forget to pour the herby olive oil that's puddled at the bottom of the foil on to the fish. Serve with a salad – it's nice with rocket and Parmesan.

You'll notice we're low on puddings. That is because one of us (India) disapproves of artificial sweeteners, especially at this stage of the diet, when you're weaning yourself off sugar. But don't worry – we'll go into your pudding options in a few days, though they are limited.

Drink your water.

Useful Tip
Make herb butters to melt on to meat or fish. Let unsalted butter soften at room temperature and add chopped fresh herbs; shape into a roll using cling film; refrigerate. Then cut off a slice or two to melt on to your steak (or whatever). You can make garlic butter this way too, and blue cheese and walnut, which is especially nice with beef.

Thought for the Day
If I can repeat failure, I can repeat success.

How We Felt on Day Two
India: *I still feel gung-ho. I also feel odd in a way that's hard to describe: I'm perfectly fine, and functioning normally, but I feel a bit speedy and there's a weird (not bad, just weird) taste in my mouth. I keep brushing my teeth. All of this so far is fine, except that earlier I really wanted a Starbucks vanilla latte, for some peculiar reason – I normally have them about twice a month. Milk aside, I don't think sugary syrup is really an option. Bummer. Never mind. Went to a restaurant for dinner. Odd to have no wine. Ate a fillet steak with béarnaise sauce and a side of creamed spinach (yummy), and then a cheese plate. Felt oddly indifferent to the bread on the table. Wonder how long that'll last.*

Was lovely to come home a: sober (not that I make a habit of getting pissed! I just mean it was nice to be clear-headed and not even a tiny bit tiddly), and b: not stuffed, but – horrible phrase – 'pleasantly full'. Just as well, as the baby was up in the night.

Told someone I was following a high-protein diet. She was delighted to tell me some ridiculous story about a woman a friend of a friend knows. For God's sake. Might not tell people I'm

dieting. They're weirdly keen to come forward with horror stories. Sisterhood, eh?

I haven't pooed since the day before yesterday, which doesn't feel great. Very slight headache before going to bed (in about two minutes), but am hoping to sleep it off.

On the plus side, though: I'm finding this diet very easy to follow. I don't have a sweet tooth, so I'm not missing the sugar (except in my tea and hypothetical latte), and I really liked the fact that I could have eaten loads of things on the menu at the restaurant. Very glad I didn't have to interrogate the waiter at length about ingredients – it's all very obvious. So far, so good. And I haven't once been hungry.

Neris: *Woke up feeling like I've got mild flu. Drowsy, irritable and blocked nose. Feeling rubbish, basically. Couldn't help but weigh myself. Wow – lost four pounds! My body is so weird. I can literally put on five pounds in one meal and take it off overnight. Anyway, still going to keep going on it. (I mustn't keep weighing myself.) Don't understand how the weight actually disappears … but it has gone.*

Had some bacon and scrambled eggs for breakfast. It's 1.08 now and I feel really full. Which is also extraordinary for me!

I did have one chunk of cheese ten minutes ago, though, which should keep me going until lunch. Desperately need a Twix bar. Life would be so nice if I could just eat one with a nice cup of normal tea.

5pm. Feeling rubbish. Sluggish. Overwhelmingly tired. If I closed my eyes now I would go to sleep (not good when I'm supposed to go in to a meeting in about five minutes). I feel a bit embarrassed by how much I'd like to go off the diet already and its only Day Two. You really have to be focused and have an excuse to go off it. Then I see myself in the mirror or look at a shop full of millions of items of clothes that I could never fit – it is those moments when I really feel angry with myself – the rest of the time I sort of feel normal and don't see why I can't eat what I want. Then I feel angry with myself that I got into this situation and

that I've wasted so much time trying to just get rid of this weight. Feeling this rubbish and fluey doesn't help the general downward spiral. Went to bed feeling not at all hungry.

Haven't drunk enough water. Only had a litre. Every time I had water through the day I felt better, though, so I'm going to try to have more tomorrow. Finding it difficult working and feeling a bit rough.

TICK

TICK

Phase One Day Three

Well, we're very happy to see you still with us. You are
very possibly not feeling that fabulous today. Or maybe
you are: Neris was practically a wreck on the third day, and
I was pretty much fine. Some people are fortunate enough
to go through this early stage of the diet feeling A-okay, and
some (the majority, I would say) find they have a couple of
rather rough days. All we can say, now we're ten stone down,
is please bear with us. And if you're feeling wonderful, please
don't panic and convince yourself you're going to feel
dreadful tomorrow, because it's not by any means a given.
I think that perhaps I felt better than Neris because I didn't
eat very much sugar (or chocolate which is Neris's thing)
before the diet, so the lack of it was less of a shock to my
system. But maybe that had nothing to do with it at all.
The point is, it'll pass. Any day now, you're going to wake
up feeling unusually fantastic. We promise.

So: you should be reasonably familiar with the morning
drill by now. Take your supplements. Drink your water,
and have another glass if you can manage it.

Breakfast

This morning, as a change from eggs, we're going to
have smoked salmon and cream cheese. Buy some smoked
salmon. Buy a tub of cream cheese – the genuine article,
please, not any 'light' version. Spread the cream cheese
generously on any number of pieces of smoked salmon,
roll up and eat, with lemon juice and black pepper if you
like. If you want to add sliced avocado to your roll-ups,
go right ahead.

Remember to go for your walk. We're still on fifteen
minutes if you can manage it.

Phase One Day Three

A Little Look Inside Your Closet

Today, we're going to go off at a slight tangent and give you an additional project. We want you to have a really good look at your wardrobe. If you're anything like us, it contains a load of garments that are only in there not because they're gorgeous, not because they make you feel fabulous, but because they fit. We've all done that kind of panicky shopping, grabbing the nearest black sack because it isn't eye-bleedingly ugly, and it's got enough Lycra in it to cover a multitude of sins.

Soon – sooner than you imagine, if you stick at it – you are going to have to acquire a whole new wardrobe. There's an entire chapter on dressing for your size coming up, but for the moment we need you to do the following:

Equip yourself with some bin bags.

If you have breasts larger than a 34C, put any round-necked tops, polo necks or T-shirts in the bin bag. You don't have to throw them away: just store them somewhere for the time being. On the other hand, if you're confident with a pair of scissors, you can cut the T-shirts into V-necks.

Put anything with an elasticated waist into the bin bag, excepting pyjamas or tracky bottoms. Elasticated waists do nothing for anyone and not having any waistbands digging into you only encourages you to pretend you don't have a weight problem.

Have a look in the mirror and work out what the widest part of your body is. It is likely to be your stomach or your backside. Now chuck out any item of clothing that ends where your widest part begins: tops that end just above the bottom; shirts that end where your stomach starts.

Put aside anything bulky, unless it's very cold outside and you have no central heating. Those classic items of comfort wear – big sweatshirts, thick, loose sweaters, baggy shirts – do nobody any favours. Get rid of them.

If you have any leggings lurking around, throw them out if you're over thirty, unless you can genuinely state that you have spectacular legs. Even if you do, beware of leggings that end at the widest part of your calf.

Skirts: if they're in any way gathered or pleated, chuck them out. Any extra fabric around the stomach is a disaster, and makes you look twice as wide as you already are. Basically, bulk makes you bulky. We're not suggesting you totter about in pencil skirts, but a narrow silhouette is what you're after, so anything floaty, 'peasanty', pleated or bunchy is a no-no. You want a really clean line, and no centre fastenings, i.e. buttons around the stomach. A hook-and-eye fastening to the side of your waist is best.

Trousers: be brutal with yourself. If they're skin-tight on the thighs, dump them (unless you're the Leggings Queen with the spectacular legs). If they're skin-tight across the butt, ditto. Be very, very careful with jeans, which can add an extraordinary amount of bulk if they're badly cut, as most are. The pleated rule above applies here, too – even more so, in fact – there is nothing – nothing – less flattering to a full figure than pleated, chino-style trousers.

Three bags full.

So what can I wear?

What you are after are thin, relatively fitted clothes. Not only are these the most flattering things to wear when you're carrying extra bulk, but they can be layered to great effect. So, dig out tea dresses, thin, form-skimming (but not tight), U-necked or V-necked cotton tops, unbulky jerseys and cardigans, tunic tops. These will form the staple of your wardrobe for the next few weeks. It is a myth that if you are fat you need to swamp yourself in loose tent-like garments: these simply make you look like an unlovely cross between Demis Roussos and Big Daddy. We don't understand why shops persist in selling them, and in urging you towards them if you're a size eighteen or above. They're hideous. Neris wrote in her diary: 'I looked at my clothes and realized they consisted of my "fat" wardrobe (going up to size twenty-four and then some maternity stuff that I still occasionally wear) and my 'thin' wardrobe (a couple of foxy size twelve suits both worn only once in 1999) and all the sizes in between. I have put everything that didn't fit me ON THIS VERY DAY into plastic bags, labelled them by size and put them in the drawers under the bed. For the first time I can actually see the choice of clothes I REALLY HAVE. And realize all I have is fifteen different types of black top and actually not much apart from that.'

On page 198 you will find photos and tips for looking the best you can at all stage of weight loss.
For the time being, it's only Day Three, and we just want you to have a think about the future. As far as dressing for now is concerned, try to remember the following simple rules:

Wrap dresses actually actively look better on curves than they do on skinny bodies. They must be the right size, though – having a gaping band of material where the 'wrap' bit of fabric has been yanked too tight looks (and feels) horrible. Every high street store stocks wrap dresses, which have become classics. Wear with a pretty camisole underneath for work, and with a beautiful necklace and some cleavage for the evening.

Reasonably tailored clothes are more flattering than shapeless sacks, even if a shapeless sack is exactly what you feel like. You need a proper waistband, too.

You're never too fat for **pretty tights or stockings**, or for pretty shoes. Don't slob about in comfy flatties all the time: a small heel dramatically improves anybody's legs, and patterned hosiery draws attention away from a hefty mid-section. We love fishnets, but again, your local department store will leave you spoilt for choice.

Scoop necks or V-necks win out over high necks every time.

Invest in some control pants. They're not by any stretch of the imagination a lovely garment, but they absolutely work. Marks and Spencer's Magic Knickers are, we believe, an absolutely essential piece of kit.

Go and get measured for a bra, if you didn't heed our advice earlier in this book. The majority of British women wear the wrong size, and a well-fitting bra can make all the difference to the appearance of your chest. If you're fat, the last thing you need is a bra that creates strange rolls of blubber by your armpits, or one that bisects your bosoms so that you appear to have four instead of two. Also, if you don't have enough uplift from your bra, your chest appears to meld seamlessly into your stomach, which is a really, really bad look, and one that is sadly very common in overweight women. We recommend Rigby & Peller, Bravissimo, John Lewis and M&S as good places to get fitted.

Wear nothing sausage-tight, but wear nothing ridiculously loose either.

Accessorize like mad, and get in touch with your inner makeup artist. It might be an idea to have a series of department store makeovers over the next couple of weeks – but do your homework: if the woman approaching you with her brushes and lipsticks has an orange face and stripes of burgundy blusher, go elsewhere.

Underwear aside, if our recommendations entail a shopping trip because you have nothing resembling the clothes we suggest, please don't go mad, and please only buy cheap things – we like H&M, whose range goes up to a size thirty, and New Look, whose range goes up to size twenty-four. The clothes you buy now will be too big in a matter of weeks, so don't go overboard.

That's probably enough to be getting on with. Incidentally, by Day Three you may very well find that some parts of your clothing – the waistband, or across the shoulders, or over the bust – feel looser. This is why we're suggesting thinking about your wardrobe. You are probably feeling a mixture of apprehension and excitement at the weeks ahead, and we have found that thinking about clothes – particularly about the sorts of clothes we wouldn't have dreamed of wearing when we started, like titchy designer jeans – was an excellent incentive. Because the truth of the matter is that, no matter how fat you feel now, you're shrinking. And if you want designer jeans, my dears, you shall have them – and look fabulous in them. But not quite yet.

Lunch

We're assuming you've been busy with the bin bags and that there isn't really any time to cook today. Have an omelette – it's delicious, it's filling, and it takes minutes to make. Choose from any of the allowed fillings – cheese, or a combination of cheeses, green leafy veg, tomatoes, onions, garlic, ham, salami, cold meats, and so on. Or go the whole hog and make a big Spanish omelette, which you can cut into chunks and help yourself to throughout the day. Drink your water.

Supper

One of the pleasing things about our diet is that it is so supremely restaurant-friendly. Tonight, we suggest you find this out for yourself, either by venturing out or by ordering a takeaway. I (India) eat industrial amounts of Indian food, which fits in with this way of eating beautifully. No rice or bread, obviously, and no mango chutney – though you're allowed pickles. Most South Indian food, with its reliance on pancakes and batter, is out for the time being, but anything else is more than allowed. Grilled meats, like lamb kebabs or chicken tikka, are made for this diet. Creamy curries, provided they contain no potato, are heaven-sent, and vegetable curries are a brilliant way of getting your greens. Chinese food is another possibility: crispy duck (and a dollop of plum sauce isn't going to kill you just this once, provided you don't make a daily habit of it), braised meats, steamed fish or seafood, all those sizzling dishes, and of course bok choi, a fantastic choice as far as green leafy veg are concerned. If you like Japanese food, go mad with the sashimi. Here are some other diet-friendly restaurant foods:

▸ chicken satay
▸ seabass with ginger and spring onions
▸ roast duck
▸ chicken liver pâté
▸ smoked salmon in all its manifestations
▸ mozzarella, basil and tomato salad
▸ omelettes (if you haven't had one for lunch)
▸ grilled meats
▸ liver and onions
▸ roast meats, e.g. roast pork and crackling, or roast chicken
▸ kebabs
▸ eggs Benedict or Florentine, without the muffin but with lots of hollandaise
▸ Caesar salad, minus the croutons
▸ most soups
▸ pretty much any fish dish you care you mention
▸ lobster, langoustines and crab
▸ antipasti – salami, cheese, olives
▸ beef or tuna carpaccio

- ceviche
- fruits de mer
- osso bucco
- moules marinières
- chateaubriand with béarnaise sauce
- sauerkraut
- oysters

And that's only the tip of a pretty massive iceberg.

Thought for the Day
Believe in yourself. You can do it.

How We Felt on Day Three
India: *I'm in the swing now. I can totally do this – to my amazement, I don't find any aspect of this diet difficult. Even my sugarless tea was much more bearable today. Marched briskly around the park for fifteen minutes – tremendously boring, especially as it was drizzling. Face went bright red, and of course I bumped into two people I knew, looking deeply unphotogenic, with crimson face and frizzy rain-hair. Went to a drinks party tonight, which would have been a great deal more fun if I could have had a drink, but am determined not to drink for at least a fortnight (famous last words). Being totally sober in a room filled with drunken people is boring in the extreme. Left after half an hour and was home by 8.30, which I took great pleasure in – a week ago I'd have stayed longer, got mildly drunk by accident, come home late, fallen into bed and woken up feeling a bit rough. As it was, had a bath and watched telly in bed, feeling very smug and pleased with myself.*

Emailed Dr S, my GP, to ask him what he thought of the whole high-protein/low-carb thing. He was extremely encouraging and in favour. I might have some blood tests done, to compare and contrast before and after. I DO still feel peculiar, but it's manageable. Low-level headache.

There is quite a peculiar taste in my mouth, but I'm getting

used to it. *Paranoid about halitosis, though A, whom I breathe on like a dragon, assures me this isn't the case. Still, though – go out and buy a Sonicare toothbrush and industrial quantities of floss. Later, discover to my horror that meat has a horrible way of lodging itself between your teeth and, uh, decaying. Am now going to floss and brush after every meal.*

Didn't poo today. I really hate not pooing. I hope there's some poo-action tomorrow.

Neris: *Stayed same weight (I did weigh. Sorry). Shouldn't have but couldn't resist. But found myself deflated by not having lost weight. Really don't want to do that again. Exhausted again. But to be honest I'm always exhausted, ever since having my daughter (maybe even before if I'm honest). Feel like I've got something wrong with me. I think I'm ill. Really irritated that I'm not organized for the day's eating. Had two eggs scrambled with double cream. And had an ounce of cheese.*

Having decaf tea with double cream. Where are the vegetables? This doesn't feel right to me. I just don't feel like I'm on a diet so it makes me nervous.

Feel rubbish and irritated. Had to get out of work today and get some fresh air ... But I still feel rubbish. Slightly snapped at someone on the phone.

I just don't have a lot of patience today.

I had sliced chicken roast and prawns for lunch with a side salad of spinach.

And have bought a cheap job lot of small water bottles in the hope I'll start drinking more and I'll feel better.

It was my friend's birthday and we did a little party for her at our house in the evening. So much cake and drink going around ... I had a tiny nibble. Not because I was tempted actually but because I just thought I should join in, but only a tiny nibble. I didn't want to draw attention to myself. Don't think that is the right way to do it though. I have such an all-or-nothing mentality. Need to refresh myself on how to deal with peer pressure. It is amazing to me how being on a diet can make so many people feel they have the licence to comment.

All is fine though. It's nearly 7pm and I'm feeling shattered again … and guess what … irritated. My poor daughter didn't get a very long bedtime story tonight.

Had some salmon fillets and some veg for supper.

Phase One Day Four

So, Day Four. You may not be feeling that fantastic. You may be wondering if this book comes with a money-back guarantee. Or, you may be thinking, 'My goodness, I have a strange idea that this may be working,' and have a sort of 'thin' feeling, best described as a kind of hollowness. Probably you're somewhere in the middle: you have faith, but, not to put too fine a point on it, you've felt better.

Well, take comfort. It doesn't get much worse than this. Apart from tomorrow. After that, it's plain sailing all the way *provided you don't cheat*. At this stage of the diet, the smallest, titchiest cheat is the kiss of death. It may seem very odd that one little mouthful of toast or a mini-bite of cheesecake should completely derail you and halt your weight loss, but it will. We can't repeat this often enough. Please stick to the programme. You're already losing weight. You have started burning your own fat. Don't stop now. If you have a headache, take paracetamol, and up your water intake. We're sympathetic to your plight, of course. But we also want to make it clear that not feeling 100 per cent is an obstacle that you just have to crash through, which you will, any second now, on your path to slimness. And once you've crashed through it, it's gone for ever.

Besides, if you are feeling rough – Neris felt really grim, India didn't – the thing to bear in mind is that you aren't feeling rough because you've done something terrible to yourself. You're feeling rough because you're detoxing from all the things that are really bad for you, which make you fat, and which will continue to make you fatter and fatter for all eternity unless you get a grip now. Your body is readjusting, that's all. Both it and you will feel much better once the readjustment has occurred. It may help to think of this period as being the equivalent of stopping smoking: a couple of days of mild discomfort in exchange for a lifetime of freedom.

Except that you're not going to fail. Listen, we did it. And we were the least-disciplined, weakest-willed people we know when it came to the question of food. Now, onwards and upwards.

Breakfast

Water and supplements first, remember. Then take your pick from the options on offer, with which you should by now be familiar. Have poached eggs, maybe on a bed of buttered spinach. Or scramble them with a dash of cream, and have some smoked salmon on the side. Or have boiled eggs, perhaps using asparagus spears as soldiers.

But what we would suggest today is that you experiment with breakfast foods which aren't so traditional – like the buttered kippers, the bacon and eggs – and have a go at trying something you would never usually associate with eating first thing in the morning. The truth of the matter is that it is quite possible to get tired of eggs, perfect and speedy as they may be. You can get egged out on this diet if you don't watch out, and so the clever thing to do is never to let yourself get to the 'eggs make me gag' stage.

How do you do this? By having something lunchy for breakfast. Remember: apart from toast and jam, none of the traditional breakfast foods are sweet – not eggs and bacon, not the full English, not salty porridge, not kippers. And yet for some reason many of us have got it into our heads that breakfast must be sugary. I (India) have never had a problem with this – as I was explaining earlier, I prefer salty things to sweet ones, so gorging on pastries, or croissants and apricot jam has never been my bag. I've often had leftovers for breakfast, even before embarking on this way of eating. Personally, I really love left-over curry – sometimes I don't even bother reheating it – but I do see that this might be a bit extreme for most people. But you could ease yourself in the gentler way, perhaps by pretending that you've woken up in Bavaria by accident and therefore have no choice other

than to breakfast on cold cuts and cheese. Half of
Europe eats this way, so there must be something in it.
Ham, smoked meat, salami, cubes of cheese: it's awfully
good, and awfully filling. Or try something relatively bland,
such as mozzarella dressed with olive oil, torn into pieces
and mixed with diced tomato and avocado, and maybe
a few basil leaves. Or have a couple of sticky, caramelized
sausages (which you could have with onion gravy, provided
you don't use flour to thicken it). Experiment. You may
very well find that last night's roast chicken dipped into
a creamy dressing makes a very excellent breakfast indeed.

Useful Tip

There is nothing less satisfying than eating standing up in
front of the open fridge door. You may be consuming the right
foods, in generous quantities, but you won't feel like you've
eaten properly – you'll feel like you've picked at things and had
a tiny snack, which means you'll feel grumpy and swizzed. So
always, always arrange your food on a large plate. You may think,
why bother – I'm in a rush, and I'm only opening a bag of lettuce
leaves to go with my Parma ham. But you'd be wrong. Put the
ham on the plate. Make a nice little pile of leaves, and dress
them. Chop up a tomato. De-stone half an avocado, and anoint
it with lime juice and olive oil. Cut yourself a couple of generous
chunks of cheese. See? You now have something proper to eat.
Even if it's only an assembly job, as opposed to something you've
cooked from scratch, eating it served up properly, rather than
grabbed on the hoof, can – and does – make all the difference.

Never eat standing up. Never, never, never. Eating standing
up makes you dissatisfied. Being dissatisfied makes you eat
some more. Ergo, eating standing up makes you fat.

Now, walking. We really hope you've been doing it. It makes
a difference, otherwise we wouldn't even suggest it. We were
lucky, in that we started our diets in the summer, when
walking was relatively pleasant, and usually rain-free. You

may not be so lucky: if you're doing this in the depths of winter, the idea of getting off your backside can appear very counter-intuitive.

BuT you've GOT to do it !

You are going to lose a great deal of weight. To be perfectly honest with you, and very un-PC, you would lose the weight at this stage whether you exercised or not.

BUT: there is no way on earth that you will appear toned if you don't exercise. You will be thin, but floppy.

Later – don't worry: much, much later – we will suggest you step up your exercise a bit if you've lost a great deal of weight, because as we discovered, failure to do so means the formerly fat bits of your body turn into thin but weirdly saggy bits, and this is – obviously – really not at all a good look. But then, we did lose five stone each: it may not be a problem if the shrinkage you have in mind is less drastic.

Still, though, you've got to move around a bit. It speeds up your metabolism, which means you lose weight faster, and walking tones your legs and bottom, which you absolutely need to do if you're planning on losing more than a couple of pounds. If you can bear to do a silly pumping motion with your arms at the same time, it'll work them as well. So get walking. We mean it. Like we keep saying, you're after a degree of breathlessness, but not so much that you huff and puff and go purple in the face.

Walking Dos and Don'ts

Wear proper trainers, even if it means taking your shoes to work in a bag. Not 'fashion' trainers, or the old moth-eaten ones you've had lying around for five years, or the ones that look the most photogenic: wear well-fitting (i.e. snug) ones that won't give you blisters, rub against your toes or flip-flop at the back. And wear socks with them.

Take large strides. You may not be used to them if you

live the rest of your life in heels, but tottery little steps aren't what we're after here. Pretend you're wearing seven-league boots.

Comedy arm movements – as if you were a cartoon of somebody walking – it will make you feel slightly embarrassed for the first few days, but then you get used to looking like a fool. They help work the upper body. We suggest you do them.

If you are quite fat, it's entirely likely that your thighs rub together when you walk. Don't use this as an excuse not to do it. Instead, wear thickish trousers rather than a dress (cotton is best – most breathable) and march away, safe in the knowledge that thigh-rub will soon be a thing of the past. If you must walk wearing a dress or skirt, use talcum powder to facilitate slip and minimize rub. Or wear loose men's boxer shorts, which go down past the worst rubby bit. Be prepared for all weather eventualities, so that you don't cut your walk short because it's raining. Buy a lightweight, foldable mac or cagoule (wooh! Lookin' good!) and keep it in your handbag.

Try not to walk carrying something heavy on one side of your body only. If you're carrying shopping bags, spread the weight evenly. If you're lugging heavy things to and from work, buy a backpack. You don't want to knacker your spine. Speaking of which, try and be aware of posture. Often, this means standing up so straight that you feel self-conscious. Do it anyway. Good posture lengthens, and can therefore be quite dramatically slimming. And you'll lose some of the benefits of walking if you do so while sporting the posture of a chimpanzee.

Music can really get you moving: make yourself a walking playlist and download it onto your iPod. All those dancy songs you're slightly embarrassed about still liking – Dead or Alive and Abba, in India's case, Scissor Sisters, Lily Allen and Beyoncé in Neris's. Steer clear of ballads, obviously, or anything that's not frenetically up-tempo. India has tried marching briskly to sonatas, but it doesn't really work. If you have iTunes, there's a ready-made 'Fitness mix' on the iTunes store that you can download, and it's not bad at all.

We swear by MBT, aka Masai Barefoot Technology, trainers. They're not beautiful and they are expensive, but we can't shake off the feeling that they have an extremely effective toning action on the legs, stomach and bottom. See www.mbtshoes.co.uk for information and stockists, but don't get too hung up on this, or think you can't walk properly without them: any well-fitting trainer will do.

Walking with a pram or buggy is great; walking with very little children less so, because they won't be able to keep up with you. You'll both feel miserable about this, so leave them at home. If you're home alone with them, wait until the evening, when you can hopefully park them with someone for a little while. Walking at dusk, or in the dark, can be quite liberating, especially if you feel self-conscious.

Walking with a dog is one of life's great joys.

Walk as fast as you like as your stamina increases over the coming weeks, but don't run. According to a couple of personal trainers we know, almost everybody runs wrongly, in a way that jars their body and impacts badly on their knees – ten years down the line, if not right away. We're not in the business of messing up your joints, or ours, so: don't run. Besides, it can be disastrous on the bust in the long term if you're anything heavier than a B-cup. However, if you absolutely insist on running, either get someone from a gym to show you how to do it properly, or take a look at the Couch (potato) to 5K programme from www.coolrunning.com.

Try to vary your walks. If you're working in the middle of town during the week, then there isn't much you can do about it. But try to find a park or bit of countryside at the weekends – or a beach, if you're lucky enough to live near one. Walking the exact same route every day can get boring (though never mind – the point isn't to thrill you, the point is to make you shrink); walking through a park is much more interesting.

Don't be lazy or complacent: if a walk becomes too easy for you, up the tempo. Wear deodorant, and plenty of it. You're going to sweat.

What we have discovered over the course of our time on this diet is this: no matter how grotesquely unfit you are (and India literally hadn't exercised since playing lacrosse, of all absurd things, at school twenty-five years ago), you can become demonstrably fitter in a matter of weeks. This feels utterly fantastic. The downside is, skip exercise for a week or so and your fitness levels plummet in freakishly dramatic fashion. So keep at it.

Lunch

FAUX SHEPHERD'S PIE

FILLING
1.5kg extra lean minced beef
2 medium onions, finely sliced
2 sticks celery, finely chopped
1 tsp fresh thyme leaves
1 tbsp tomato puree
sea salt and black pepper
2 tbsp butter
230g mushrooms, chopped

TOPPING:
900g trimmed cauliflower
230g grated cheddar
60ml sour cream
2 tbsp butter
1 egg
8 cooked, crumbled bacon rashers

Put the beef in a large pan and cook over high heat until it stops looking red and raw. Add onions, celery, thyme, tomato puree. Season. Cover, turn heat right down and cook for thirty minutes, stirring from time to time. Add some water if it looks too dry.

Fry the mushrooms in the butter and add to beef; cook for fifteen minutes more.

Meanwhile, make the topping: steam the cauliflower until almost mushy, about fifteen minutes. Blend in food processor, adding cream, cheese and butter. Add the egg and whizz again. Mix in the bacon. Assemble the shepherd's pie and bake at 180°C, gas 4, for forty-five to fifty minutes. Can be made the night before and reheated in the office microwave.

Phase One Day Five

(This may fall on Days Four or Six for some people.)

This was the day we felt *really* bad. On the other hand, some of our guinea-pigs felt absolutely fine – actively great, in a few cases – so here's hoping you do too. See how you feel this morning, and go with it: if you're feeling crap, it may be time to throw a sickie, or call for help with childcare if you're at home with babies. Be absolutely sure to drink your water today, and up the intake a bit if you can bear to – you'll feel better for it. And take things easy: if there's the possibility of spending some time reclining on the sofa in front of the telly, grab it.

Remember, it doesn't get any worse than this. From now on, the only way is up. Also remember – we've said this before, but we'll just say it again – you're not feeling bad because you're doing something terrible to yourself. You're feeling bad because you're detoxing from all the sugar, caffeine and processed rubbish that was clogging up your system and making you fat and unhealthy. Bear with it.

If you're anything like us, today might very well be the day when you have an overwhelming urge to give up. Your mind starts playing funny tricks on you: 'I'm fine as I am,' it tells you. 'So I'm on the podgy side. So what? I'm happy. Life's too short for these kinds of sacrifices. And I want a biscuit.'

It is important that you see this for what it is: a trick. Self-sabotage, to be precise – a talent most serial dieters have in spades. It's time to knock it on the head once and for all. If you were happy with the way you looked, you wouldn't have picked up this book. That's the truth of it. The other truth is that you've nearly completed Week One, and that with this way of eating, as with others, your body is reprogramming itself every day, every hour, every minute. Soon it will barely register irritation (or furious rage) at not having sugary snacks shoved down its gullet every half an hour. So stick with us.

Breakfast

Water and supplements, needless to say, followed by anything from the allowed list. Or a protein shake, if you don't feel much like eating. You need one scoop of whey protein powder, which you get from any health food shop – check the label, please: some are carbier than others. To your scoop, add a glassful of *unsweetened* soya milk, and any flavouring you like and are allowed: vanilla essence (the real thing, not the extract); peanut butter; a sprinkling of nuts; double cream for added richness. Whizz it all up (you can do this with a fork – it doesn't go all lumpy) and drink. This is a useful breakfast if you're in a hurry, too – it takes ten seconds to make, is protein-packed, and easily keeps you going until lunch.

Oh, for God's sake, I really want something sweet! Like, NOW!
Yeah, we know. We personally chose not to go down the artificial sweetener route, simply because we don't entirely trust them – we actively despise aspartame (which causes cancer in rats, and there is, to say the least, a huge question mark over its safety) and we're not 100 per cent convinced about the safety of the newer ones, either. But you may feel differently. In that case, you can have Splenda, which is actually made from sugar (one carb per sachet). Sweeten the protein shake above with some, or have sweetened, whipped double cream with a dusting of cocoa powder and/or nuts. Just don't go making too much of a habit of it. Sugar got most of us into this mess in the first place. We think it's better to tell your body that sugar simply no longer features, but we do realize that this is quite hardcore. Do as you see fit, but be on your guard. And do try to butch it out for the time being, at least during Phase One.

Today is a day when you deserve some cheering up. We hate to venture into women's magazine territory, but sod it, we're going to. The following suggestions may sound like desperate old chestnuts, but we find they work for us. Try not to huff cynically as you read through them. They may very well work for you, too.

Read a book. Go to the bookshop and buy the fattest, trashiest, most engrossing-looking volume you can find. Or buy *The Brothers Karamazov*, by all means, if that's what works for you, or an atlas, or the entire Booker Prize shortlist, or whatever. We like a bit of trash-lit every now and then, ourselves. Make a cup of tea, lie on the sofa, and extract said book from its bag. Not the most original suggestion in the world, granted, but we do guarantee a couple of hours of utter (and distracting) contentment.

Buy some flowers. Flowers make us really happy. Disproportionately so, really, considering that a cheap bunch costs the same as a ready-made cake. Sit and stare at the flowers. Suddenly, life is beautiful. And you're beautiful too. Wussy, but true. Hooray!

Have a hot, fragrant bath. Line the edge of the bath with candles. Put music, or the radio, on. Lie there for hours, until you go all wrinkly. Bliss.

Listen to music. Or tune your radio to BBC 7 and recline, listening to some marvellous old thesp reading stories to you. This works especially well if you're in bed at the time, though your comfiest armchair works well too.

Keep your mind occupied. Obvious, but essential. If you've got nothing to think about other than how not-brilliant you feel, and how you fancy a doughnut, you're actively helping the self-sabotage.

If you can't keep your mind occupied, **do something that requires concentration.** India is a knitting fiend – in fact we'd go as far as saying that, for her, buggering around with wool has been a really marvellous diet aid. Crochet, too – and you can crochet your child (or yourself) a beanie in an evening. Neris paints. Do what you like, even if you haven't done it for years. Sketching is a heavenly thing to do,

Watch the telly. Rent a DVD, but preferably not *Babette's Feast*.

Lunch

THAI SALMON FISHCAKES

(Serves two as a starter or main, depending on how hungry you are.)

200g salmon	2 teaspoons finely chopped
1 red chilli, sliced	lemongrass (I use 'lazy'
4 spring onions	lemongrass in jars)
handful fresh coriander, chopped	salt and pepper
1 egg	olive oil

Put everything but the salmon in the blender until finely chopped. Add salmon, salt and pepper to taste, and blend again until similar to mince. It will be quite sloppy, but don't panic!

Heat a good puddle of oil in a frying pan.

Blob tablespoons of the mixture into the pan (makes eight little cakes, or four large ones). If it starts to spit, turn the heat down. Let one side really seal before trying to turn over (like an omelette). When firm and golden brown, they are ready. Delicious served with a squeeze of lime juice and black pepper and stir-fried cabbage.

Supper

DELICIOUS ASPARAGUS

1 big bundle asparagus	2 hard-boiled eggs
50g unsalted butter	black pepper

Steam the asparagus until done. Meanwhile, gently melt the butter. Mash the eggs into it, add pepper. Dip the asparagus into the egg-butter mixture. Total heaven. Serves one greedy person, or two more restrained types.

How We Felt on Day Five

I think we've covered this. We felt really, really crap.
We felt like Mrs Crappy from Crapville, Crapland, United
Crapdom. Appropriately enough, Day Five was the day India
finally pooed, so there was some rejoicing. But not much.

However ...

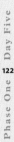

Phase One Day Six

(This may fall on another day for you.)

On Day Six, we felt fabulous. F-A-B-U-L-O-U-S. Fabulous enough for it to be nothing short of miraculous. There we were, dragging ourselves around on Day Five, with the nasty headache and the achy limbs and the weird taste in the mouth and the general 'I'm dying' and 'I can't do it, what's wrong with being fat, anyway?' melodramatic vibe going on, and then, suddenly, on Day Six, we leapt out of bed feeling wonderful and curiously energetic. Hallelujah! And about bloody time, too, frankly.

You may, by the way, experience this first week in a different order from us. You may not have a bad Day Five – you may not have a bad day at all, in which case you can skip this entry. Or you may have more than one, in which case re-read it, for strength. And remember, all the advice and recipes in this section are interchangeable. You don't have to cook the recipes we give you: they're just suggestions. This is a diet book, not a cookbook: cook what you like, sticking to the rules. Just because we don't give a method for crab with spring onions and ginger, or braised belly of pork with star anise, or double-bacon cheeseburgers (sans bun, naturellement, mais avec mayo, gherkins and salsa) doesn't mean you can't eat them. As for the stuff you used to eat: be ingenious about recreating them in a diet-friendly way. Steamed cabbage leaves, for instance, make a nice substitute for lasagne sheets.

But anyway: here we are on Day Six. The sun is shining a little bit more brightly. There's a spring in our step and a song in our heart. For Neris and me, there was also a distinct and unmissable 'thin' feeling. It's hard to put this into words – we just felt lighter, cleaner, better. Whether you are experiencing the thin feeling today, or whether that was yesterday, or whether you've got it to look forward to tomorrow, well done. But be careful. The thin feeling can cause serious wardrobe malfunction. Because it's so pleasing to feel lighter – and tomorrow is weighing day, by the way, so try and resist the temptation to weigh or measure yourself today, no matter how well you feel – the temptation to celebrate the thin feeling sartorially can be overwhelming. I (India) decided on Day Six that I felt so great I should maybe wear a little flouncy above-the-knee dress. Big mistake, because I still weighed fifteen-odd stone. So remember: you will be feeling great, and the chances are that your skin and eyes will have taken a dramatic turn for the better too, but feeling great doesn't mean it's time to slip into the gold lamé hotpants just yet. Bide your time.

Breakfast

Have your supplements, your water and breakfast.
Here are some Phase One-friendly 'muffins'.

EGG AND SAUSAGE 'MUFFINS'
(makes twelve, which is a lot. Recipe works halved.)

455g sausages
groundnut oil
12 eggs
120ml double cream

120ml water
sea salt
170g grated Cheddar

Preheat the oven to 180°, gas 4. Oil a twelve-cup muffin tray. Remove the sausages from their skins and fry until browned (with onions if you like; they're nice caramelized). Divide the meat equally between the muffin holes.

Whisk together the eggs, cream, water, salt. Pour over the sausage and top with the cheese. Bake for twenty minutes until golden and fluffy. Cool slightly before attempting to remove from tin.

Feel free to vary this, adding herbs, bacon pieces and so on, and feel free to use any cheese you like.

Now go for your walk.

Today is probably a good day for a little pep talk.

We hope you're discovering for yourself that this diet, or way of eating, is easy to stick to. We hope you're not hungry – if you are, eat more. We hope you've found out that one of the diet's virtues is that it is portable, i.e. that it doesn't ruin your social life; that you can go to restaurants and feast as usual; that cooking at home doesn't involve an unmanageable palaver.

But this is a diet that needs sticking to. You can't (at this stage) go wandering off. You can't think, 'Oh, just this once.' And so today is a good day to ask yourself how you feel vis à vis eating this way in the long term.

Take a good hard look in the mirror (but step off those scales! That's for tomorrow). You should see a distinct improvement. Lie flat in bed and have a feel: there may be some action around your hipbones. Your stomach should be way flatter than it's been for a while. You may even be developing a waist, assuming you thought yours was gone for ever.

Don't stop now. You have achieved all of this in under a week. You are retraining your taste buds, your metabolism, the way your body processes food. You are melting your own fat – and at the rate of knots. You're doing an amazing thing. And if you think you feel good today, just wait another week – and then another month. The results will be jaw-dropping. We promise you.

Don't get complacent. Develop a will of iron. Resist the urge to stick your finger in the Nutella jar. You are going to look fantastic very, very soon. You probably feel pretty great already. Hang on to that feeling, and savour it (as though it were a rose-petal macaroon). You have a choice: either to have that feeling every single day, or to go back to feeling fat, bloated and miserable in changing rooms. The choice is yours, and yours alone.

I went to the health food shop this morning and came across an array of low-carb energy bars. Please tell me I can eat them. They're all chocolaty-looking and I feel I deserve a reward!

We wouldn't advise eating them this week or next, i.e. during the stages of Phase 1. To be perfectly honest with you, we wouldn't advocate eating them ever – ditto low-carb shakes. The whole point of this diet is to eat 'clean', wholesome food, and to junk the junk, even if the junk ingeniously presents itself as being 'healthy'. The bars you refer to are full of weird stuff – check the ingredients list – and we've yet to find one that tastes anywhere near as good as it looks: nice packaging, but seriously disappointing contents. We also think they can dangerously derail you at this stage – by providing sweetness, which you're trying to teach your body to lose the taste for. They also stall a number of people who follow low-carb, high-protein diets, and the only way to find out you're one of them is to eat them and then watch the scales refuse to budge. But don't panic: another week, and you can have chocolate – real chocolate, not some chemical-laden approximation. We think it's worth waiting for.

Lunch

TZATZIKI

½ cucumber
1 crushed garlic clove
sea salt and black pepper

300g Greek yogurt
good olive oil

Grate the cucumber on a cheese grater. Put it in a sieve and squeeze out as much of the juice as you can.

In a bowl, mix together the crushed garlic with some salt and pepper. Add the Greek yogurt and thoroughly mix.

Now mix the cucumber with the yogurt. Put in a bowl and drizzle over one tablespoon of olive oil just before serving. Delicious by itself, but also as an accompaniment to any kind of lamb (especially kebabs). This tastes better if you can leave it in the fridge for a minimum of one hour.

Supper

COMFORTING BEEF STEW

1kg lean braising steak
1–2 cloves garlic, sliced or in chunks
   if you feel brave
A pinch or two of dried chilli
2 large onions
3 courgettes
4–5 field mushrooms

200g broccoli
200g cauliflower
Beef or vegetable stock, approx.
   1 pint (depends on size of your
   cooking pot)
2 tbsp olive oil

Chop all veg into big chunks and set aside. Heat the oil in a large saucepan and brown the meat. Keep frying to seal the meat on all sides until golden brown. Remove from the pan and set aside on a plate. Fry the onions and garlic in the pan with the meat juices, allowing to colour slightly. Return the meat to the pan, adding enough stock to cover. Bring to a light boil and stir to loosen all the flavour from the bottom. Leave to simmer gently for one hour with the lid off, until the meat is tender.

Add the veg. You can use any of the vegetables from the 'allowed' list for this – but remember to put the harder vegetables in first, and the softer ones last, otherwise they'll turn to mush. Put the lid on and simmer for a further fifteen to twenty minutes. Serve with a salad and faux-mash (see page 87 for recipe).

How We Felt on Day Six
Fan-flippin'-tastic!

Phase One Day Seven

We would clasp you to our bosoms if we could, and give
you a bone-crushing double hug. WELL DONE! You're
on the last day of your first week. You have achieved a really
wonderful thing. And the hardest bit is over.

We hope you're feeling really, really pleased with yourself.
If you're anything like us, you'll be practically mad with
joy. We repeat: well done, hooray, hats off and bravo. If this
book were interactive, we'd pause for a little triumphant
trumpet tune.

Breakfast

Have your supplements, your water and your breakfast.
We suggest sausages. Perfect Fried Sausages.

Here's how to cook them (no, we haven't gone mad,
giving you a sausage recipe. It's just that a lot of people
don't cook them for long enough, with the result that they
taste unpleasantly pink 'n' porky. There's nothing worse
than a sausage that's rare in the middle, plus it can make
you mighty sick).

So: your frying pan. A nut of butter, a dot of groundnut oil. Get it nice
and hot. Add the sausages. Now turn the heat down to the minimum
and leave them alone for at least twenty minutes. Then turn them over
and repeat on the other side. The result is a really regal sausage, sticky
and caramelized on the outside and cooked properly within. While
they're cooking, if you can be bothered, very finely slice some onions,
fry them on a very gentle heat in some butter (with our friend the dot
of oil to avoid burning) until they've gone brown at the edges; toss in
some herbs (thyme is nice) and a little liquid – leftover stock, leftover
gravy, a corner of stock cube, or even just water, and simmer the whole
thing until it's all melted and melded together. Eat with the sausages.
Very, very nice. But failing the onion marmalade, try dipping your
sausages in any creamy dressing you like, in shop-brought salsa, or
in mustard thinned down with sour cream, to which you might add
snipped chives.

As you are no doubt aware, today is weighing day. 'O frabjous day! Callooh! Callay!' Less poetically, please make sure you've pooed before you step on the scales.

And away you go. Go on, step on them. You have nothing to fear. If you have been following our instructions, you'll have dropped a load of weight. And, by the way, it's not all water-weight – that only happens for the first few days. You've dropped a combination of water-weight and FAT. Congratulations.

Weighing's not enough. Get out the tape measure, too, and measure the parts of your body we mentioned on page 72. Nice, innit? We told you it worked.

If you haven't lost any weight, you haven't been following the diet properly. It's as simple as that. You've either cheated, or some carbs have snuck in when you weren't looking – your sausages, for example, may have contained bread or other carby fillers; you might have eaten your fish battered without thinking; that jar of shop-bought sauce may have contained starch and sugars. Vigilance, my dears, at all times. We mean it when we say, as we have been over the past week, that the smallest indulgence will completely derail the diet at this stage. Consider yourself chastised and go back to Day One. And don't feel too sad: just put it down to experience. It's not going to happen again. The thing about our diet is, it works. All you have to do is do it properly.

The rest of you will be feeling jubilant. As you should be. And it's only Day Seven. Just wait. Your process of transformation has only just begun.

Now go for your walk, skippety-skipping with joy. Why not add on an extra five or ten minutes? The diet's working, you're already looking and feeling better: go on. You have nothing to lose but your flab.

By the way, just because you've lost weight DOES NOT mean that you can take it easy in terms of food today. No sneaky rewards, please. Have a salon-quality facial instead. Here are some tips, courtesy of celebrity uber-facialist Amanda Lacey:

Home Facials
A Step-by-Step Guide
It is always best to perform your pampering facial last thing in a busy day. Put aside twenty to thirty minutes and remember, when it comes to massage, this should be for at least ten minutes at a time.

Fill a very clean bathroom basin with hot water and throw in a couple of pure cotton-towelling face mitts.

Use a natural oil-based cleanser so as not to dry out the skin too much – we like Amanda Lacey's own cleansing pomade, Eve Lom's eponymous cleanser, or Vaishaly Patel's wonderful cleansing balm, but we're a bit deluxe about cleansers – your local chemist will stock plenty of cheaper alternatives. These waxy cleansers will have a far more effective action on the skin than cream or frothy cleansers, plus they keep skin soft and supple, not stripped and tight feeling. Do not fear them if your skin is oily – it may sound counter-intuitive to use an oily-feeling, waxy product on oily-feeling skin, but trust us, it works.

Warm the cleanser between the palms and massage onto dry skin using upward circular movements.

Grab your mitts and gently exfoliate in small circular motions to remove any dead skin cells from the epidermis (top layer of the skin). This will revive sluggish, sallow complexions and brighten the skin.

Wash your face in a new basin of warm water and make sure every trace of cleanser has been removed.

Pat dry and leave your face alone for one minute. Then sit down and hold your face gently in the palms of your hands. The reason for doing this is that you have just

stripped the skin of its pH balance of 5.5. By holding
your face you are keeping it warm and therefore retaining
the moisture and preventing it from feeling tight (this is
especially important in winter months).

Take a drop of facial oil – any kind: most cosmetics
companies do one – and warm it between your palms.
Then begin to massage it into the skin. If you have time,
try to lie on your bed as this will relax you and your facial
muscles. Tissue off any excess oil, though there shouldn't
be any. At this point you can either go straight to bed or ...

If you have extra time, you can use a hydrating mask
to nourish and soothe dry or irritable skin. The best thing
to do is wrap your hair up, put the mask on and soak in
a hot bath, removing the mask before you go to bed and
finishing off with another drop of face oil.

Amanda's products can be bought from
www.amandalacey.com, Vaishaly Patel's from
www.vaishaly.com, and Eve Lom's from www.evelom.com.
We also recommend Liz Earle's products, available from
www.lizearle.com.

Lunch

INDIAN SCRAMBLED EGGS

2 eggs	pinch ground cumin
small handful chopped coriander	pinch ground coriander
1 small onion, very thinly sliced	butter
1 green chilli (less if you fear heat)	drop of groundnut oil
1 tomato	salt and pepper

Melt the butter with a drop of oil. The smaller the pan, the less contact
with direct heat, and the fluffier the eggs will be. When hot, add onion
slices and fry until coloured and crispy around the edges. Meanwhile,
mix all remaining ingredients. Tip into the pan containing the onions
and scramble for a couple of minutes, or until set. This makes a
fantastic brunch dish. Makes one generous portion.

Supper

MARINATED SPICED LAMB

2 French-trimmed racks of lamb	2 tsp ground cumin
3 garlic cloves, crushed	2 tsp ground coriander
2 tsp ginger, grated	1 tsp chilli powder
2 tsp white wine vinegar	150ml yogurt
handful finely chopped mint leaves	sea salt

Put the lamb in a shallow dish. Blend together the garlic, ginger, vinegar, mint, cumin, coriander, chilli, salt and yogurt in a food processor. Pour this mixture over the lamb, cover, and refrigerate for at least three hours (overnight is best).

When ready to eat, preheat the oven to 200°C, gas 6. Lay the lamb on a lined baking sheet and cook for twenty minutes if you like it pink, longer if you don't. Remove from oven and allow to rest for ten minutes before cutting into cutlets. Serves four.

How We Felt on Day Seven
Happy, happy, happy.

Phase One Day Eight

Look at the time, already. You're on the first day of your second week. No mean feat, you know.

Basically, what happens now is that we carry on as we were. Week Two is a repeat of Week One. You've presumably got the gist by now. Keep sticking to the rules, keep drinking your water and taking your supplements, and keep walking. Remember, if it starts feeling too easy, up the tempo and add on five minutes.

We're not going to give you any more recipes for this second week. Repeat those for Week One, if you're not tired of them, and if you are, use your existing cookbooks, or improvise.

Here are some breakfast ideas:

- Eggs and bacon
- Vegetable omelettes
- Cheese and ham omelettes
- Scrambled eggs with crab
- Pigs in blankets
- Poached eggs on spinach, with hollandaise sauce
- Poached eggs on ham, with hollandaise sauce
- Frittatas
- Creamed mushrooms
- Grilled tomatoes
- Avocados – sliced into an omelette if you prefer
- Buttered kippers
- A cup of vegetable soup, with added olive oil and/or parmesan, and added crunchy bits of bacon, if you like
- A cup of instant miso soup
- A handful of nuts
- Leftover roast meats with dressing
- The antipasti option – hams, salamis, cheeses, olives

Anything at all, really, from your list of allowed foods. As we've been saying, there is no law that decrees that breakfast must be bready, or sugary, or grainy. You want prawns dipped into mayo for breakfast? Go right ahead. It's not as odd as it sounds, as you're hopefully discovering by now.

And if you're in a rush, remember the protein shake recipe on page 118.

Time to look, now, at swapping bad habits for good. We've established that you'll soon be able to have some fruit, porridge for breakfast (or whenever you prefer) and even the odd chunk of chocolate. All of that happens next week. In the meantime, here's what to do when you crave a particular thing.

FRUIT! I want fruit! And fruit is good for you, so why can't I have it?

The truth of the matter is that fruit is only good for you up to a point. Vegetables are much better. This is because fruits contain sugar, as fructose, and we're trying to steer clear of sugars for the time being – which means steering clear of anything that ends in '-ose', including fructose. Citrus fruits – the breakfast orange juice which we believed for so long was incredibly good for us – are now avoided by many people and by many complementary therapists, not least because they're awfully acidic, especially on an empty stomach: hello, reflux. Bananas are yummy, but they're the fruit equivalent of the potato: carb city. From next week, you'll be allowed berries and melons, so don't get your knickers in a twist and just bear with us. In time, when you've lost the bulk of your weight, you'll be able to have any fruit you like, though we'll encourage you to choose your fruit with care and not to go guzzling vast quantities willy-nilly.

PORRIDGE! I want porridge! And porridge is good for you too, so why can't I have that either?

It is good for you, yes – and it keeps you going, as well. But it's still too carby for Phase One. However, you can have it regularly from Phase Two onwards, so hang in there.

I want a pudding.

Do you really, though? It's Day Eight and you've done brilliantly so far. But if you must, then have whipped double cream sweetened with Splenda, to which you can add chopped nuts and vanilla essence. Have this in a normal-sized bowl please, not a trough. From today you're also allowed sugar-free jelly, with whipped cream (but NOT the stuff out of a can).

I want something crunchy, like crisps or biscuits.

Make Parmesan wafers. Coarsely grate Parmesan, or cheddar, or a mixture of the two. Add cayenne if you like a bit of heat with your crunch. Cover a baking sheet with baking parchment or those clever silicone non-stick sheets (good investment, plus they last for ever). Pile on the cheese in little clusters – space them far apart, because obviously they're going to melt. Stick them in a preheated oven (190°C, gas 5) and watch them like a hawk – they only take a few minutes. Cool them (this is crucial). Peel them off. If they've all melted into one big sheet, break it apart. And lo: we have crunch. Keep in an airtight box, if they last that long – they're very moreish.

You can also have nuts, for crunch. And very crispy bacon rashers. And, should it be your bag, pork scratchings.

I want a proper drink. All this water is getting me down.

And you shall have one next week – it'll be double voddies all round. Clean spirits contain no carbs, but we're taking them out of Phase One because we didn't find it helpful to drink while we were at this stage of the diet. Spirits may be carb-free, but when there is alcohol present in your system, your body will burn it for fuel first, i.e. while it's doing this, it won't be burning your own fat. Also, there is always the danger of having one drink too many and thinking, 'Ah, sod it, I want a bag of chips' and acting on that slightly drunken impulse. Which would be disastrous at this stage.

So for the moment, please stick to the water and tea or coffee. The water is your friend. The water is helping you get thin.

Remember, you can use soya milk to create your own version of a latte. And here's how to make a homemade chai latte: put a big mugful of soya milk in a saucepan. Add two crushed cardamom pods, half a stick of cinnamon, a clove, a slice of fresh peeled ginger, two teabags (or two scoops of tea-leaves) and a pinchlet of Splenda. Heat until just before boiling point. Strain. Heaven.

I feel like I'm eating industrial quantities of meat. I know I'm a carnivore, but this is ridiculous.

Well, then eat less of it. India ate a lot of seafood but not much fish before embarking on this diet – something to do with being nervous about cooking it. No more. Fish rocks, It's easy to cook, and it takes hardly any time to prepare. Do not fear it. And do not fear tofu, either.

I want chocolate.

Us too. Would it help if next week we made chocolate truffles?

The point here is that it's not only your body or taste buds that we need to re-educate. It's also your mind that needs reprogramming. We bumble along through life thinking, 'This is just the way I am,' or, 'This is just the way I think,' so that when our mind says, 'Time for biscuits,' we just think, 'Oh, okay,' and mindlessly reach for the cookie jar. It's all well and good, thinking this is just how we are – but when it comes to food, it's also not true.

Eating two Danish pastries for breakfast is not the way you are meant to live at all. It's not the way you were born. It has very little to do with anything, except habit. And all habits are breakable. If people can get off heroin, you can get off thinking that you're doing yourself a favour by eating fattening crap. Be the boss of yourself, as my children would say. When you have the thought that says, 'Bugger it, I want to eat the garlic bread,' don't just give in to it spinelessly. Hold it up for examination (the thought, not the bread) instead of frantically trying to push it aside. Have a good look at it, and then dismiss it. Don't try to push the thought away halfway through having it, or get in a panic about it – that's how obsessions are created, and how you end up feeling deprived instead of in control.

Hold it in your head and examine it. All you have to tell yourself is, 'Actually, that's a crap idea. I'm getting thinner. Why would I have the garlic bread? I'd be mad to.' If you do this enough – and admittedly it is quite boring, but also important – it becomes second nature. What we're basically saying is, never take any food-related thought you have for granted. Ever. Examine it. Show it who's boss: you, and you alone.

Some More Ideas for Lunch

The antipasto plate, but this time including a couple of semi-dried tomatoes (delicious: they taste almost candied), artichoke hearts, bottled peppers in olive oil, some more olives, and a big side salad, with cheese if you like.

Any salad – but be butch about it, and not namby-pamby. Salads don't have to be wimpy rabbit food. Add grilled chicken, poached eggs, crispy bacon, hunks of cheese, our old friend the avocado – whatever takes your fancy from the allowed list. A little gem salad with roast chicken and lots of fresh tarragon leaves in a creamy dressing is a very delicious thing indeed. As is a Caesar salad without the croutons. And you're allowed pesto, so either drizzle it on fish or chicken, or use it as a salad dressing.

Vegetable soup, to which you add extra virgin olive oil and Parmesan – and bacon or pancetta, if you like. This is a very useful thing to make a big pot of twice a week, because then you barely have to think. Plus, it freezes beautifully and reheats in minutes. Chicken soup is also very useful, and marvellously comforting.

If you are fortunate enough to live near a fishmonger's, a dressed crab or six oysters make a really wonderful and luxurious treat – and there's no preparation required. Also, those jars of French fish soup are pretty delish (if sometimes a bit salty), especially if you have them with grated Gruyère.

Those low-effort lunch ingredients from the deli aisle are also very useful: don't discount them because they're more traditionally eaten with bread. Have the chicken liver pâté, or the smoked mackerel; the smoked salmon or trout or eel; the soft cheeses. Either train yourself to eat them as they are, or use celery or another robust green vegetable, such as green beans, to scoop.

Guacamole (chop up avocado, tomato, coriander, onion, chilli, squirt with lime juice), see above for dipping materials. Also quite nice scooped out of the bowl with your finger, actually.

A big pot of chilli con carne is a very useful thing to have lurking around in your fridge. Don't include the kidney beans at this stage – but do decorate your portion(s) of chilli with sour cream and chopped avocado if you fancy them.

Supper

GRILLED PORTOBELLO MUSHROOMS WITH BLUE CHEESE DRESSING
(serves four)

100 g Gorgonzola or other blue
   cheese, crumbled
4 tbsp sour cream
1 tbsp mayonnaise
1 tbsp red wine vinegar

1 tsp minced garlic
4 portobello mushrooms
extra virgin olive oil
salt and pepper

Mash the cheese to a paste. Stir in the sour cream, mayonnaise, vinegar and garlic. Season to taste.

Remove the stem from each mushroom and scrape out the gills with a small spoon. Score the tops in a cross-hatch pattern. Season the mushrooms with the olive oil, salt and pepper. Grill, two to three minutes on each side until cooked through. Drizzle the dressing on top.

Serve with a green salad.

How We Felt on Day Eight
Optimistic.

Phase One Day Nine

We're really rolling now.

Eat breakfast. Take your supplements. Drink your water. Go walkies.

Being Prepared, and Why It Really Matters

We can't emphasize this enough: preparation is all. This diet is incredibly easy to follow if your fridge is ready for it, and not so easy if it isn't. If you work long hours, or live miles away from the shops, your new way of eating is going to require forward planning. You do get hungry on this way of eating, and if there's nothing suitable to hand, you're likely to grab the wrong thing, simply because your body is telling you to eat. And that's a big fat disaster.

Unfortunately, the kind of food you're eating is the opposite of the kind of stuff you can keep in the cupboard – no rice, no pasta, no other useful starches or grains. Pretty much everything you're eating is made from scratch and involves fresh ingredients. It may sound like advice from the Good Housekeeping Institute in the 1950s, but with this diet, it really, really pays to sit down on a Friday evening and plan your meals for the following week. That way, your time spent at the shops on Saturday will be intelligently spent. The alternative, if you're me (India), is to do a mad, hurried dash round the supermarket and end up with far too much food, bought on the basis that it's bound to come in handy and it's allowed.

We don't know what your own personal tastes are, obviously, but here is a sample shopping list that should last you a good few days. We like this shopping list. If anyone tells you that the way you're eating is unhealthy, show it to them. We bet it's a great deal healthier than theirs.

- Organic eggs
- Rooibos tea, or herbal tea of your choice
- Two cartons unsweetened organic soya milk
- Butter
- Large carton double cream
- Bacon, smoked or green, preferably cured without nitrates
- Ham, any kind, preferably cured without sugar
- Salami, chorizo, quails' eggs to snack on (with celery salt)
- Walnuts, pine nuts, almonds to snack on
- A hunk of Parmesan
- A hunk of cheddar
- Mozzarella
- One organic chicken
- Another meat of your choice – anything from minced beef to veal cuts for osso bucco
- Fresh fish or seafood (but eat it the day of purchase)
- Firm tofu
- Fresh spinach
- Fresh mushrooms
- Fresh tomatoes
- Fresh salad, and salad vegetables, including chives, cucumber, radishes
- Fresh avocados
- Fresh cauliflower
- Fresh broccoli
- Any extra seasonal green leafy vegetables you fancy
- Fresh herbs of your choice
- Onions
- Garlic
- Olives

- Good olive oil
- Groundnut oil
- Mayonnaise, if you don't make your own
- Sour cream
- Canned tuna (you'll never starve if you have canned tuna to hand)
- Canned tomatoes (but watch out for added sugar)
- Splenda, if you use it
- Whey protein powder
- Vanilla extract

Now here's what a non-dieter might purchase instead:
- Battery eggs
- Normal tea or coffee
- Cow's milk or artificial creamer
- Margarine or 'fake' butter spread
- Large carton ice cream
- Crisps to snack on
- Biscuits to snack on
- Chocolate to snack on
- Processed cheese
- Battery chicken
- Mechanically recovered 'meat' products
- Fish fingers or frozen battered fish
- Frozen peas and another vegetable or two if you're lucky
- Canned fruit in syrup
- Canned soup
- Sugar
- Cakes
- Bread

QED. Anyone who tells you this diet isn't healthy – because they believed all the scare stories about Atkins and eating mince fried in lard three times a day – has not got the full picture. And remember: good plans shape good decisions. The contents of your fridge are the foundation of this diet.

I buy ready meals a lot. I live alone and they're just really convenient. You're going to tell me to give them up, aren't you?

Not necessarily. But you are going to have to turn into Miss Marple and scrutinize the packaging with enormous care. The majority of ready meals use starches as fillers, and they're usually full of flour and sugar, as well – to say nothing of really bad trans-fats. Obviously, this won't do.

However, they're not healthy, and so it's no great loss. On the other hand, they are massively convenient. We suggest you eat better ones less often. The most expensive ones (they would be, wouldn't they?) are the ones formulated with the least additives and the fewest chemicals and E numbers. We particularly like Marks & Spencer's Cook! range. At the time of writing, about seventy per cent of its products are suitable

I do a weekly supermarket trawl for things like water and loo paper, but then I rely quite heavily on the corner shop. Is there anything at all I can eat that's quick to make and buyable from my local convenience store?

To be honest, your options are going to be really limited – also, it's a really expensive way of shopping. You can buy the ingredients for an omelette, or a cheese plate (maybe), or for a big tuna salad, but beyond that things are probably going to get a bit repetitive. If you like shopping daily broaden your net and find a street with a good grocer and a decent butcher or fishmonger. Then it becomes simple: a piece of grilled chicken, some roast pumpkin to go with it, and a salad on the side. Easy.

Useful Tip

If you physically go to the supermarket rather than ordering online, avoid the biscuit, cake and crisp aisles for the first few weeks of this eating plan. There's no point at all in putting yourself in temptation's way. Sooner rather than later, these aisles will hold no fear for you. We now blithely skip about every aisle of the supermarket, and buy 'forbidden' foods for our families without batting an eyelid.

Needless to say, it is a really, really bad idea to go food shopping on an empty stomach. Don't make life difficult for yourself: eat first. If you've forgotten, head for the nut aisle, grab some shelled pistachios, or whatever nut you like best, and eat them before you carry on. Remember to hold on to the empty packet, as you still have to pay for them!

Here are some more basic takeaway-style lunch and dinner ideas:

Almost any Indian curry, served with pickles but without rice or bread: chicken tikka masala, for instance, with a side of fragrant spiced spinach and another of cauliflower bhaji

- Thai green or red curry
- Clear Thai soups/broths, such as Tom Yum
- Satay
- Stir fries
- Chicken with cashew nuts
- Chinese-style spare ribs
- Lemon chicken
- Chicken or prawns or fish or crab with spring onions and ginger
- Beef or chicken or pork in satay sauce
- Tiger prawns
- Wok-fried scallops
- Bok choi, or any Chinese greens, either with garlic or with oyster sauce

As you can see, eating this way is not difficult if you're after something yummy to scoff in front of the telly. Having said that, though, try not to scoff in front of the telly. You end up eating in a completely absent-minded and repetitive way, which means that you usually end up eating far more than you needed to. Eat at the table, like a normal person.

How We Felt on Day Nine

India: *I used to do a funny thing when I was really fat: I was incapable of eating by myself, just looking at my plate. I had to have distraction, in the form of either a book or magazine, or the telly. It was as though I knew that physically seeing the amount of stuff I was proposing to wolf down would probably freak me out a bit. Stands to reason, really – I was in denial about what I was eating. So I shovelled it in without actually properly looking at it, staring at a magazine instead. Weird, isn't it? This is one of the many reasons why we would really encourage you to eat sitting at a properly laid table, with a napkin, with cutlery, with a jug of water, whether you are eating alone or with somebody else. You need to focus on what you are doing, and that can't be done with distractions other than conversation. It also means that you'll know when you feel full, rather than just mindlessly carrying on chomping long after you might have stopped.*
Neris: *I felt okay.*

Phase One Day Ten

Good morning. We hope it's getting easier, that your clothes are getting looser, and that you're feeling better than you have done in years.

Drink your water. Take your supplements. Eat your breakfast. Walk. If you haven't upped your walking time by at least ten minutes over the past week or so, do it now. If you're marching away for half an hour or more, well done. You'll get to goal (aargh! what a phrase) much faster.

This chapter is especially for you if you have children. As we were saying much earlier on in the book, having young children in particular is often the beginning of the end as far as your waistline is concerned: somehow, mothers feel duty-bound to hoover up their children's leftovers – even if they don't normally particularly like apple purée or fish fingers and chips. Maybe it's some strange biological imperative. And when you add those leftovers to the three adult meals a day you're also eating – well, it's a wonder every fertile woman in the country isn't Zeppelin-shaped.

Obviously, you haven't – we most sincerely hope – been hoovering up those cold, congealed titbits for the past nine days. But here are a few coping strategies to see you through the coming weeks.

First of all, always, always have a snack – or your meal – before you start cooking for children. You're unlikely to lust after their leftovers if you're feeling stuffed.

Secondly, ask yourself if your children really need to eat that differently from you. The truth of the matter is that, Jamie Oliver notwithstanding, we still feed our children an awful lot of junk – we know it's not especially good for them, but every once in a while, we feel we're giving them a treat. But if you cook home-made burgers rather than frozen ones, you know exactly what's gone into them, and you can eat them too. If you swap fish fingers for, say, lemon sole strips pan-fried in butter, you can hoover up all the leftovers you like. If they're having fresh vegetables rather than oven chips, you're more than welcome to help yourself. It makes it all so much easier – and you are dramatically improving your children's health in the process. Leave them to chomp on their bread, potatoes, pasta and rice – they're growing children, and it's not doing them any harm, although if you are seriously concerned about optimizing their physical well-being, swap anything they eat that's white for the brown equivalent – that way, you'll soon be able to join in with those bits, too. So: wholemeal bread, stone-ground; brown or wild rice; and whole foods instead of processed.

If you persuade them to eat this way now – and nothing is more persuasive than leading by example – they'll not only grow up having a healthy idea of what eating well means, but they'll be in peak form physically. And hopefully the patterns that turn us all into fat adults won't ever be in place. Especially if you ensure they cut down on the sugar.

There isn't a recipe in this book that our children would be unhappy to eat, but obviously it's all subjective. Develop your own repertoire of family-friendly recipes that you can all eat together. That way, you don't feel like you're sitting there in miserable, self-imposed exile – you eat what they're eating, but without the stodge.

Eating out with children needn't be tricky either. If the pizza restaurant you're in won't run to a salad, you can eat the pizza topping provided you leave the crust (we don't recommend you do this every day, but once every now and then won't hurt). It doesn't look especially charming, but it's not going to ruin your diet. If you're at a burger joint, tuck in, but leave the bun (and the ketchup, which is mostly sugar). Fried chicken isn't recommended, but provided you pick away the batter, it's not going to harm you – ditto battered fish. Like we keep saying, this is a sociable diet. You're never going to starve – not unless you're locked in a sweet shop or a potato-processing plant.

Back at home, there is an ultra simple solution to not being tempted by the children's crisps, biscuits and cakes: don't buy them. They can have them at friends' houses, but it won't kill them not to have them at home.

Having said that, everybody's different, but we found we didn't have to go to these lengths: once the weight begins to fall off – as you are experiencing right now – the temptation to cock it all up for a mouthful of something sugary fades.

How We Felt on Day Ten
Like we were getting there.

India: *Day Twenty* [India may have been further along in the diet than you are, but we hope this will prove to you that it is possible to feed your kids those forbidden foods without giving into temptation yourself.]

Baked a cake! How perverse is that. Didn't even lick the spoon clean of batter. Have developed a sort of revulsion towards doughy things. Don't know if this is because I have been reading so many low-carb texts and books, but now I just see them as empty and puffy and fatty and bleh. Must watch out for this – don't want to develop a weird nutty obsession about the evils of carbs.

We actually bought exactly what we'd usually buy for our children. This is a way of eating that's life-long, and we felt that the sooner we got used to it, the better. Part of getting used to it means ignoring the three kinds of cereal sitting on top of the fridge. Anyway, we don't really believe that the cereals, or the biscuits, constitute 'temptation'. The idea that some foods are more 'tempting' than others is another clever trick by the diet industry. We believe that everything is about choice: about choosing to make a difference to the way you look by choosing to eat a certain way. If you feel like you're the one wielding the power – which you are – then no amount of sugary carbs will deter you from your chosen path, because the choice is stark and simple: follow the diet, and you lose weight and look great. Ignore the diet because you feel 'tempted', and you get fatter and look worse. It's a no-brainer.

Phase One Day Eleven

Take your supplements. Drink your water. Have breakfast.
Go for your walk.

By Day Eleven India was in the swing of things; Neris had
a down day and was majorly fed up. Chances are that you may
be too. This diet is easy, and this diet works, but that doesn't
mean that, in its early stages, it can't feel repetitive and
slightly monotonous. We wouldn't blame you if, by today,
you're beginning to think, 'That's enough of that.'

Neither would we blame you if you were thinking, 'This
is great – I could go on for ever.' But for the purposes of this
chapter, we're going to assume that you may be struggling.

It's more an emotional struggle than a physical one – after
all, you're eating, your body is functioning, and you're losing
weight. You should also have noticed a marked improvement
in your energy levels: all that feeling tired at around 4pm is
on the way out. And all of this is good. But one of the really
boring things about diets in the long term is that the pounds
only come off as a result of you making thousands of right
decisions, and sometimes hundreds of the wrong ones. And
all of the onus is on you: you're the only one there for every
single one of those choices/decisions. It can feel quite lonely,
or quite overwhelming, or emotionally exhausting.

Neris: *I always feel a bit short changed when I've got to the end
of a really successful day and just managed to stay on track. What
I remember is all the opportunities that I've turned down. The slice
of birthday cake. The crisps in the bar. The drink at the leaving
do. So many times I could have slipped up – and I didn't. But you
don't really get praised for that. And sometimes you feel like a pat
on the head.*

First, consider your head patted. Secondly, we share your
pain. Getting through a day when there are more obstacles
to surmount than usual can feel like you've climbed Everest,

except that instead of there being a celebratory party waiting for you at the summit, nobody's noticed. And that can make you feel quite resentful. And when you feel resentful, if you're anything like us, the temptation is to reach for your comforting little friend, food.

We'd expect your weight loss by now to be visible. Not dramatically so – nobody's going to come running up to you and exclaim, 'Oh my goodness, how much have you lost?' But it should certainly be visible to you. As far as other people are concerned, you may be getting a number of those 'You look well, what have you done?' comments. Enjoy them. In another fortnight, there will be a physical difference in you that you'd have to be blind to ignore – especially if you have a great deal of weight to lose. This is the image that you have to hold in your head when you're feeling wobbly. Weight loss is no longer an unattainable ideal: you're experiencing it right now. It's no longer pie in the sky. Your clothes should be feeling looser already, and pretty soon you're going to have to chuck them away because they'll be ridiculously big on you. That's not wishful thinking; it is fact. You've got to hang on in there.

If you're feeling that the diet is monotonous, take heart from knowing that you only have another three days to go before it broadens out a great deal and allows you, among other things, alcohol and chocolate. Three days out of your whole life is not a high price to pay for being the shape you want to be.

While Neris was feeling irritated on Day Eleven, I knew I'd cracked it. The point of telling you this isn't that I was a good girl and that she was naughty. It is that we both got there in the end, following different routes. You're allowed to have wobbles, to feel annoyed or restricted or both, just as (obviously) you're allowed to find this way of eating pretty effortless and simple. Whether you're finding things easy or hard doesn't really matter when it comes to the end result, because provided you don't waver, you will lose all the weight you want to lose. Sure, there's an easy way to do this – which is just to do it, without questioning anything. And there's a harder way – which I expect occurs when people (Neris being a prime example) are dieters of many years' standing. The harder way involves feeling deprived and querying everything you aren't allowed to put in your mouth – 'But WHY can't I have a cup of hot chocolate?' Well, you know the answer to that one, so my advice would be, don't even go there. You might as well ask, 'But WHY can't I inject my eyeballs with heroin?' You could, you know. You are a free agent – if that's what you really want, go ahead. But you'll have failed to look after yourself, and you'll have cocked up. You'll also be setting a dangerous precedent. And if you cock up, you have to start all over again.

Okay. You know what? I'm happy to start all over again, provided you allow me to cock up today. You said I could go off-piste in the introduction, after all.

We simply can't emphasize this enough: at this stage of the diet, going off-piste is fatal. Your body is getting used to this new way of eating, and getting into the swing of burning your own fat as fuel. If you give it extra carbohydrates to use as fuel instead, it'll go off the rails. It is entirely possible that you will put on up to five pounds overnight, or within twenty-four hours. Seriously. We really, really advise you not to go there – because on top of everything else, those extra pounds won't just fall off when you get back on the diet; they'll hang around for a while and may prove hard to shift.

Phase Two of the diet allows you to fall off the wagon occasionally. Phase One doesn't. So don't. If you already have, and are reading this too late, go back to Day One and start all over again. Here's another thing you should know about the diet: it works brilliantly the first time. And it works okay the second time. By the third time, your metabolism doesn't quite know what to do with itself; everything slows down dramatically, and the diet only half works. Alarming, but true – it's true of every diet. Let's not even go into the fourth or fifth time: it'll still work eventually, but we're talking months and months rather than weeks. Don't mess it all up for the sake of a Twix.

I don't know what you're talking about in this chapter. I feel really inspired.

We're delighted to hear it. I (India) felt really inspired too, especially when I noticed a difference in the way my clothes fitted around the waist. After horrible Day Five was over, and to this day, I like everything about this diet. I like how it's easy and I don't have to think – only occasionally read labels carefully; I like how it's easy to incorporate into my social life; I like – love – the way it makes me feel; and above all, I like the fact that it works. I've always liked cooking, and I like ploughing through my recipe books to find more and more things to cook. I have to say, liking cooking – which Neris doesn't, particularly – has made this way of eating 100 per cent easier: I really enjoy the fact that I can go through my favourite books and find literally hundreds of recipes that work just as they are, and which don't even need adapting. So if you're feeling inspired, good on you. Carry on. You have a huge advantage over the people who are struggling a bit. But you'll both get there in the end.

So what did Neris do? Deep breath . . .

So you're well into the second week. Hopefully you've thought about why you got fat in the first place, learnt the rules of what to eat, and started the actual diet. But now comes the tricky bit – sticking to it. I failed many times before I succeeded, always promising myself that 'this time it's going to be different'. So what has changed?

Here is my diary entry from thirteen months ago:

I can't do this. I don't know what's wrong with me. Oprah Winfrey's epiphany came when she was standing on the verandah of her new-colonial mansion in Hawaii, celebrating her fiftieth birthday. She looked at everything she had achieved, and how far she had come, and finally it clicked. However rich she was, she would never be truly happy while she was overweight.

I wanted my epiphany, when everything would suddenly make sense. I was overweight and unhappy as well. I didn't even have the mansion in Hawaii. To be honest, my biggest revelation was that I was really, really, really bored. I was bored with dieting for eighteen years – and actually putting on thirty pounds in the process. I was bored with not being able to stick to something that I wanted so much. I was bored with being a grown-up who wasn't able to control herself. I was bored with putting things off. I was bored with imagining how life would be better if I lost weight. I was bored with not being able to wear what I wanted. I was bored with always imagining the future, when I would be at so-and-so's wedding, looking great – and it never happening. I was bored with seeing my amazing friend Ruth never eating her child's leftovers – when I couldn't stop hoovering them up. I was bored with failing.

    I was brought up by two schoolteachers, who were big on the ethos of learning, so being bored just wasn't part of the deal. And even now, saying 'I'm bored' makes me feel guilty. But that is what I felt. I'm a pretty intelligent person. I got ten O levels, five A levels, a degree, and a diploma in landscape photography. I have an amazing family and friends who I like being with a lot. I have a house that makes me happy when I walk through the front door and is filled with nice things. I'm achieving most of what I want in my career. My husband makes me laugh and is lovely. He and my daughter are the loves of my life. But I can't bloody stick to a diet. WHY?

Okay, so here is my small moment of epiphany after feeling this overwhelming boredom with myself. Imagine this:

I am at home again in the evening, one month into the diet, and I'm literally about to eat a three-cheese pizza. I believe this pizza is what will make me happy. When I dial the delivery number it's like I'm not consciously doing it. I'm on autopilot. I just have a need for pizza. I'm not happy. I'm not sad either. I just want my lovely pizza. Even as I eat my pizza I am thinking to myself that I shouldn't have it. But I do.

I'm watching **The House of Tiny Tearaways** *and the quite extraordinary Dr Tanya Byron is working closely with a young mum and dad and their two young children. They are sitting around a table and one of the kids is refusing to eat anything at all apart from yogurt, and is throwing the fit of the century. Scary stuff, to see the child so irate and the parents so helpless. As Tanya unravels the problem, it turns out that the mother can't have any more kids and is sad about that, and also underneath it all she doesn't want her children to grow up. She's happy with the baby stage and wants the children to have everything they want. Tanya tells the parents that this extreme eating disorder is really nothing to do with the child but is all up to the parents. Until the mother makes the decision that 'THIS IS IT, little Johnny is going to be a normal little boy and eat properly,' then nothing is going to change. The boy is getting away with it because HE CAN. Tanya tells his mother that she has to be 100 per cent totally sure that this is what she wants, and to change her focus, accepting no excuses; not caving in to the easy route and allowing the boy to do what he wants. Instead, she must make a decision and stick to it. Without that decision nothing will change. It is pure mind over matter stuff: if she sticks to it and is strong then her life will get so much easier.*

The transformation was unbelievable and extremely quick. Once he was faced with no get-out clause and a mother who was determined to change things, the little boy transformed his eating and the pasty look on his face disappeared almost immediately.

I am sitting eating my pizza and for some reason the programme has totally struck a chord with me.

*Beside the television is a rack full of fashion magazines, and I love to look at the clothes I don't believe I'll ever be able to buy but really hope one day I'll fit into. But I'm eating pizza. Helpless. Unable to control myself. It is like there are two parts of me. I want to be slim (my heart), but I want to eat what I want (my head). So I eat the pizza. But as I do, I suddenly come to realize that maybe **this is not about what goes into your mouth. It is about what goes on in your mind.** That little boy could eat healthily, just like I can if I decide that is what I'm going to do.*

Think about the split second between doing it and not doing it. Those precious moments of looking at a cake and deciding whether you are going to eat it or not eat it … It's your decision. It's your brain and your thoughts that will either get you through this or not.

There is this whole level of discussion going on under the surface all the time. But the truth is, there's no magic formula, and no time for discussion, either. Over a period of time I have had to teach my brain new tricks. I've had to outwit it and think two steps ahead of it. Miss Marple would be proud.

We are what we think. We think – then we do it. This may sound like psychobabble but it is true.

The lazy part of the brain that tells you not to bother – that niggling voice that tells you it's okay to eat the cake – I don't want to waste any more time listening to it. Nor do you.

But what do you do? How do you stop all the rubbish going on in your head?

First of all, you have to make a decision that you're going to do this. And nothing is going to stop you. You have to grab yourself by the scruff of the neck … I AM GOING TO DO THIS ONCE AND FOR ALL AND NOTHING IS GOING TO STAND IN MY WAY.

Accept that your head is trying to rule your heart and be strong. Battle with your subconscious niggles and win. Maybe your mind tells you, 'You can't stick to your diet. You have never done it before ... why would you do it now. Have those chips over there.' Realize that it is your mind telling you this and you can say no to it. Because you are in charge.

Tell yourself, 'I don't want those chips because I want to lose weight. I'm bored with my situation always being one where I'm not happy with myself. From now on I'm going to change my situation.'

Think through properly what eating that chip will mean to you : chips = not sticking to my diet = going off my diet = failing = eating more = putting on more weight = feeling worse about myself and unable to do what I want and feel the way I want.

You have to give yourself a strict talking to.

What do you really want in your life? Make a decision. Stick to it.

NOW WRITE IT DOWN AND PUT IT IN YOUR PURSE.

My bit of paper has two things that make me immediately focus on the decision I've made.

I want to be
Fit, Fit, Fit.
I WANT TO WEAR
Size 12 Jeans.

The first bit is from a kids' programme called *Boogie Beebies*. Whenever that song comes on my daughter jumps up and sings it and does the actions. So it makes me think of her as well. And the bit about jeans may sound superficial but I just want to wear nice jeans. India and I are looking for the perfect jeans to reward ourselves with.

Look at your bit of paper every time you're troubled by food. Look at it and think about what you're doing. It may sound over the top, but who cares? It will work if you want it to. You can do it. India and I did it. And we're still doing it – every day.

India's Secret for Being Little Miss Sunshine

This is entirely subjective, and I apologize if it sounds smug given Neris's *cri de coeur* above, but it worked for me. After the first few days were over, and after I'd stopped feeling strange, which was on the morning of Day Six, I stopped thinking about being on a diet. Unless I was with Neris, when obviously we'd discuss what we were doing and how we were getting on in microscopic detail, I just got on with my everyday life. I treated dieting rather like I'd treat going to the hairdresser's to have a radical change of colour: it would take a few days to get used to it, but after that I wouldn't constantly be thinking, 'Oh my goodness, I have red hair now.' My hair would just be my hair. In the same manner, the way I ate just became the way I ate. Not eating carbs simply became what I did. This has made the diet very, very easy for me to follow. It's not a diet, to me. It's how I eat. And I eat really well (I'm writing this just having had crispy courgette rosti for lunch). My family eats what I eat, with mash or rice or pasta on the side. It's not a big deal.

How We Felt on Day Eleven

India: Up.
Neris: Down.

Phase One Day Twelve

The usual. Water. Supplements. Breakfast. Walk.

You know how yesterday we were saying that people might be commenting on you looking somehow better? That's today's topic. First of all, don't be depressed if those comments haven't yet come your way. They will. But one of the incredibly frustrating things about dieting is that sometimes you feel and see a dramatic difference in the way you look – and you know you're not hallucinating, because your scales or tape measure back you up – and yet there is a distinct and demoralizing failure to notice on the part of the people around you. It makes you feel like grabbing a marker pen and writing 'I'm ten pounds down, actually!' in capital letters across your forehead. The truth of the matter is that the usual pattern, at least for us, is that you get the odd 'You're looking well,' and then nothing for a while, and then a sudden avalanche of 'My god, you've lost so much weight.' (Happily, the people you sleep with on a regular basis are usually a little bit quicker on the uptake, which is cheering.)

We touched on the subject of unhelpful friends much earlier in this book, but we think it's a topic that's worth revisiting. If you remember, we mentioned the 'friends' who said, 'You look fantastic, you don't need to lose any more,' when we weighed a hefty fifteen stone. Whether you're doing this diet in private, as we suggested, or in public, the comments may start any time round about now. And you need to be braced for them. As we've said before, there are people who may love you dearly but who aren't entirely at ease with the idea that trusty, reliably fat you are in the process of morphing into something unknown, i.e. something less reliably comfortable, or indeed comforting.

A great number of people – and we're sorry to say that when we say 'people' we mean 'women friends' – have serious difficulties with that concept. It may be that, as the designated fat friend, you're their excuse to pig out every now and then. The unlovely thought process behind this is, 'Well, she doesn't watch her weight, or care that she's fat, so if I have this chocolate cake with her, she's not going to make me feel bad about it. Besides, how could she? She's the size of a house.' By removing that possibility, since you're not eating chocolate cake any more, you're also removing your friend's excuse to binge. And that's quite likely to really piss her off, whether it's at a conscious or a subconscious level.

We're not saying it's an enormous deal, but we are telling you to be aware of it, and to get wise to it. When this friend suggests you go off the diet for a night, and join her for dinner, with pints of Baileys and a bag of chips on the way home afterwards, she isn't thinking about you; she is thinking about herself. Know this, and you've got the winning hand. Fall for it – thinking, she's my friend, she cares about me – and you've lost. Of course your friends care about you. But a lot of women also care quite a lot about their self-image, and as the fat friend you are an integral part of it.

The long and the short of it is that by losing weight you are going to look better, and by looking better you are going to make some people feel threatened. When I (India) was very overweight, nobody (mercifully) ever called me fat to my face, but I had a reply ready in my head – for decades – just in case. It was, 'At least I can go on a diet. What are you going to do – have a face and body transplant?' Childish, I know, but it cheered me up to know that I had a riposte if I was ever to be aggressed by one of those horse-faced twigs who assume that everybody would really rather look like them. Thin I can deal with; pinched and lollipop-headed, no thanks. And there are an awful lot of women around who equate physical beauty with near-anorexia. We hope you're not one of them – we like pretty faces better than spindly arms. But those spindly women aren't going to like you for losing weight and, by so doing, becoming prettier. We're not suggesting they're your closest girlfriends, obviously (and if

they are, please get yourselves some new ones, pronto).
They may be your boss, or a colleague, or the friend of a
friend, or whatever. They exist in quite considerable numbers.

So, What to do About Them?

Ignore them. However, this is much easier said than done.
If it is your misfortune to sit opposite someone at work who
has an almost forensic interest in what you do and don't put
in your mouth, things can get very trying. In which case:
be blunt. We know we said to try to diet on the sly, but that
can become impossible if you've got Sherlock bloody
Holmes on your back for ten hours a day. Either be polite
and say, 'I'm watching what I eat,' or be impolite and loudly
say (smiling), 'Do you have food issues? Because I find your
interest in what I eat obsessive and weird.'

If that doesn't work, or if it sparks off World War Three –
always a possibility – play the same game. For every 'Oh,
you're eating ham and cheese again,' come back with 'And
I see you're gorging on chocolate for the third time today.'
If your colleague comments on your snack of nuts,
comment (unfavourably) on her snack of crisps.

Force her to pay you a compliment. Hold out your
trousers and say, 'Look, my waistband's become really
loose.' She'll hardly be able to deny it.

If anyone tells you that low-carbing is unhealthy, refer
back to pages 66–8. Or laugh out loud: who's healthier –
the person having grilled salmon and salad for lunch, or
the one chomping down on a lard-burger and fries?

Being honest is a good policy, too. If you're offered
something you know you can't eat, say, 'I'm doing so well
today, I'm feeling pleased with myself, and I don't want
to spoil it, so no thanks.'

If you genuinely feel hurt by a comment ('Bloody hell!
You've put on so much weight!'), then say so. 'That's not
a terribly helpful remark,' you can say, which puts the ball
back in their court.

Neris is a big fan of love-bombing. If someone makes a remark you don't like, bombard him or her with insanely positive things. Instead of acting hurt, say, 'You're so lucky to have such a beautiful figure.' Heap compliments on their lovely shiny hair, or nice clear skin, or beautiful hands, or whatever. It will take them by surprise and throw them off guard. They've been bitchy to you, but you've been heavenly back, and now they're confused. And you feel mighty fine.

If all else fails, tell them to fuck off.

Be aware, though, that the nightmare friend/boss/ colleague scenario outlined above is quite an extreme example – though food does make people behave in extreme ways. Also be on your guard for the more subtle forms of sabotage that come from closer friends. A good, non-aggressive but guilt-inducing line to have at the ready is, 'I'm very good at sabotaging myself. I don't need your help.'

Here's a similar situation from Neris's journal:

Some 'slim friends who like to see people eat' came to see me and they were really on at me about being on a diet and it being a fad. They kept trying to get me to eat what they were eating but I resisted.

How, I don't know! Actually it was sheer bloody mindedness and the fact that I really need to have a good day behind me now where I get on with everything. I need to remember that you have to be careful with some people. They don't always have your best interests at heart.

I was having dinner at my friend's house. She knows I'm low-carbing, but she cooked pasta for starters and potato gratin to accompany the main course, and then there was pudding. I felt very embarrassed, and had the smallest possible quantities of food I shouldn't have eaten at all. But I couldn't not eat – it would have been so rude. Right?

Well, congratulations on having nice manners. But no, it's not right. You should have passed on the pasta, and had the meat and vegetables but not the potato. At pudding time, you could have said, 'I don't suppose you have any cheese lurking in your fridge?' If you'd done this, chances are your friend would have smacked herself theatrically on the forehead, and loudly exclaimed, for everyone else to hear, 'Oh God, I forgot, YOU'RE ON A DIET.' We don't blame you for wanting to avoid this scenario. But you have to decide what matters more: your ten seconds of embarrassment, or your weight loss. Besides, you hear those words and mentally add, 'BECAUSE YOU'RE SUCH A GIANT FAT HEFFALUMP', and feel anxious and humiliated in advance. But you know, the other people sitting at that table wouldn't have added those crazy words, or sniggered, or thought to themselves, 'Yeah, she looks like she could do with going on a diet, the big fat hog.' They'd have been admiring. We know, because we *really* admired people who had the self-control to look after their weight – and we admired them doubly for sticking to their guns in social situations.

Whether your friend cooked a carby meal accidentally-on-purpose or whether it was a genuine oversight, people don't ask people round to dinner to stuff them with food – they ask them round because they enjoy their company. Be good company. Don't make a fuss about not being able to eat certain things: just eat what you're allowed to eat, and enjoy yourself.

How We Felt on Day Twelve
Better.

Phase One Day Thirteen

Bravo! You've only got today and tomorrow to go, and then Phase One is over.

OR is it ?

Today – following water, supplements and breakfast, naturally – we want you to spend your walking time having a little think.

It's time to be honest. Brutally so. If you feel you've followed the diet to the letter, consider yourself garlanded with laurels, skip the rest of this chapter, and have a nice day.

Still reading? Hmm. Okay. So we're assuming you've cheated.

Don't despair. It doesn't mean you're doomed to failure. Flip forwards a couple of days and read Neris's journal entries for proof. She was the queen of cheating – but she didn't come clean about it for a good long while. Of course, it was only when she was able to look her cheating in the eye that the weight started really coming off. There's trying to diet, and there's lying to yourself about succeeding. Neris knows all about this.

We'd meet for lunch and talk about the diet, and I'd say, 'I'm so pleased, I weigh such-and-such at the moment,' and she'd say, 'That's great! So do I.' And – I'm sure she'll forgive me for writing this – it was transparently obvious to me that, give or take the odd pound or two, she looked identical to how she'd looked a fortnight previously. And yet here she was claiming to have lost half a stone. It made me feel very confused, for a while. She was wearing the same clothes, and they fitted her the same way – so where was the weight loss she was claiming had made her so delighted? I've never known Neris lie about anything in all the time I've known her – she is a realist, not a fantasist. And yet here she was – every time we met up – claiming to have lost weight when she clearly hadn't. She also perfected quite a nifty trick, which was to stand up, beam, and say, 'Can you tell I've lost weight?' When it's put like that, it's very very hard to say, 'Er, no.'

So, yeah. We know about lying to yourself. We know about sticking to the diet all day and then ordering a pizza and wolfing it down and pretending it hasn't happened. We know about the two bottles of wine that seem to have found their way down your gullet when you weren't looking. We know about the chocolate bars that somehow fail to register if you're keeping a food diary with fitday.com. Here's Neris, writing once she'd got over her cheaty phase:

I'm scared to admit failure. I want to succeed but I've got the ghosts of old – failed – diets weighing down my neck, and that means that sometimes I'm not quite brave enough to be completely honest. Did I really just have a bit of bread? Nah. It was only in my mouth for second. Does that count? And will anyone notice that I just had too much of that cheese?

Believe me when I say that I've been in denial for years. Sometimes I would speak to India and for some reason just tell her that I was sticking to it and that it was going great. I have talked to friends and said I was on a diet, and gone home and eaten a ton of carbs. I know what it's like to lie about it. And I was lying to myself. I'm not leading people up the garden path for no reason. I know what the reason is. It is that I literally can't be honest with myself. I am too scared to admit that I can't stick to something I want to do. I've sat in Weight Watchers classes in the past and sworn blind that I have stuck to their diet all week. I've done food diaries for nutritionists and amended the contents so it would say what I thought they would want to see.

But it is all rubbish. The only way I have been able to stop doing this is just to be completely straightforward and say, 'I ate that bit of bread because I felt sad and nothing else would satisfy my needs.' When you can admit that, you're getting somewhere. You have to be completely up front. Good or bad. You are what you are, and you have to stop beating yourself up and just say the truth: I ate that because I wanted to. At a certain point I had to get real. You have to get real. You are overweight because you eat too much. Honesty is the only thing that will get you through.

under siege, and hold on to its reserves of fat. That would be the opposite of a result.

Do not attempt to move on to Phase Two if you've been cheating. It won't work. Go back to the beginning, and start again. It's only two more weeks out of your life. And you'll thank us in the end.

It might help to re-read the whole of this book until now. Really read it. Ask yourself questions. Absorb information. Get yourself in the right frame of mind. There is nothing unique about you, and that means there is absolutely no reason why you should fail – even if you weigh 400 pounds. The past is the past. Forget about it. Tomorrow is the future. And your future is thin. You deserve it. It's within grasp. Now, go for it.

Phase One Day Fourteen

You've made it! How brilliant is that? We take our hats off and throw them in the air, whooping with delight on your behalf.

You're looking and feeling miles better. Your clothes are getting looser by the day. You may even have dumped those horrible tent-dresses and gone to the shops to buy something more fitted (one of the great, great joys of this diet for us was when we could suddenly wander into any High Street shop and buy clothes – not stretchy clothes, or things made of cotton jersey, but real, proper clothes, in real, proper sizes).

Congratulations. We really mean it. We know how far you've come, just as we know that the whole process may have been a bit up and down emotionally. But we hope you're now firmly entrenched. We hope you've got the bug. Now, a confession. We lost five stone each. Obviously, we didn't do this in two weeks. It took us a year. And this is what we did: we repeated Phase One for several months – six, to be precise.

Now, you're either thinking, 'You've got to be joking,' or you're thinking, 'Okaaaay...I can live with that.' Your reaction will determine what you do next. If you didn't have that much weight to lose to start with – two stone, say – move on to Phase Two tomorrow. If you have more than that to lose, do consider staying on Phase One for a while longer. How much longer? Only you can tell. We suggest moving to Phase Two when your goal weight is within reach – say when it's a stone away. Things slow down very slightly on Phase Two, and you have to ask yourself whether you're happy for that to happen in exchange for a broader menu and a wider variety of things to eat.

However, if you do decide to stay on Phase One – and really, you could stay on it indefinitely if you were so inclined – we're going to allow you alcohol. From tomorrow,

you may drink DRY white wine, red wine and champagne (not all at once!). Better still, develop a taste for vodka, and have it with either diet tonic or with soda water and a twist of fresh lime. This equals zero carbs.

Whatever your decision, pour yourself a drink. Cheers! You've achieved an amazing thing.

Time to buy a full-length mirror, if you don't own one already.

The Stakes

Neris:
- ▸ I wanted to buy nice underwear.
- ▸ I wanted to wear V-shaped T-shirts at the gym, not old baggy crappy ones.
- ▸ I wanted people to notice more weight loss and I wanted more compliments.
- ▸ I want to lose my tummy fold.

India:
- ▸ I wanted more compliments too – they became addictive.
- ▸ I wanted to look hot in a swimsuit.
- ▸ I wanted my stomach to shrink more.
- ▸ I wanted to buy smaller bras.

What are your stakes?
Write them down here.

Part Three
The Diet – Phase Two

Phase Two Week One

Once again, congratulations. You may be coming to this part of the diet after only a fortnight, or it may have taken you several weeks or months (as was the case for us) to get here. Either way, welcome, and well done. Please weigh yourself again before commencing Phase Two, and take your measurements again (see page 72).

So what happens now? Well, you still need to watch your carbs, obviously. Low-carbing, as we said earlier in the book, is a way of eating that is for life. But we're now going to take you away from the restrictive confines of Phase One, and broaden out your eating quite dramatically over the coming weeks.

To recap: this is basically what you have been eating so far:

- All meats, including hams, bacon, pâtés and salamis
- Eggs
- Green leafy vegetables
- Many other veg, provided they're not starchy
- Fish and shellfish
- Cheese
- Nuts
- Double cream
- Butter and peanut butter
- Olive oil
- Groundnut oil
- Olives
- Tofu
- Soya milk
- Whey protein powder
- Splenda sugar substitute
- Lemons and limes

That list is still valid, and will still be the bedrock of most of your meals. However, we're going to add to it. In Phase Two you will also be allowed:

▸ Non-leafy green vegetables – onions, for instance – in increased quantities
▸ All the berries – blueberries, raspberries, strawberries, etc.
▸ Cantaloupe and honeydew melon
▸ Seeds, as well as nuts
▸ Dark chocolate
▸ Coconut milk
▸ Plain yogurt
▸ Alcohol (hooray!)
▸ Soya flour – which means you can now bake (double hooray!)
▸ Ground linseed – ditto
▸ Stone-ground, wholewheat bread

All of the above need to be eaten in moderation. In moderation. In moderation. Once more: in moderation. That means twice a week to start off with. Otherwise you will be thrown off-course in a spectacular way.

Furthermore, Phase Two allows you – eventually, not straight away – to fall off the wagon occasionally. Given that you're going to be eating this way for the rest of your life, we don't expect you to be saintly at all times. This is not, however, a licence to slip up: going off-piste at Christmas is one thing; doing it weekly is another. And anyway, there's no need to do it weekly – or at all – when you can now have chocolate mousse for pudding, provided you're happy to use Splenda. A celebratory evening menu might look something like this:

STEAMED CLAMS IN GARLIC AND HERB BUTTER

**FILLET OF BEEF WITH BÉARNAISE SAUCE
ROCKET AND PARMESAN SALAD, GREEN BEANS AND ROAST TOMATOES**

RASPBERRY PAVLOVA

CHEESE

Hardly unbearably strict, we think you'll agree. In fact, almost crazily fabulous. And not something you'd feel shy about serving to non-dieters, either.

Now, we're not going to add all of the above new foods in one fell swoop, because that would clearly have disastrous results. Your body needs time, and plenty of it, to adjust to each new food – and bear in mind it'll adjust much more happily if you eat the new food with some fat. We're not going to lie to you: you will be able to eat these things in moderation, and from time to time, but not at every meal. While having scrambled eggs on toast every once in a while is one thing, sitting down to a mound of buttered toast every morning is always going to be a disaster. You're going to have to make some choices, but don't worry: we'll be there to guide you through them.

We'll work our way through the new foods in this order:

▸ Alcohol – because we think you deserve it (if you don't drink, move down the list)
▸ Dark chocolate (ditto if you don't like chocolate)
▸ Porridge oats
▸ Soya flour and ground linseed
▸ Extra vegetables in increased quantities.
▸ Coconut milk
▸ Berries
▸ Melons, and other summer fruit
▸ Seeds
▸ Plain yogurt
▸ Wholewheat, stone-ground bread

In the final phase of the diet, we will reintroduce:

▸ Other fruits
▸ Legumes
▸ Starchy veg
▸ Whole grains (i.e. brown things, not white)

But don't even think about these four items for the time being. We're just letting you know for future reference.

The idea is to introduce one new thing at a time and give it a week to see how it goes, and how it impacts on your metabolism. Your scales, and the way you're feeling, will be able to tell you all you need to know. If you bloat instantly and feel like you're bursting out of your clothes upon reintroducing wheat, for instance, learn from it. We're against people believing they're allergic to everything all the time, but in the case of wheat there does seem to be cause for concern.

If you work through everything on the list too fast, you will put on weight. So don't. Take your time. You're still on a diet, and you still want to lose weight. If you feel one week isn't enough to gauge whether one particular food agrees with you or not, give it two weeks.

Having said that, we believe it is enormously cheering to reintroduce alcohol and chocolate in the same week (but for heaven's sake not at the same time, please – it's hard to keep control of how much chocolate you're eating if you have a couple of glasses of wine inside you). So, go ahead. At some stage today, pour yourself a drink.

You may reintroduce the first nine items on the above list in any order you like, provided it's one at a time, each for a period of one week (or two). Leave the bread until last. For the purposes of this book, we're following the numerical order as it is above, so it may be easier if you do too. But if you desperately crave berries above alcohol, then go right ahead and have berries first. They'll taste amazing, by the way – almost unimaginably sweet.

Alcohol

When you say alcohol, do you mean any drink at all?

No. Not any drink at all, at all. You need to know two things: the first is that spirits have zero carbs – that's 'clean' spirits, 'hard liquor', rather than the sugar-laden ones such as Southern Comfort or Bailey's, which are and always will be completely forbidden. So don't even go there. (A pina colada, for example, has thirty-two grams of carb per serving – which is, freakily, more than you've been eating *in a whole day* during Phase One.)

But you can have gin, vodka, rum and whisky. Our tipple of choice is vodka, the cleanest spirit of all, and – we find – the least hangover-inducing. (Beware of hangovers, by the way. If you've been following our instructions and not drinking for the past fortnight – or more – then go easy with the alcohol. One drink is usually plenty to start off with. India went to a wedding a week into Phase Two, had three glasses of wine over two hours, and had to leave to throw up. Gross but true. So pace yourself, and don't forget your water.)

Mixers

Mixers, as you are no doubt aware, are awash with sugar. My (India's) pet hate, Diet Coke, is awash with appalling amounts of artificial sugars, and we're not talking relatively safe Splenda. It's also awash with monstrous amounts of additives and chemicals, which have no part to play whatsoever in this way of eating. Do you know, everyone I know who has a weight problem is addicted to this stuff – and none of them think it's bad for them, or a contributing factor in any way, because it's 'diet', innit? I say, DO NOT DRINK DIET COKE. Always remember, you are not following a calorie-controlled diet, which means that 'diet' products are irrelevant. Actually they're worse than irrelevant – they are actively NO GOOD. They are evil. They have horns and a tail.

Quite aside from anything else, Diet Coke's artificial

sweeteners alone can stall weight loss indefinitely in a great number of people. You have been warned.

By the same token, don't drink Irn-Bru, Fanta, Sprite, or any of those sweet, sugary, rubbish-laden drinks – even if they are the 'diet' version. Ditto lemonade, limeade, lime cordial (or any cordial: they're primarily sugar). Ditto fruit juice of any description. Cranberry juice may be great if you have cystitis, but it's full of sugar. Orange juice is also full of sugar, plus it's horribly acidic.

So, what does that leave you with? Soda water or diet tonic. Of these, soda water is the best, though diet tonic isn't the end of the world (and is the only exception to our rule about not eating or drinking anything 'diet', ever). If that feels bland, add a slice of lemon or a squirt of lime juice (not cordial). We won't lie to you; we had to train ourselves to develop a taste for vodka and soda. At first, it seemed awfully bland. Now, we love it. There's a reason why vodka, soda and fresh lime is the models' drink of choice.

You may also drink wine of either colour, red (two carbs per glass) being marginally preferable than white (one carb, but none of the known benefits of drinking red wine in moderation). If you're going to drink white wine, it's got to be dry: if your tipple of choice is Gewürztraminer, you're going to have to bite the bullet. Champagne is okay in moderation, meaning two glasses.

And please remember: being allowed alcohol doesn't mean you now have to go and drink excessively every night. Drinking in moderation doesn't stall anyone that we've come across. Drinking loads does. This is because your body will burn alcohol for fuel when it's available before it burns your own fat. Do bear this in mind: every drink, even if it's carb-free, means a small delay. Small delays we can live with. Big ones, not.

Chocolate

Now, on to chocolate. You can only have the dark stuff, with the highest cocoa content possible, and you can only have it in moderation. By 'moderation', we mean a square or two a day. If you think you don't like dark chocolate, think again. If you've been following Phase One properly, it will taste sweet and delicious. If it doesn't, cook with it – add Splenda if you're okay with it – and make things like chocolate mousse (NOT every day! Once a week, tops!).

On with the first day of Phase Two, then. You know the drill: Water. Supplements. Breakfast. Walk. Today, we'd like you to increase your walk by an extra fifteen minutes. We would also like you to think about upping your exercise. Don't panic: it's not imminent. But do have a think about what you might find bearable: yoga, pilates, the dreaded gym, swimming, whatever. This isn't because we're mean. It's because we don't want you to sag.

See previous entries for lunch and supper ideas, if you still need them: we hope that by now you're into the groove and understand that the easiest way to eat is by adapting your own family recipes.

If we were you, we'd save the alcohol until tonight, and don't forget to keep the chocolate and alcohol separate – you don't want to get tiddly and consume a family-size bar. Before we go, one last thing: congratulations again for getting to this stage.

The structure of the book changes from here onwards: what you now do is introduce the new food of your choice on a Monday, and carry on eating that way all week. Watch your body. Weigh yourself the following Monday. If the weight is still falling off, great – though please note that, with the reintroduction of more carbs, it will slow down a little. If it stalls altogether, first of all remember that weight loss is not linear and that it is entirely normal, in Phase Two, to lose nothing for a couple of weeks – or longer, but not more than four weeks – and then suddenly drop a load almost overnight. If the new food causes you to put on weight, even eaten in moderation, drop it immediately.

So this week, for instance, you will be eating everything you were eating in Phase One, plus alcohol (but see above for restrictions) and a limited amount of chocolate. You will still start the day with water, supplements and breakfast, and you will still be going for your walk which should, from today, take a minimum of thirty minutes. Carry on for the week; we'll see you again in Week Two.

Phase Two Week Two

Hello again. We hope you've had a nice week and not too many hangovers. And we hope you've managed to be intelligent about the chocolate, and not indulged in any crazy choco-binges. If you've found the reintroduction of chocolate difficult to manage, i.e. if you've had any trouble at all with controlling the amount you eat, now is the time to be honest with yourself, do yourself a favour, and ration it properly: have it only on Friday nights, or – if it's proving to be a complication too far – stop having it for the time being. Bear in mind that I (India) am writing this from the point of view of someone who doesn't have a sweet tooth, and who is perfectly happy nibbling at one square of dark chocolate a few times a week. You may be different. If you are, know it, and do something about it. Take control. You've been dieting for weeks, with great results – don't chuck it all away because your cravings for chocolate have returned, big time. This applies to all of the foods we'll be reintroducing. If you find yourself eating them excessively and can't seem to control your appetite for them, chuck them off the list. Life's too short to get fat again.

Neris wrote in her journal about chocolate:

Compelled to go to garage to buy a paper and a chocolate bar. Don't know what it is but this has been a combination that fits me and it is a difficult one to break. I am driving to the garage. Not feeling particularly bad or good, just focused on needing a little bit of chocolate.

Just called India from the forecourt … she has talked me into to having dark chocolate. Really not as nice and satisfying, I'm sure, as milk chocolate … I know it is a lot better for me and it still is chocolate (I suppose). I'm going in to get some. They don't have any! There is a gap where it says Green and Black but they have all gone. Crisis. What do I do now?

I need a bit of chocolate. Call India again. She's talked me down. And now she says I need to drink some water … from my bottle. Uuhhhhhh so boring. I've done it. It works for a few moments. I've got to distract myself. I'm beginning to get strange looks from the people at the garage.

I'm going in to look at a slimming magazine and get inspiration. All the time drinking my water ... okay ... panic over.

Rest of the day stuck to it.

Now, weigh and measure yourself. Do this every Monday.

Porridge oats

This week we are introducing porridge – that's real porridge oats, not anything that's 'instant' or comes in microwaveable sachets. You are now allowed a small mugful of raw oats two mornings a week, three once you're exercising. (Not yet! Don't panic and see pages 206–10.) Tip the oats into a pan with double the quantity of liquid (soya milk, water or a mixture of both), simmer for ten minutes or so, and eat. You can add Splenda (or salt), vanilla extract, two chipped squares of dark chocolate, a glug of double cream, ground cinnamon, nuts, and so on. I like having it with cream, crushed cardamom seeds and the merest droplet of rosewater.

You may only have porridge once during twenty-four hours – i.e. don't have two bowlfuls in a day. We strongly suggest having it at the obvious time – first thing in the morning – and following it with your brisk walk immediately afterwards. Never have porridge after midday.

Don't forget: always try and eat fat with the new food. This lessens its impact on your blood sugar.

Think yourself slim

Neris and I found it very difficult to imagine ourselves slim. Or slimmer, even. It felt like a really delusional thing to do, to be standing in a department store ogling a skimpy dress or a pair of skinny jeans and thinking, 'One day soon, that piece of clothing is going to look great on me.' 'Yeah, right,' a part of my brain would pipe up. 'In your dreams, Fatty.'

I have to say, Neris kept the faith to a greater extent than I ever managed: I remember one lunch when we met and she announced – being roughly a size twenty-two at the time – that she couldn't wait to be a size twelve.

Part of me greatly admired her – there is something very empowering, to use one of my least favourite words, about being so vocal about your ambitions: if you say it out loud, it's much harder to go back on your word.

Nevertheless, part of me also thought she was mad.

You are now getting to the stage where, having already experienced dramatic weight loss, the goal should be clearly visible, rather than pie (as it were) in the sky. Today, we want you to concentrate on visualizing yourself slim, even slimmer than you are now, at your dream weight. You may find this easy...or you may not. In which case, here is some stuff that we hope will be useful. Some of it's quite hippyish, I'm afraid. But it all helps.

Today's instruction is to get back in touch with your body, man. Seriously. It has been our misfortune (in a sense – in another it has been the most life-enhancing experience ever) to have spent considerable amounts of time in hospital wards full of very sick children. After the merest five minutes in such an environment, you become truly and pathetically grateful for the things you take for granted every single day: the fact that you can breathe without difficulty, and go to sleep at night without a canister of oxygen by your side. The fact that you can walk, run, skip, dance, without getting blue and tired within ten minutes. The fact that your limbs obey the commands from your brain; and the fact that the wiring in that brain works perfectly. The fact that you can talk and sing. That you can laugh. That you can move, and don't rely on someone pushing your wheelchair. That you are free, and happy, and not in pain. That your life expectancy is good, and that you are well. That all you have to worry about, as far as your body is concerned, is dropping some weight. Which you are doing.

Broaden it out: your amazing body may have borne you amazing children, and it's easy to lose sight – especially if those children are now surly teenagers – of how utterly miraculous that was, and remains. Your body nourished those children, both inside the womb and out. Your body is your friend, at all times, and it works indescribably hard for you, every second of every minute of every day.

When you're overweight, it's incredibly easy to lose sight of all of this – especially if, like us, you reach a stage where looking down makes you feel uncomfortable (neither of us looked in a full-length mirror for about ten years). But now it's time to re-connect. Have a long, steady look at yourself. Every bit of you. Because every bit has a story to tell, and every bit – every scar, every dent, every wrinkle – is part of you. Never mind if you hate your upper arms, or your stomach, or your chin. It's all there, in working order, and working for you. We really want you to love yourself more with every day of Phase Two that passes. This is probably happening anyway, because with the dress sizes dropping and the large amounts of weight you've already lost, it would be difficult not to feel better about yourself. But we want you to love the inside of your body as well as the outside. We even want you to love your internal organs. Your lungs, your kidneys, your liver, your heart – they're all there, beavering away, keeping you well. So don't just love the new way your body looks. Love the way it works, too.

Here are some of the things you can look forward to eating during Phase Two:

- Pancakes made with soya flour, to which you can add berries
- Muffins made with soya flour, ditto – though savoury ones are pretty nice too
- Quiche with a soya-flour crust
- Crustless cheesecake
- Courgette chips
- 'Spaghetti' made using spaghetti squash, dressed with your favourite sauce
- Strawberries and cream
- Home-made chocolate truffles
- Deep-fried onion rings, using soya flour
- Brownies, made using soya flour and Splenda

And so on. The list is only as limited as your imagination.

As I (India) have mentioned before, I really like cooking. And I want to make it clear that even though you can create your own modified recipes, you can also use 'normal' cookbooks and create feasts based on this way of eating. We could give you dozens of recipes, but it's pointless, because you'll find dozens yourself – and besides, we're not professional chefs writing a cookbook. One of the things we dislike about diet books is the idea that you can only cook the (usually rather grim) recipes at the back. The opposite is true in our case – you can use whatever recipe you like, provided it adheres to our rules. You'd be surprised at the number that do.

So I thought I'd go through three cookbooks I often use to illustrate the truth of this. When I embarked on this way of eating, I was keen to order special low-carb cookbooks, and felt that I would probably never eat 'normal' food again. I was completely wrong. The low-carb cookbooks served their purpose, but I soon returned to Nigel, Nigella, et al., and I haven't looked back. Here's the proof:

From Annie Bell's *In My Kitchen*:
- Cocktail sausages with mustard dip
- Devils on horseback
- Quails' eggs with saffron salt
- Smoked salmon with keta
- Crudité dips
- Potted crab
- Prawns with chorizo and sherry
- Squid and tomato stew
- Mackerel rillettes
- Red peppers stuffed with Gorgonzola
- Portobello mushrooms wrapped in Parma ham with goat's cheese
- Spinach soup with ricotta
- Chilled courgette soup
- Cheat's chicken Kiev
- Stuffed tomatoes
- Greek beef casserole with feta
- Kleftiko
- King prawns and mussels with basil purée

…and so on.

From Rose Gray and Ruth Rogers's *River Café Cook Book Easy*:
- Mozzarella and red pepper
- Green beans and anchovy
- Asparagus and anchovy
- Porcini and Parmesan
- Crab and fennel salad
- Beef carpaccio
- Roasted langoustine
- Roast whole squid
- Monkfish spiedini
- Grilled scallops
- Dover sole with capers
- Grilled tuna with fennel seeds
- Chicken with nutmeg

- Guinea fowl with fennel
- Roast quail with sage
…and so on.

From Nigel Slater's *The Kitchen Diaries*:
- A salad of fennel, winter leaves and Parmesan
- A salad of winter cabbage and bacon
- Stew
- Clear, hot mussel soup
- Chicken patties with rosemary and pancetta
- Roast pumpkin, spicy tomato sauce
- Pork chops, mustard sauce
- English cheese salad
- Pork burgers with lime leaves and coriander
- Roast fillet of lamb with anchovy and mint
- Chicken with mushrooms and lemon grass
- Mackerel with cumin and lemon
…and so on.

My point is, you don't need any special cookbooks to do this diet: what you have on your shelf will be ample, and will produce delicious meals that will delight everybody you feed them to (including your dear self), without giving anyone the impression that this is diet food. Which it isn't, you know. It's clean, healthy, home-cooked food that just happens to be low-carb.

Phase Two Week Three

Water. Supplements. Breakfast. Walk. You know. Now weigh and measure yourself.

Soya Flour and Ground Linseed

This week we will be introducing soya flour and ground linseed (the latter has the advantage of being a known 'superfood'). Again, we're not going to go crazy and start our very own soya bakery. But we will be eating the flour/linseed in moderation. This means all sorts of things, primarily that you can now have pancakes for breakfast, and make low-carb 'bread'. If you've missed squidgy things over the past few weeks, your agony (except it wasn't that painful, was it?) is over. If you haven't missed squidgy things, congratulations: your palate is re-educating itself beautifully.

FAUX-WAFFLES/PANCAKES

You can get ground flaxseed (aka linseed) from your friends at the health food shop. If you try to do it yourself in a coffee grinder or blender, it won't be fine enough. Flaxseeds are very good, because of their high Omega 3 content.

40g ground flaxseed	4 tbsp Splenda
60g walnut pieces	4 large eggs
50g finely ground almonds	240ml unsweetened soya milk
2 tsp ground cinnamon	1 tsp baking powder
¼ tsp sea salt	groundnut oil for frying

Blend the flaxseed, walnuts, almonds, cinnamon, salt and sweetener in a food processor until the walnuts are finely ground.

In a bowl, whisk the eggs and half (120ml) the soya milk. Add the walnut mixture and combine well. Cover and refrigerate for at least an hour, or overnight (but no longer).

When you're ready to eat, add baking powder and the remaining milk, then stir well.

Heat an oiled greased frying pan and drop blobs of the mixture on to it. This makes US-style fat pancakes, not crepes. Cook for about two minutes or until browned, then flip. You can have them slathered with butter, and you could also add vanilla extract to the batter.

You are allowed two of these twice a week.

MICROWAVED LINSEED 'BREAD'

25g butter	4 heaped tbsp ground linseed
2 medium eggs	1 tsp baking powder

Melt the butter, let it cool a bit, add the eggs and mix. Add the linseed and baking powder. Mix again. Let it sit for a couple of minutes to thicken. Pour into a small microwaveable container (about 5 x 4 inches/12 x 10cm) and blast on full power for three minutes. Leave to cool for improved texture. You can also add cheese, bacon pieces, herbs or whatever.

You are allowed two slices of this twice a week.

You will find many other recipes involving this week's foods on the net – we only mention this because neither of them crop up very often in ordinary cookery books. For more ways to use them, try looking up recipes on www.lowcarber.org, www.stellastyle.com or www.lowcarbluxury.com, to name but the tip of a most enormous iceberg. (Make sure you check out the before/after photographs, where applicable. We think we've done well, but some people lose literally hundreds of pounds eating this way and the photos are jaw-droppingly impressive.)

Building Your Confidence

From India's journal:

My mother made a remark about my having lost weight. A miracle of sorts, really – if she's noticed, it must really be showing.

3. It's not a good idea to spend too much on new clothes, since this weight loss is an on-going project – but on the other hand your old clothes should be hanging off you by now. This is probably the perfect time for a raid on a cheap shop – buy a couple of season-appropriate outfits and rejoice! rejoice! rejoice! at the way they fit you. Don't go mad: the best is yet to come, and you'll only have to give the clothes you buy now to Oxfam. Learn to clothes-shop cheaply. Topshop became India's best friend at this stage. Primark was Neris's, although she never forgot M&S.

4. Revisit the makeup situation. We did, and it was great. Here is one of Neris's early journal entries.

Stuck to it all day but felt sad. I think it only needs one thing to set you off. Felt better after emailing India. But basically, it's because I'm going out tonight. I have nothing to wear. I feel like a loser. Am going to an awards thing with my husband and I don't feel like he is going to be proud of me.

Writing this a few hours later. I decided to make a real effort getting ready. Spent more time than I have in years doing my makeup. I really decided to put myself first and act confident. So I put on my heels which I hardly ever wear any more because they are so uncomfortable, and put on some red lipstick. The evening went well. And I stuck to the diet. Except for four glasses of wine.

5. Don't neglect your hair. A slimmer face needs a better cut. We revere our hairdressers. If you want to wait until all the weight's gone, then at least go for a trim and learn how to execute a decent, professional blow-dry. See opposite.

▸ Towel-dry your hair.
▸ Most important bit: section your hair with clips, making six sections at least, with three each side of your head.
▸ Blow dry each section, pulling down your hair with a brush.

6. Establish what your best bit is. We very much liked the appearance of our collarbones, and went necklace-crazy, but you may be seriously into your legs, or arms, or face (more makeup). Once again, don't make the mistake of wandering around in minute clothing because you were a size twenty-four and are now an eighteen. Yes, it feels fabulous. And yes, you do look great. But hold your horses, and, for the time being, concentrate on accentuating one area you are especially pleased with; ideally not the upper thigh.

7. Consider heels. In the past, they may have struck you as seriously uncomfortable. Things should have lightened up by now. And there isn't a leg in the world that doesn't benefit from a bit of a heel. Even if they do make you look like a drag queen (India in modestly high heels is 6'2"). Speaking of shoes: we dropped a shoe size, so try everything on instead of blithely buying your normal size, and bear this possible reduction in mind if you shoe-shop online.

Phase Two Week Four

Hiya. Continue with the usual routine this week: water, supplements, breakfast, walk. Weigh and measure yourself.

Extra Vegetables
We hope you're feeling great and that you're enjoying the wider variety of foods you're no longer forbidden. This week we're upping the quantities of vegetables you're allowed. Not wildly thrilling, no, but it does help with variety cooking-wise. Up until now, we have encouraged you to eat up your greens; and to use, say, onions and tomatoes in moderation – where a recipe calls for a little of it. From now on, you can eat them more freely. We still urge you to keep at it with the green leafy veg: they're the lowest in carbs, and the best for you. But if you now want a couple of stuffed tomatoes for lunch, go right ahead. You still need to avoid potatoes – carb-city – altogether. Carrots are very carby also, but from now on you could, for instance, add a couple to minestrone – just don't eat three bowlfuls of carrot purée. Sweetcorn remains problematic, but you could certainly add a spoonful to your tuna mayonnaise. Treat peas, also very carby, as you do carrots: a handful here and there shouldn't be a problem, but more than that might be.

Coconut Milk
From this week, you can also cook with coconut milk – especially useful if you like fragrant vegetable curries, or Thai food.

Socializing and Sinning Sensibly
This week we're going to look at socializing. As we keep saying until we are blue in the face, this is a sociable diet. The foods you are eating are not what are traditionally considered diet foods, which is good news a: because you can diet on the sly if that's the way you like it, and b: because it exempts you from having to stand around at parties not being able to eat anything. You should have worked all of this

out for yourself by now, but here's a handy guide just in case. Some parties are more diet-friendly than others, and what we're going to do now is teach you how to sin sensibly if you're forced to go off-piste for one night.

The Drinks Party

Usually pretty straightforward, unless the only things on offer are sugary cocktails and baked potatoes.

Drink: DRY white wine, champagne or red wine; you can also drink clean spirits with diet tonic or soda water. We find that following each alcoholic drink with a glass of water is helpful on all counts – one wine, one water, another wine, another water, and so on. Not only do you remain relatively sober, but the water flushes out and rehydrates your system in a useful manner.

Eat: crudités, sausages on sticks, cheese on sticks, cold meats and antipasti, mini burgers without the buns, smoked salmon, cream-cheese-based spreads, little mozzarella balls, sashimi.

If all else fails: dismantle your food. This applies to all social situations. Have the quiche but leave the pastry; have the topping of the canapé but not its bready base; pick apart the sandwich and have its filling. Admittedly this isn't going to win you any awards for poise or chic, but hey – it's better than overnight weight gain.

If you're going to break your diet: don't have the baked potatoes, or the crisps or chips, or the Twiglets. Always head for the protein, even if it's accompanied by a carb, but be intelligent about it. Sushi, for instance, is a far better thing to eat, diet-wise, than a ham roll, even though both contain a mix of protein and carbohydrate. A little bit of sushi rice will hardly impact on your weight loss at this stage (it would be disastrous in Phase One); a great stonking white roll will. If you're confused, go for the option that you instinctively consider healthiest, bearing in mind what you've read in this book, and the allowed foods that are coming up in the rest of

Phase Two. A buckwheat blini topped with smoked salmon and sour cream is always going to make more sense than a chocolate éclair, because you'll eventually be allowed whole grains (like buckwheat) but not white sugar or milk chocolate.

The Children's Party

Trickier, because children's parties are usually based on sugar and other highly processed/refined foods – biscuits, cupcakes, crisps and the like.

Drink: water, tea, coffee, dry white wine, red wine, champagne. Or a triple whisky on the rocks, if you're India, who finds children's parties slightly challenging.

Eat: you shouldn't feel too much pressure to eat anything at kids' parties – the few occasions when I have nicked a crisp or two, I've been given filthy looks by the mum who organized it. At the end, when the hostess is trying to palm off the leftovers on the other mums, that's another thing, but by then it's all so soggy or dry the temptation just doesn't exist! 'No thanks, I've eaten,' works pretty well. If you feel obliged to eat something, try the following. The insides of sandwiches. Mini sausages. Dismantled sausage rolls. Scotch eggs (easy on the breading). Burgers without the bun. Pizza without the base. Hummus.

If you're going to break your diet: try and do so with savoury foods rather than sweet ones. As we keep saying, sugar is your number one enemy, and as addictive as nicotine. If you absolutely have to, because it would be bad form not to, then have a sliver of birthday cake, but leave the icing. Don't have sweets, biscuits, cakes, muffins or anything similar. And drink plenty of water to help flush out all the sugar.

The Wedding

Easy-peasy.

Drink: clean spirits and mixers, dry white wine, red wine, champagne. And water. You don't want to be pissed like a

mad auntie because you're not quite used to alcohol yet.

Eat: whatever's on offer: it is extremely unusual for wedding meals to be entirely carb-based. Ignore the bread basket, as usual, but have the soup, the meat or fish, the cheeses, the vegetables and salad.

If you're going to break your diet: don't. You really shouldn't have to. Weddings don't warrant it, unless you know a lot of bakers who wish to celebrate their special day by forcing three dozen different kinds of bread and pastries down your throat. There is always something you can eat at weddings, and given that you are now free to drink, the day really shouldn't be a problem.

The Funeral

Difficult, because wakes and the like are very often sandwich-based.

Drink: the usual.

Eat: what's on offer, unless you can wait until you get home. If you're going to break your diet: well, we don't blame you. You can't go to a funeral and start picking sandwiches apart, or scraping the insides of quiches out. If you have to eat, eat, but do try to stick to the basic breaking-out rules: don't go for the highest-carb option possible on the grounds of 'If I'm going to break my diet, I'll break it in style,' and steer well clear of sugar. See below if the post-funeral event takes place in a pub.

The Dinner-Party

It ought to be entirely possible to leave out the carbs, unless your host is vegetarian and serves up a giant bowl of pasta. In which case, if it's actively rude not to, have a small helping, don't angst about it, drink tons of water and up the length of your walk tomorrow morning. NB: pasta used to make up a large part of my (India's) diet: I literally couldn't imagine living without it. Now, I find it has a really weird and slightly sinister texture – I prefer foods that require more chewing. Double NB: eat pasta – when you're allowed it again, or if you're slipping up – the way the Italians do, which is in small, starter-size quantities, not in industrial-sized horse troughs. And keep it al dente – overcooked pasta means a higher GI.

Restaurants

There is absolutely no reason to break your diet because you're at a restaurant. You could do this diet for two years and eat out three times a day, and you'd still lose all the weight you need to lose. With this way of eating, restaurants are a help rather than a hindrance. Tuck in, but stick to the rules.

The Pub/The Office Party

Pretty easy, really. You can't have crisps, but you can have salted nuts and – waah – pork scratchings, should you fancy them (we can't say we do). And you can drink the usual drinks. You can even have a kebab on the way home afterwards, sans bread. Nice.

Abroad

Very easy – really, the only country that has a catastrophic record when it comes to processed carbs and sugar is America. Happily, they also have copious quantities of meat, fish and vegetables. But be super-vigilant: nearly everything ready-made you buy from a supermarket is going to be laden with sugars, trans-fats and corn syrup. No wonder they're so blimmin' fat, frankly. They're also really big, as it were, on low-carb substitutes – low-carb meals, low-carb pasta, low-carb bread, blah di blah. Avoid these at all costs. EAT FRESH FOOD!

And when you're abroad, eat what the locals eat: tapas, not fish and chips, for instance.

From India's journal.

On holiday. Lovely day at the beach. We took a picnic and I stupidly forgot to pack anything for myself, so then was starving. Must remember to plan. Managed to score some nuts at the beach shop. Had a latte with normal milk and vanilla syrup – thought, ah, why not. Had to swap it for normal latte. Vanilla syrup nauseatingly sweet – literally, I spat it out. I used to have one of these every day!

We came back from the beach and R was making dinner, and suddenly I was OVERWHELMED with hunger. Really rudely said sorry, I can't wait for your food, I have to eat NOW. Which I did. then I felt great. Long lecture from B about how boring it was of me not to drink.

Christmas

Christmas is really nice, but we don't quite understand why it's become an annual binge-fest – not just on the day, but from mid-December onwards. The whole country goes completely mad, and then feels really ill and out of shape, and it's all very puzzling. As you understand by now, bingeing until you feel sick has nothing to do with celebrating anything. The party season shouldn't bother you diet-wise – see above for canapé advice. You are, of course, allowed to drink. Christmas dinner itself is not remotely problematic either – just pass on the roast potatoes and double up on the turkey and vegetables. You may have bread sauce, once a year, in moderate quantities. And if you really, really love Christmas pudding, you can have a small helping of that as well.

You'll notice that we are suggesting breaking the rules every now and then in this chapter. Are you ready to break them? Only you know the answer to that one. If you still feel anxious about things like portion control, then try to stick to the rules. But if you know that one serving of Christmas pudding/a couple of illegal canapés/a small bowl of pasta aren't going to send you into a carb frenzy and destroy your eating plan, then just use your gumption and go off-piste when you really have to.

Please note, we are not saying 'whenever' you have to, or 'when you really want to'. Rule breaking is okay every once in a while, but it is not okay done regularly. It must never last more than one meal. You must never, ever stretch it out into the next day or, God forbid, week. You would be *amazed* at how quickly the weight you've spent weeks or months shedding will come back on. Amazed, and probably suicidal. So don't even go there. Have the odd bad thing – in isolation and, crucially, with your eyes wide open. Don't stick your head in the sand and feel all panicky. Do it deliberately and with your head firmly above ground. Know that it will delay you. Ask yourself if you'd rather have on-going weight loss, or delay it for the sake of a slice of birthday cake. Make knowing choices. You're no longer a ninny who just crams food into her mouth without thinking of the consequences. Thank goodness.

Phase Two Week Five

Okay – we can't put it off any longer. We're going to have to talk about exercise.

Berries

Before that, the food we are reintroducing this week is berries – all of them. Scatter them about gaily, with wild abandon: in your smoothies, on your pancakes, in sugar-free pavlovas. Have strawberries and cream – for breakfast, if you like. Speaking of which: water, supplements, breakfast, walk. Weigh and measure yourself.

Exercise

The walking should be a piece of cake by now: at the bare minimum, you've been walking every day for five weeks, though you may have been walking for months if you followed Phase One for longer than a fortnight. You will by now have dropped a considerable amount of weight. And you may be noticing that, although you can fit into clothes that are several sizes smaller, you may not be massively toned.

Here's the bummer: that particular issue is going to get worse with time, not better. The only way it's going to vanish is if you work out.

We know. That sentence sucks donkey butt. Or maybe it doesn't – maybe you're not as gym-phobic as we were. We're going to assume you are, though. Very few people with a history of fatness enjoy deporting themselves on stair machines on a daily basis.

Neris and I went down two different routes here, with similar results in the end. Unlike her I am, or was, really phobic about exercise, and thought I needed something fairly hardcore to keep me interested, plus I knew that I needed a person standing next to me forcing me to work out. So I signed up for the most brutal programme I could find: the Bodydoctor's intensive six-week course. I can't claim it was fun. I was hoping I'd become one of those

people for whom exercise becomes addictive, but I didn't –
although my attitude to it has changed: I now see it's a
necessary pain in the arse, and that with the effort come
serious rewards. The point is, the programme worked –
and how. My waist shrank dramatically. Everything became
harder and leaner. I dropped another half a stone. My
clothes got too big again. And I suffered: remember, I hadn't
exercised since school, twenty-five years before. But it
worked. The basic gist is fifteen minutes of cardio on torture
machines, half an hour of target-specific weights, and a
further half an hour of cardio. David Marshall, aka the
Bodydoctor, has a website – and dozens of celebrity
endorsements – at www.bodydoctor.com. Have a look.
If you despair when it comes to exercise, and want serious
results, you can buy the entire programme online and do
it at home. It's pared down, precise, and it gets results. And
no, you won't need to buy two tons of special equipment.
Neris joined a gym ... and for the first time in her life actually
went there regularly. She kept going by meeting her old friend
Mari-Claire there three times a week. Mari-Claire guided
Neris through the sessions and encouraged her all the way.
You need a really inspiring trainer or exercise class teacher
at some point just to keep you going. It is great to have
someone to talk to and to spur you on and make you laugh.

Whatever you choose to do, gather information first.
We're not personal trainers, and we can only tell you what
worked for us. My understanding is that a minimum of three
sessions of cardio is unbeatable if you want to burn fat.

Neris wrote in her diary:
My husband told me that now I've started exercising a bit, the
most noticeable thing about me ... even though I'm moving more
than I've ever done before ... is that I'm not exhausted all day
every day like I used to be. Even when I was watching telly this
evening I had an urge to do a deep muscle stretch ... unheard
of and strange. I didn't actually do it but I had a strong urge.

Phase Two · Week Five

Another benefit of exercise is that it enables you to eat more – and that it clears your conscience if you've overindulged. It is an absolute fact that the weight comes off faster if you're working out at the same time as dieting – but it needs to be the right kind of workout. I know lots of quite fat people who are marvellously supple through yoga, but they're still fat. I know fat people who cycle every day, and they're fit – but still fat. I know fat swimmers, and fat people who go to the gym religiously, but stay fat. You really, really need to know what you are doing, and what works best at shifting the weight. Our advice would always be to go to your local reputable gym, have a consultation, make your goals crystal-clear, and probably hire a one-on-one trainer for a session, to ensure you're using the equipment properly (it sounds obvious, but there is a right and a wrong way of using those machines).

You need to bear in mind that muscle weighs more than fat, which means that when you've been exercising for a while, your weight may stop dipping as dramatically as it has in the past. At this point, we suggest using a tape measure to keep track of your changing figure – and, as always, relying on the way your clothes fit you. As you firm up and build lean muscle, the scales may no longer be your new best friend. The tape measure, on the other hand, will always bring you joy.

The Bodydoctor's Top Tips
Exercise as early in the day as possible, so that your metabolism stays elevated for longer and burns more calories when you're not exercising.

In an ideal, non-dieting world, you would eat a carb meal before you exercise (to give you energy) and a protein meal after exercise (to replenish lost muscle proteins). In your case, it's fine to eat protein twice, until you get to the stage of the diet where porridge is allowed.

Never rely on the scales, use a tape measure to chart your progress – the tape measure never lies, scales can.

Make sure you drink plenty of water before and during exercise. If you wait until you're thirsty you're probably already dehydrated.

Make sure you warm up thoroughly. Your muscles are like an engine that needs to be the correct temperature to operate efficiently.

Concentrate on your breathing. You should always exhale on the positive movement of exercise (exertion) and inhale on the negative (return).

When you begin any exercise programme, start very gently to pre-programme your muscle memory and avoid soreness and stiffness. New exercises need to be a gentle introduction – not a blind date.

Do not concentrate on working 'harder' (quantity), but on working 'smarter' (quality). Channel all your energy positively as opposed to 'huffing and puffing', which wastes up to seventy per cent of energy expenditure.

Perform all resistance exercises slowly and smoothly. When you work quickly, momentum takes over and your muscles become the passenger instead of the driver.

Perform your cardio-vascular exercises at a moderate intensity so that you burn fat and not glycogen (blood sugar) – working at a high intensity does not burn fat.

Work with weights that exhaust you at between twenty and twenty-five reps.

Work within seventy and eighty per cent of your maximum heart rate. Any higher than this, a build-up of lactic acid will leave you very tired.

So, the time has come. This week, go and sign up for whatever form of exercise you have chosen to take. That probably means acquiring a gym membership, and going no less than three times a week. And it doesn't mean giving

up on your morning walk, either. That just carries on.
Don't forget to up your water once you start working
out; it's very important to keep hydrated during, and after,
exercise. One more point: when you start working out, it
may help your energy levels to do so after a carb breakfast,
i.e. after porridge. India always worked out after a pure
protein breakfast, and found she still had plenty of energy,
but trainers do recommend porridge. You're allowed
porridge twice a week, which can be before two out of
three workouts. Eat protein before the third. So you have
no excuse!

Phase Two Week Six

Welcome back. We hope you're not too cross with us for suggesting a gym membership. Some of you may even be enjoying going there. Even if you don't, you will not fail to notice the dramatic difference going to the gym (or whatever other proven fat-burning exercise you have committed to) makes to your body. If you still hate the gym, we sympathize. But we guarantee that you will LOVE the way it makes you look. As I (India) was saying earlier, six weeks was all it took to notice a dramatic difference.

Melons and Other Summer Fruit

This week, we are reintroducing melons, apricots, plums and peaches, which we hope for your sake are in season (bear in mind that, as a general rule, summer fruits are by and large lower in carbs than winter ones). Melon means cantaloupe or honeydew, and not watermelon, which scores very highly on the Glycaemic Index, being mostly fructose, fibre and water. Enjoy these fruits in moderation, every now and then: don't start having fruit salad three times a day. As we've already explained, all fruits have carbs and all fruits have sugars, in the form of fructose. Also bear in mind that your body is not used to fruit. Go easy. Don't have this week's fruits more than twice a week.

You know the drill: water, supplements, breakfast, walk, exercise. Weigh and measure yourself today.

This week, we'd like you to take stock.

How's the weight loss ?

As we've explained, the carbs that we've been adding over the past five weeks do slow down the process, which is why we only suggest starting Phase Two when you're within reach of your ideal weight. If you have three more stones to lose, you shouldn't be here, but still on Phase One.

However, assuming you're on this page for the right reasons, we need you to have a good long think about how you're doing. Are you still happy at the speed with which you're losing weight? If so, all well and good – and we found the increased variety of foods we could eat compensated for the slowing down in shrinkage.

If you are not happy, though, you should be able to identify the food(s) which have caused you to slow down: if you were happily losing weight until, for instance, you reintroduced soya flour, and then suddenly nothing much happened, then you need to ask yourself whether things got moving again after a few days, or whether they're pretty much at a standstill. If they're at a standstill, then drop the soya flour until a later time. All dieters have foods that will cause them to stall; we can't tell you what yours are because we're not you. But the point of reintroducing foods slowly is for you to look out for the ones your body finds tricky.

Remember: weight loss is not linear. At this stage of the diet, it is normal – though unbelievably irritating – to plateau for a while. We define a plateau as four weeks with no weight loss or inch loss whatsoever, no matter how small, which is not caused by anything identifiable, such as eating too much chocolate or suddenly deciding to make up your own rules. There are ways out of the plateau, but first we need to establish whether you've actually hit one.

India writes in one of her diary entries:
Another half a stone down. This diet is a miracle. It has quite honestly changed my life. Am worried about Neris. She doesn't seem to be losing the amounts she would be losing if she was sticking to the diet. Which she swears she is. Hmmm. I don't know how to say it to her.

Cheating or Plateauing: a Guide
All the foods that you have reintroduced need to be eaten in moderation. Moderation does not mean 'at every meal'. Nor does it mean 'several times a day'. It means 'a couple of times a week, more if I know for sure that it doesn't affect

my weight loss'. If you've been having linseed bread morning, noon and night, you are not eating it in moderation. If you've gone fruit-crazy – easily done, since our brains are hard-wired to think that fruit is good for you and that there's no such thing as having too much – then you're not eating it in moderation. (Fruit *is* good for you, but not if you're low-carbing. Then, *certain* fruits are good for you in moderation; vegetables are way better.) Ask yourself honestly whether you've sneakily been upping the quantities of these new foods to the point where you are no longer eating them moderately. If the answer is yes, STOP doing it: you may be plateauing now, but one morning soon you're going to wake up and find you've put on weight.

You still need to watch out for hidden carbs, especially in restaurant foods, prepared products (e.g. mayonnaise) and ready meals. Just because you're in Phase Two doesn't mean you can magically forget about reading the labels. Low-carbing means always being on your guard – which is why it's easiest to cook fresh foods yourself, from scratch. That way, you know exactly what's gone into them.

You really, really need to keep up with the water, now more than ever.

You can, as we've told you, go and eat a fast-food burger and leave the bun, or pick the topping off a pizza. But this is only to be done in extremis. If you find yourself lurking round the front door of McDonald's on a regular basis, you're sabotaging your diet. Don't. Make your own bacon and cheese burgers at home. That way, you'll know what's in them. And if you have a thing about fast food, you might like to scoot to the bookshop or library for a copy of *Fast Food Nation*, by Eric Schlosser. Parts of this book made India throw up.

Have you thought, 'I've got the gist of this way of eating now. What I'll do is, I'll just have some rice and a naan with my curry, and go super low-carb tomorrow and the next day'? You know what? That doesn't work. It's not going to

send you running off to Fatland if you do it once in a blue moon. The problem is, lots of people do it twice a week. And then three times. And then four. And then one morning they wake up in a state of panic, wondering what's happened to the collarbones they worked so hard for.

We allow you to cheat *occasionally*, where the social situation calls for it. That doesn't mean we allow you to deliberately put yourself in that situation on a regular basis. Yes, you can have a tiny slice of cake on your daughter's birthday. But no, you can't then make a point of doing the same thing every time you pass a cake shop.

We sincerely hope that your eating is no longer emotional, and that you no longer run to the fridge when you're feeling bored, happy, upset or lonely. The thing is, we can hope all we like, but you're the only person who knows the answer to that question. Sneaking the odd chocolate finger and then eating 'by the rules' for the rest of the day is not the right thing to do. You're not plateauing, you're cheating.

Never pick and mix diets. You're eating low carb. Don't throw any other diet method into the mix, no matter how appealing or trendy it sounds. Deciding, for instance, that you're ready for the fruit-juice detox you've just read about in your Sunday supplement is going to be FATAL. Stick to one diet (this one, hopefully), and one diet only.

Never weigh or measure yourself just before or during your period. You'll get a false reading, due to water retention, among other things. If you weighed a certain amount last week and now you weigh more and your period is due, don't panic: just weigh yourself again once it's ended.

Now, if you can honestly say that none of the above applies to you, that you have been following the diet to the letter, and that nothing has happened scale or tape-measure wise for four weeks or more, then, very annoyingly, you have indeed hit a plateau. Don't be demoralized: we've all been there. Here's what to do. And, by the way, it won't work unless you've hit a genuine plateau – it's not a fast-fix for on-going cheating.

Know that this phase is surmountable. Don't despair. Don't give up. Don't think, 'the diet has stopped working'. It hasn't. It's a phase, albeit an exasperating one, and it will pass.

Check and re-check for hidden sugars in the foods you're eating. Read every single label on every pack of food you own. If it's got sugar in it, or anything that ends in '-ose', give it away or chuck it out. Ditto anything with an unseemly number of additives. Those weird E numbers and mysterious additives stall a large number of people.

Eat more. Remember, we're eating three full meals a day, and as many snacks as it takes to keep us satisfied. If you've started skipping breakfast, or forgetting about lunch because you feel full – very easily done, since protein is so much more filling than carbohydrate, and keeps you going for longer – then please stop doing so. Skipping meals doesn't work on this diet. You must have breakfast, lunch and dinner, and as many snacks as you need in between. During a plateau, those snacks should always be a combination of protein and fat, for example cheese dipped in a creamy dressing, or smoked salmon and cream cheese wraps.

Eat more fat. Remember, this isn't a low-calorie eating plan. By this stage of the diet, now that your diet is more varied, it is easy to forget about the need to eat good fats. But you need to remember that it is the fat + protein combo that's causing the weight loss. Stick some cream and butter in your morning porridge. Don't have your steak or fish 'naked' – make a sauce.

Drink more water. Yes, even more than you're drinking already.

Cut down on coffee or tea. They stall some people.

Cut down on drink. Alcohol stimulates insulin and your body uses it – instead of your stored fat – as fuel.

Have a think about quantities. The 'free' foods you are allowed – i.e. the proteins – are free because it is almost impossible to eat them in massive quantities. But if you have been – if one fat steak isn't enough for you, and you eat three, with three lots of béarnaise, then you're going to get stalled. The 'in moderation' foods are easy to eat in excess too, especially cheese and nuts.

Up your exercise.
Still plateauing? Sure you've upped your visits to the gym?

Okay. Go back to the very beginning of Phase One for one week only, but cut out cheese and nuts. It's hardcore: it means basically eating meat, fish and eggs, plus good fats and green leafy veg and masses of water. We pretty much guarantee that this will break your stall. When you come back to Phase Two, have berries but not other fruit, and work your way up from there. The main thing to remember is that nobody plateaus for ever. There is no such thing as an eternal plateau. Sooner – we hope – or later, your weight loss will kick in again.

From Neris's journal:
My poor husband … his face is a picture every time I ask him if he can see a difference (in my weight). Last night he answered, 'Yeah, it's amazing how much you've lost between leaving the bathroom and getting into bed.' Maybe I'm asking him a bit too much!

Everything all right? Revisit pages 49–50, which cover emotional eating, if you're feeling even remotely wobbly.

Phase Two Week Seven

To recap: you should now be at the gym, or at the fat-burning class at the community centre, or wherever, at least three times a week. You should be drinking your water, having upped your daily intake to reflect upping your exercise. You should be taking your supplements and having a brisk morning walk. You should eat breakfast, lunch and dinner, and as many snacks as you need to keep you going in between. You should be looking pretty damned hot.

Weigh and measure yourself.

Seeds

This week we're adding seeds to the menu – that's sesame and sunflower seeds to go with the nuts you're already allowed. You can have a couple of handfuls a week. Any other seeds, such as pumpkin, are also fine.

You're nearly there, you know. You've nearly done it: another two weeks of Phase Two and you'll be eating pretty much everything.

We know we've become world-class bores on the subject of water. We're just going to do it one last time, because when we were at this stage we found that we weren't as careful about drinking water as we had been in the earlier stages of the diet.

Here's Neris's take on the subject:

Water: Your New Best Friend

Everywhere you look in all the magazines and on the telly you can't get away from somebody talking about the virtues of drinking more water. It has been going on for years now. Did people bother so obsessively about water before? Well, I don't know, but I've read it and seen it and sort of taken it in. I'd not done much about it before I started this diet.

Sometimes something as simple as drinking one more glass of water just doesn't factor into your day, does it? Also you hear people giving you so much advice that it goes in one ear and out the other.

I think I really started thinking about water when I began observing a couple of my friends who have absolutely lovely figures and are also luckily not obsessed with their weight. They really are both very fortunate. I started to notice that the one thing they have in common is that they both really knock back the water.

Take case number one: Faye, who works at a desk all day, keeps a one-and-a-half-litre bottle of water by her side and always manages to finish it by the end of the day. If she has had a late night she'll drink a bit more. When I asked her about how she keeps her Julia Roberts-like figure, she put it down completely to the amount of water she drinks. When she was younger she went to America to live and work for the summer and said that she just got out of the habit of drinking as much water as she had been. She got home again three months later and her friends couldn't believe the difference: she just looked so BLOATED and 'fat' (possibly not fat as we know it – but 'fat' comparatively speaking).

Then take case number two, my darling friend Ruth. She just sips all day, every day, and is never away from her small bottle of water. She is a mother who looks after two children all day long, and we know the stresses and strains of that, but I find it extraordinary that she has so quickly managed to regain her figure after two pregnancies in quick succession. Plus she is very, very upbeat and positive and has a ridiculous amount of energy. Again, when quizzed about her amazing physique and her healthy energy levels, she puts it down to sipping water throughout the day.

Then my hairdresser told me her golden rule for staying energetic while on her feet all day... loads of water. At this point, I just thought I MUST GIVE IT A GO.

I went to my local gym and they did a water level test and to my surprise they seemed shocked that I could even put one step in front of the other, because I was so dehydrated.

I went home and decided to do a mini experiment. I wrote down my energy levels for a day when I didn't drink enough water. On that day, which was quite a hot one, I only drank two cups of decaf tea and about three glasses of water in total all day.

7am: Woke up feeling tired.
12pm: Not completely awake yet and slightly irritable.
3pm: Just had lunch an hour ago and now I'm ready for a sleep. Can't concentrate on the computer screen.
6pm: Okay, I'm counting the hours now till I'm home and have my feet up. Feeling irritable.
10pm: I'm loving my sofa.
Another unpleasant thing is that my urine is darkish, not clear and not much of it.

The next day I did the same experiment. Admittedly with a walk as well. And I had ten glasses of water: eight, which is what everyone should have, and two extra because I was walking. The change was ridiculous, in a good way.

7am: Woke up feeling tired (I hadn't had my water yet). Had a glass first thing. By the end of the breakfast even my husband couldn't help commenting on my 'upness' for this time of the morning.
12pm: Have been sipping through the day. Have had many a visit to the loo.
3pm: Just feel so much more energetic than I usually do. I went for a walk after lunch. I came back to my desk and genuinely felt I was more focused on what I was doing.
6pm: Okay I'm not on drugs but I just feel so energetic and happy. I've been to the loo so many times today it is extraordinary but my wee is much lighter and so much more of it. Sorry for the details.
10pm: Still loving my sofa.

I did this experiment a while ago. I'm really not exaggerating. Water works. Your mind feels more alert. You feel much more energetic. Your whole system just flushes through so much better. It sort of makes sense, if you consider that your body is made up of around two-thirds of water.

I'm a convert

I must admit I've spent a few years waking up in the morning and feeling tired before I've even got out of bed. I now drink more water and have become Miss Water-bore of the century. I feel like I have so much more energy. If you feel a bit tired, lethargic or irritable, the change you will feel is almost instant. And you'll never go back to the shrivelled, dry old days.

I now buy a small bottle of water everyday and keep it with me in my handbag and on my desk and sip it all the time, whenever I can. Then I fill it up again and keep filling it all day.

You do get a bit obsessed but I promise you, you will feel the difference.

If you are prepared to read someone who is even more obsessed about the benefits of water, try *Your Body's Many Cries for Water*, by F. Batmanghelidj.

Are you a butterfly yet? Have you emerged from your cocoon? Then don't hang on to it. Chuck out – or sell – those binbags full of fat clothes.

Phase Two Week Eight

Nearly there now. Don't forget to weigh and measure yourself today.

Plain Yogurt
This week, we're reintroducing plain full-fat yogurt in moderate quantities. You may have a bowlful three times a week, which is, as I'm sure we don't need to point out, especially nice with fruit. It also means you can have raita with your curry (try adding toasted cumin seeds).

We've looked at how to get out of plateauing. This week, with the end of the 'diet' bit of this way of eating in our sights, we're going to look at how to get out of habitual cheating.

Cheating
Listen, don't feel bad. We've both done it. I (India) had some Christmas dinner one year, one thing led to another, and somehow I didn't get properly back on track for a couple of months – not because I was cheating every day, but because I'd somehow got it into my head that the odd thing occasionally wasn't going to hurt. I was right – but my understanding of 'occasionally' was wrong. It ended up meaning 'once or twice a day', more in the case of normal cow's milk in my tea. No, I didn't balloon and suddenly put on two stone. I put on half a stone, though, over those two months, and it made me very unhappy indeed. And Neris, as you've already seen from her journals, was a champion cheater for a while.

What We Have Learned About Cheating
The crucial thing about cheating is knowing you're doing it. The worst possible way of approaching the problem is to metaphorically close your eyes to it by pretending it's not happening. This is also the most fattening way.

The second crucial thing about cheating is to understand that there's always a price to pay. There is no such thing as

free cheating. And you pay in pounds. That's pounds in weight, not pounds Sterling.

The third thing, bearing in mind the first two, is that, armed with this information, there is really stupid cheating and there is intelligent cheating. We say, if you're going to cheat, be clever about it.

Spontaneous cheats are the worst. They're terrible. What happens is this: you're coasting along quite happily, and you suddenly start obsessing about something or other – for the sake of argument, let's say roast potatoes. You love them. You crave them. You miss them. And everywhere you look, people seem to be eating them. It's doing your head in, but you try to push your roast potato fixation – because that's what it has become, a fixation – aside.

You don't listen to it. You ignore it. And then one weekend you're having Sunday lunch at a friend's house. You've had a couple of drinks. And there, coming out of the oven, golden and puffy and perfectly crisp, is the biggest tray of roast potatoes you've ever seen in your life. You can't stand it. You have a plateful. And then seconds. And then you feel so depressed that you think, 'Bugger it – I've completely cocked things up. I'm behaving like some mad binge-eater. Oh God. What have I done? Ah well. I'll just dunk this roast potato – my sixth – into the bread sauce, and then I'll just have some chocolate cake, and some ice cream, and another drink, and I'll think about it properly tomorrow. I'm only human. And while I'm at it, I might as well have fish and chips for supper tonight.'

The solution is this: when you are in extremis, don't push things to the back of your mind. Don't obsess about what you can't have, because that's just stupid – like spending your life in a state of abject misery because you're not Angelina Jolie and living with Brad Pitt. What's the point in moaning about that? After all, you're not thirteen years old.

But if a serious craving – one that simply won't go away – rushes to the fore, accord it the respect it deserves. Spot it coming from a distance, before it assumes mythical proportions and gets too big to manage. Say to yourself: 'Okay. Well, I *could* eat some of that. It would set me back. There would be a price to pay. But I *could* do it. I am the boss of myself. What I choose to do is up to me.' This way, you are in control – you, not the stupid roast potato.

Neris wrote in her journal one day:
Went off it today ... got really stressed about my daughter going into hospital (which is coming up soon) and the only thing that was ever going to make me feel better was a piece of Victoria sponge cake. My favourite cake of all time. I devoured it and you know what ... I really, really loved it, and felt better, and instead of beating myself up I just thought ... that was lovely!

If you've somehow wandered over to this page from earlier on in the book, please go away; this doesn't apply to you yet. Now, what we would suggest at this stage of the diet is as follows: plan your cheat. Don't get to the point where you can't stand it any more and go mad with longing. If you want a roast potato, have one. Or two. Or even three. But don't allow yourself to get to the stage where you're so desperate that you have three platefuls followed by a ton of other stuff you're not allowed. Nip your craving in the bud by indulging it in a moderate way. Remain in control. Know what you're doing. Accept the consequences – and have as few carbs as possible for twenty-four hours from the next meal onwards by doing a day of Phase One.

Also, ask yourself why you are obsessing about a potato.

Another example: say it's your fortieth birthday, and a big group of you are going out for a fancy dinner. You know this is happening. You know that, just this once, you'd really, really love, on this celebratory occasion, to have anything at all you like from the menu. We say, if it's really going to enhance your life, do it. But do it cleverly. Plan ahead. Go back to Phase One for a couple of days before the event,

Forty and a hundred? That's a bit vague, isn't it?

It's vague in the extreme, yes. That's because we're not you. We don't know how many carbs your body can ingest without putting on weight again, or whether you're more or less likely to be at the upper or lower end of the scale.

But I don't know either!

Ah, but you do. You've been watching yourself, and will continue to do so. And that means that at some point – probably not yet, though – your weight loss will stop. You may even put on a couple of pounds. When this happens, provided you've been sticking to the diet, you know you've reached your critical point. At this stage, get out the carb counter, work out how many carbs you were eating a day before your two pesky extra pounds arrived, and stick to that number as your daily limit.

What, so now I have to start counting everything?!

No – only the new, carbier stuff. You know you lose weight by eating protein, good fats and green veg, plus the foods allowed in Phase Two – if there's a Phase Two food that stalls or bloats you, you'll have identified it and cut it out by now. Therefore, you will know at this current moment in time that you are not eating anything that throws you off course. That may change in Phase Three, when you are offered even more variety. So we're just saying, be prepared. Know what's what. You could eat several racks of spare ribs and ingest fewer carbs than you would by eating one doughnut. As the diet ends and the way of eating for life begins, we think that's worth knowing – and the way to know is to buy a carb counter.

Please now spend a moment thinking about how much you've achieved. How different you look. How different you feel. How much lighter you are. How energetic you've become. Never forget these feelings. Write them down here.

The Stakes

Neris:
- ▸ I like feeling light.
- ▸ I like having more energy. I never want to have NO energy again.
- ▸ I want to do up my size twelve trousers that I bought last week and for them not be too tight.
- ▸ I want my daughter to never remember me being frumpy and tired.

India:
- ▸ I want to continue with feeling energetic.
- ▸ I want to laugh with pleasure at fitting into a smaller size.
- ▸ I want to believe that one day my stomach will be flattish.
- ▸ I might want to get married.

What are your stakes?
Write them down here.

Part Four
The Diet – Phase Three

Phase Three: The Home Run

This is not a complicated diet, and from here onwards,
it becomes almost absurdly simple.

What's Missing From Your Diet?
The following:

- Legumes, aka pulses
- Other fruits
- Starchy vegetables
- Whole grains (aside from the whole wheat in your
occasional toast)

So they're what we're going to reintroduce next. Except
that we won't be trying them out for a week or two and
seeing how you do with them. We know that all of the above
foods are extremely high carb, and that if you eat them on
a frequent basis you'll fatten up again. There's no point
in experimenting: the result is guaranteed.

So this is what we're going to do instead: not have
them very often. That means once a fortnight, tops. You
want lentils? You can have them, once every two weeks
and in moderate quantities. You want an apple? Ditto
(remember: the sweeter the fruit, the higher the fructose
(sugar) content). You want a plateful of carrots? Go ahead,
twice a month. Yes, it's that simple. And if you want whole
grains – we're afraid white, processed grains are out as
things to eat on a regular basis, though you may choose
to cheat with them once in a blue moon – then do the
same thing: twice a month.

That's it. And if, having consumed these things twice
a month, you see no decrease in your weight loss, you may
have them once a week.

What about potatoes, bananas, sugar, pasta, white rice, white flour, biscuits, cakes and crisps?

What do you think? We don't recommend that you eat them. We have certainly eaten them during our planned cheats, but we would never in a million years make any of these foods a staple part of our diet. And we don't think you should, either.

Potatoes: nothing monstrous is going to happen if, having reached your target weight, you have the occasional potato. Let's not get phobic here. But bear in mind at all times that potatoes are ridiculously carby, and that eating too many carbs is part of what got you fat in the first place.

Bananas: rich in potassium, but then so are green leafy veg, various fish and meats, apricots, tomatoes, lettuce and parsley. But then again, the world won't collapse if you eat the occasional banana.

White sugar: this remains the crack cocaine of the food world. It does absolutely NOTHING for you except make you really fat. We say, avoid at all costs, in all of its forms.

Pasta: you can have it occasionally, say a couple of times a month, cooked al dente and served starter-size. Try to make it brown, not white.

White rice: we're not going to crap on the food that keeps half the world alive. Eat, cautiously, once or twice a month.

White flour: try to avoid (but see below). It's really not good for you, and so many people – thin people as well as fat ones – have issues with it, from IBS to bloating.

Biscuits and cakes: see white sugar. Try not to. We know you will, though – but please: there's no faster way of getting fat again than to scoff down biscuits and cakes. Not unless you have them with a side of chips, at any rate. So be ultra-aware, and if you absolutely must, have a couple once in a blue moon.

Crisps: No. Sorry. Completely pointless food. Seriously avoid. Have nuts instead.

Do bear in mind that one of the many virtues of this diet is that you eat 'clean', unprocessed, additive-free food, organic where possible. The protein + fat equation is what causes the weight to come off, but eating clean food – food that hasn't been faffed around with or chemically altered or God knows what else – is also part of it. Don't ever again clog up your system with Frankenstein-like foods that make you fat and unwell, even when you've reached your target weight. Other than those, though, the world is your oyster. Eat sensibly and wisely, follow our basic rules, and fatness will be a thing of the past. If at some point in the distant future, you ever feel your weight creeping back up – though the only way this will happen is through extensive cheating – return to Phase One for a week or two. Keep working out, keep drinking your water, keep taking your supplements … and remember to eat and never skip meals.

Finally, we could make all sorts of claims for this way of eating. Following a low-carb regime is, according to many people, supposed to have a positive and occasionally dramatic effect on a number of complaints and conditions, from depression to polycystic ovary syndrome, and from fertility problems to general aches and pains. The anecdotal evidence is persuasive, but we're not going to go there – we're not doctors. All that we can tell you is that this way of eating worked incredibly well for us when it came to weight loss, renewed amounts of energy and general well-being. We think this is remarkable enough. If you suffer from any of the complaints above, please consult your doctor.

As the journal entries scattered throughout this book have shown, we have not always formed a united front. We went about our diets in different ways. Neris was the funny, naughty one, unable to resist the lure of the bread bin; I (India) was the boring by-the-book, square one, dutifully munching on nuts. It took Neris a while to be able to follow the diet to the letter; I did so pretty much immediately. She lied to herself (and to me) for some time; I didn't (I'm hating myself, I sound so hideously pious). I think it is fair to say that Neris's relationship with food has been indelibly marked by her dieting history, a history that stretches back a couple of decades. I don't have a dieting history. Well, I do now, obviously, but I didn't at the start of this project. Neris really beat herself up whenever she strayed. When I went off-course, I basically felt one emotion, and one emotion only: annoyance at myself. What Neris's journals show is that her reactions were far more complex (and far more interesting) than mine: she didn't just feel annoyed but angry, sad, like a failure, hurt, out of control, panicky, despairing, pathetic, concerned about the impression she was making on her daughter; occasionally devastated. Her self-esteem plummeted dramatically every time she cheated, or even wavered; mine stayed pretty much the same. She is, I think, more self-analytical than I am, and far better attuned to the vagaries of dieting than I will ever be, but this hasn't necessarily worked in her favour: it's made her journey harder, not easier. It has also made it more impressive.

Of course, there comes a point where the diet stops being a diet and starts becoming a new way of eating – for life. I understand now, finally, that my overeating was for the greater part emotional. The way I think is not sophisticated: after I have identified a problem, I am able to sort it out and move on, without looking back. It's quite a brutal approach – Neanderthal, really. I can't really help it. I always think I'm unattractively and rather freakishly mannish for thinking and behaving this way, like some gnarled old bloke. But it does mean that, loath as I am to try to peer into the future, I don't anticipate encountering many difficulties in my eating life over the coming years. For me, overeating belongs to the past, and eating to mask an emotional issue is, well, no longer an issue for me. Being fat is over. It's not coming back if I have anything to do with it. And of course, I have everything to do with it.

I think food will continue to be more of an issue for Neris, simply because it has always been. And although I'm guessing here, I suspect that this will be true for the majority of readers of this book. If thinking about food has been a feature of your life for any length of time, if you're used to using it as both carrot and stick, you're unlikely to stop doing it overnight, despite your best intentions.

But do you know what? It doesn't matter. Because the point I am rather circuitously trying to make is that we both got there in the end. And you will, too – whether you choose to do this the hard way or the easy way; whether you come to this diet with a head stuffed full of preconceptions about calories, about carbs, about eating, and about food; or whether you come to it as a dieting virgin. Every overweight person is overweight because they eat too much of the wrong stuff. For the majority, that has less to do with greed than with a less easily identifiable hunger, a hole that needs filling, an emptiness that food somehow makes better for a while. If you are one of these people, chances are that food may continue to feature in your thoughts more often than it does in mine. Accept it. It doesn't matter. If you follow our diet, you will lose weight. And losing weight is as simple or as complicated as you want it to be. Whatever your choice, know that we did it both ways. Simple, and complicated. And we both lost five stone. You can do it too.

Here is Neris:
Losing weight has been without doubt the most difficult thing I've ever done in my life. It has been so tough. Talk about highs and lows.

I've never felt so vulnerable one week and then so strong the next. Realizing that losing weight isn't just about what you eat was a big step for me, and one I have to keep thinking about all the time. But now, I feel like for the first time I understand why I got fat. I feel like I've stopped talking to myself in such a critical way. Or at least I know

when I'm doing it. I know I want to stay healthy and slim.
I know it is up to me. No more excuses. What happens is
completely down to me and only me. I've done it and I'm
going to stick to it and nothing will stop me. And I feel
so much happier.

If you ever feel yourself slipping, pick up this book
again. It contains everything you need to know in order
to lose weight.

That's it. We're done. Whether you've read this book all
the way through before embarking on our way of eating,
or whether you're done too, and have reached these final
pages during your own final stages of doing our diet, thank
you for reading. This diet has worked beautifully for us –
it wouldn't, I don't think, be melodramatic to say it's
changed our lives. We hope it changes yours, too.

And, once again: congratulations ... for recognizing
that you had a problem; for having the oomph to do
something about it; for picking up this book; for following
its instructions; for looking great and feeling better; for
taking control. We know how hard it is. We knew you could
do it. We admire you more than words can describe, and
we salute you.

India Knight and Nen's Thomas.

July 2006.

Inspirations

'Always bear in mind that your own resolution to succeed
is more important than any one thing.' Abraham Lincoln

'A discovery is said to be an accident meeting a prepared mind.'
Albert von Szent-Gyorgyi

'To follow, without halt, one aim: There's the secret of success.'
Anna Pavlova

'If your success is not on your own terms, if it looks good to
the world but does not feel good in your heart, it is not success
at all.' Anna Quindlen

'It is possible to fail in many ways ... while to succeed is possible
only in one way.' Aristotle

'I don't know the key to success, but the key to failure is trying
to please everybody.' Bill Cosby

'The person who makes a success of living is the one who sees
his goal steadily and aims for it unswervingly. That is dedication.'
Cecil B. DeMille

'The man of virtue makes the difficulty to be overcome his first
business, and success only a subsequent consideration.'
Confucius

'Aim for success, not perfection. Never give up your right to be
wrong, because then you will lose the ability to learn new things
and move forward with your life.' Dr David M. Burns

'We succeed only as we identify in life, or in war, or in anything
else, a single overriding objective, and make all other
considerations bend to that one objective.' Dwight D. Eisenhower

'Success is counted sweetest by those who ne'er succeed.'
Emily Dickinson

'To freely bloom – that is my definition of success.' Gerry Spence

'My mother drew a distinction between achievement and
success. She said that "achievement is the knowledge that

you have studied and worked hard and done the best that is in you. Success is being praised by others, and that's nice, too, but not as important or satisfying. Always aim for achievement and forget about success."' Helen Hayes

'Men are born to succeed, not fail.' Henry David Thoreau

'If you wish success in life, make perseverance your bosom friend, experience your wise counselor, caution your elder brother and hope your guardian genius.' Joseph Addison

'There's no secret about success. Did you ever know a successful man who didn't tell you about it?' Kin Hubbard

'Formulate and stamp indelibly on your mind a mental picture of yourself as succeeding. Hold this picture tenaciously. Never permit it to fade. Your mind will seek to develop the picture ... Do not build up obstacles in your imagination.' Norman Vincent Peale

'Success is not the result of spontaneous combustion. You must set yourself on fire.' Reggie Leach

'A minute's success pays the failure of years.' Robert Browning

'Many of life's failures are people who did not realize how close they were to success when they gave up.' Thomas A. Edison

'Eighty percent of success is showing up.' Woody Allen

'Walking is the best possible exercise. Habituate yourself to walk very far.' Thomas Jefferson

'Exercise ferments the humors, casts them into their proper channels, throws off redundancies, and helps nature in those secret distributions, without which the body cannot subsist in its vigor, nor the soul act with cheerfulness.' Joseph Addison

'Why do strong arms fatigue themselves with frivolous dumbbells? To dig a vineyard is worthier exercise for men.' Marcus Valerius Martialis

'All we actually have is our body and its muscles that allow us to be under our own power.' Allegra Kent

'Safeguard the health both of body and soul.' Cleobulus

'…but the body is deeper than the soul and its secrets inscrutable.' E. M. Forster

'I live in company with a body, a silent companion, exacting and eternal.' Eugene Delacroix

'The body is an instrument, the mind its function, the witness and reward of its operation.' George Santayana

'Every man is the builder of a temple called his body.' Henry David Thoreau

'I stand in awe of my body.' Henry David Thoreau

'Our own physical body possesses a wisdom which we who inhabit the body lack.' Henry Miller

'A sound mind in a sound body is a short but full description of a happy state in this world.' John Locke

'He who loves the world as his body may be entrusted with the empire.' Lao-tzu

'There is but one temple in the universe and that is the body of man.' Novalis

'Choose rather to be strong of soul than strong of body.' Pythagoras

'If any thing is sacred the human body is sacred.' Walt Whitman

'Nothing has a stronger influence psychologically on their environment and especially on their children than the unlived life of the parent.' Carl Jung

'Act as if it were impossible to fail.' Dorothea Brande

'Our bodies are our gardens to which our wills are gardeners.' William Shakespeare

These Are a Few of Our Favourite Things

We love our products and thought you might like to hear about some of our favourites.

Hair

We both went to the same hairdresser for years without realizing. Great minds think alike when it comes to Susan Baldwin at John Frieda (020 7491 0840). She has the magic touch.

Neris uses Aveda hair products. The blow-dry lesson in the book was done at the Red Chat Chiswick Aveda salon (020 8994 3022), which is fantastic, using Aveda products. Order the products online at www.aveda.com.

We love Neal's Yard Remedies hair products. Buy online at www.nealsyardremedies.com.

We also love Bumble and Bumble Hair Powder for a quick touch-up when your hair is looking a bit 'two days ago'. Stockists 01768 891 394 and available at www.spacenk.com.

Another great hair product is Kiehl's Crème with Silk Groom. Kiehl's mail order number is 020 7240 2411.

Face

Cleansers and Toners

India introduced Neris to Shu Uemura's cleansing oils and they are amazing. Take off your make-up with it as well. Shu Uemura's mail order number is 020 7240 7635.

Tesco do a fantastic beauty balm called Skin Wisdom Deep Cleansing Balm. See nearest stockist 0800 505 555.

India swears by Vaishaly's whole range of products available at Harvey Nichols nationwide (mail order 020 7235 5000, extension 2322) and direct from her clinic on 0808 144 6700 or at www.vaishaly.com.

We really love all the face products Amanda Lacey makes, especially her evening oil. They are very natural and very simple. www.amandalacey.com.

Clarins' Water Comfort One-Step Cleanser is a cleanser and a toner and is fuss-free. You don't even need water. 0800 036 3558 or www.clarins.co.uk.

Moisturizers

We love Dr Hauschka's Rose Day Cream. It is made with extract of rose petals and is really light and smells so lovely. For more details or to buy online: 01386 792 642 or www.drhauschka.co.uk.

We love Origins' Dr Andrew Weil range, especially the Mega-Mushroom Face Cream. It sounds like it is going to smell weird but is actually really lovely. 0800 731 4039 or www.origins.co.uk.

We really like Dermalogica's range of moisturizers – available in lots of salons nationwide and via www.hqhair.com.

Exfoliators

Origins' Modern Friction is great. You feel scarily clean after using it. 0800 731 4039 or www.origins.co.uk. Clarins' Gentle Facial Peeling is absolutely brilliant. 0800 036 3558 or www.clarins.co.uk.

Eye Creams

These work:

Elemis's new Pro-Collagen Eye Renewal. 01278 727 830 or www.elemis.com.

Ren's Active 7 Radiant Eye Maintenance Serum. www.renskincare.com.

Bliss's Wrinkle Twinkle. www.blisslondon.co.uk.

The Minimal Makeup Bag for Every Day

We struggle with anything capsule-like in our lives but there are a few make up essentials.

Foundation

The most important thing to do is get a good foundation for smooth, even, luminous skin. A few of our favourites are below.

We worship at Laura Mercier's makeup altar. Her range

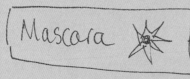
Mascara

includes foundations, tinted moisturizers, etc. 0870 837 7377 or www.lauramercier.com.

Prescriptives make up the colour exactly for your skin tone. No excuse for tide marks ever again! Custom-made foundation, concealer and powder available nationwide. 0870 034 2566.

Chanel's Pro Lumiére range with SPF15 is beautiful. 020 7493 3836.

Hydrotint Duo from Pixi is an amazing multi-tasking product. Tinted moisturizer with a blusher on the lid. WE LOVE PIXI. www.pixibeauty.com.

Eyebrows

Artist's Brow Stylist Mobile Essentials by Estée Lauder. This kit includes eye and brow pencils, mini tweezers, even a tube of brow gel, and is the same size as a mascara. 01730 232 566 or www.esteelauder.co.uk.

Laura Mercier also does a fantastic brow powder duo. 0870 837 7377 or www.lauramercier.com.

Mascara

Barbara Daly has created a fantastic smudge-proof mousse mascara, available at Tesco. 0800 505 555.

Of course we love Lancôme's mascaras. Their bestselling mascara is Hypnôse and it is brilliant. www.lancome.co.uk.

Sisley make great mascaras. www.sisley-cosmetics.co.uk.

Maybelline Great Lash Mascara really works. www.maybelline.co.uk.

Lipstick

Pixi Lip Booster. Put it on in the morning and it stays in place for ages. Love it. www.pixibeauty.com.

Chanel's Rouge Allure lipsticks are fantastic. 020 7493 3836.

Estée Lauder lipsticks. We love them. Classic. 01730 232 566 or www.esteelauder.co.uk.

Lancôme's juicy tubes. Light and lovely. www.lancome.co.uk.

Body

Deodorants

We are strict about using only deodorants free from parabens and aluminium.

We like Pit Roc at www.pitrok.co.uk, Dr.Hauschka (01386 792 642) and Organic Base at www.organicbase.com.

Shower

REN's Moroccan Rose Otto Shower Wash. www.renskincare.com.

Clarins' Relax Bath and Shower Concentrate. 0800 036 3558 or www.clarins.co.uk.

www.thisworks.bathandunwind.com do fantastic shower gels.

The Art of Bathing

Scrub first:

Exotic Lime and Ginger Salt Glow Scrub by Elemis. 01278 727 830 or www.elemis.com.

Origins' Incredible Spreadable Scrub. 0800 731 4039 or www.origins.co.uk.

Then relax in:

REN's Moroccan Rose Otto Bath oil. This is amazing. www.renskincare.com.

You can buy the wonderful organic range Abahna online at www.abahna.co.uk.

We really like Thalgo's Micronized Marine Algae sachets. One hundred per cent natural and detoxing. 0800 146 041.

Body Creams

Frankincense Toning Body Cream by Neal's Yard Remedies is gorgeous. www.nealsyardremedies.com.

We really love all This Works' range, especially the Enjoy Really Rich Lotion. www.thisworks.bathandunwind.com.

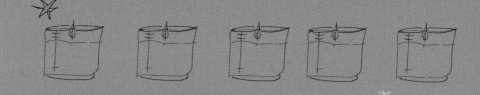

Candles

Put aside that money for a takeaway and buy a candle instead.

We love, love, love Natural Magic candles because they smell incredible and they are a hundred per cent organic. 0870 460 4677 or www.naturalmagicuk.co.uk.

Rigaud from Les Senteurs. The Cyprus one is utterly amazing. 020 7730 2322.

True Grace candles are really lovely and reasonably priced. www.truegrace.co.uk.

Facial Treatments

Eyes

We have a brilliant lavender eye mask made of pure organic lavender. No more mascara smudges, the lavender pouches cleverly zip in and out and the rest is fully washable. You should get a great night's sleep. www.laterre.co.uk.

Facials

Here are some of the best, for when you want to treat yourself:

All of Amanda Lacey's products. Amanda is fantastic and refreshingly down to earth. www.amandalacey.com.

The Dr Hauschka facial treatments last two hours and are amazing nationwide. 01386 792 642.

Clarins' one-hour facial makes your skin feel young again. 0800 036 3558.

Groom. Brilliant idea. One hour and two therapists. Both luxurious and efficient. 020 7499 1199.

Vaishaly's amazing facials. 0808 144 6700 or www.vaishaly.com.

I'm sleeping

Body Treatments

Elemis' body treatments rock. Find out where your nearest treatment is nationwide. 01278 727 830.

Thalgo are all sublime and fantastic. Call 0800 146 041 for your nearest treatment centre.

Other Things You Might Find Useful

Sports Bras

Whatever size you are, you should be wearing one for any amount of exercise. If you don't wear one check out www.shockabsorber.co.uk/bounceometer/shock.html. You will after seeing that.

www.boobydoo.co.uk stock every type you could ever want in any size and if they don't fit properly you can send them back. Our favourite is Shock Absorber.

Sports Clothes

Sweaty Betty have fantastic and flattering sports clothes. Order online at www.sweatyBetty.com. Neris wears her 'sweat pants' all the time.

Marks and Spencer of course do lovely stuff right up to size 24. www.marksandspencer.com.

Boots for Bigger Calves

You can look great in boots as well. In any size. Try www.duoboots.com or www.vivaladiva.com.

Tights

www.mytights.com is absolutely brilliant and has everything including Falke and Spanx. They stock not only every style of tights imaginable but also control pants. They deliver the next day.

Fitness

Here are some people we know and trust:
Mari-Claire Turley (07950 626 521 or

m.c.turley@fsmail.net). The woman behind Neris's behind. Mari-Claire is fantastic, professional, fun and lovely. She will change your attitude to fitness.

Sharon Saker (07970 258 527). Seriously experienced and inspirational. Highly recommended.

India loves Tom and Paul and Grays Fitness, London NW8, 020 7483 4130.

Makeup for Special Occasions

Sarah-Jane Froom. 07725 585 476 or www.sarahjanefroom.com.

Amanda Wright made us up for this book's jacket. amandasmakeup@aol.com.

Wardrobe Makeover

Ann Hamlyn is the stylist who gave both of our wardrobes an overhaul. She is great. Her company is Dress Me. 020 8208 4281, 07734 870 567, www.dressme.biz or info@dressme.biz.

Journals

Don't forget to write everything down, either on a computer or on paper. We don't care, just write.

If you're not on www.fitday.com then buy a journal at www.paperchase.co.uk or, for an amazing journal, go to www.bookery.co.uk and look at the 'Journalest' range. There is a journal there specifically for health.

Acknowledgements

India would especially like to thank Neris, who made working on this book such a fantastic laugh from start to finish. You're a beautiful person, in every sense. Thanks also to Georgia Garrett and Juliet Annan, as ever; to my family, for the support and encouragement; to David, Tom and Paul for the excruciating but effective workouts; to Sophia Langmead for looking after my children so brilliantly – without you, there would be no books; and to Andrew for the lurve, and for finding me hot whether I'm fat, thin, or somewhere in between.

Neris wants to thank her buddy and partner-in-crime, India. Time has flown. What a laugh we've had, and what a really great friend you are.

Thanks to Juliet Annan from Fig Tree who is quite simply brilliant, and Georgia Garrett who is a fabulous agent. Thanks also to Carly Cook, Jenny Lord, John Hamilton, Tom Weldon, the lovely English rose Louise Moore, and everyone at Penguin.

Thank you so much Mari-Claire Turley for being such a great friend and getting me to move. Thanks also to The Hogarth Health Club for putting up with us and Sharon Saker, Gill Sanders and the Chiswick Pilates Practice.

Thank you to Shirley and my amazing sisters-in-law Michaela Plaice and Eve Stokes and your families for the love and support and to our lovely Emma Kirby – I simply couldn't operate without you!

A girl needs friends to lose weight. Thank you Trudie for the inspiration, Lara Turner Tomkins, Juliet Rice, Catrin Jones, Sarah Taylor and MARISA, Alison, Richenda, Samantha, and Iona and my 'forum' girls Madeleine, Charlotte and Katie T. So many thanks to Mark and Zivi, and thank God for Dixie Linder, Fay Lapaine and my rocks Jo Laurie and Ruth Joseph.

Thanks to my incredible mother, father and sister Philippa, for literally EVERYTHING and to Bruce and my gorgeous nephew Thomas as well for making our family complete.

But most of all, this is ALL for Rich. As everything is. My beautiful husband, my absolute pal and love of my life.

From us both. We both want to thank John Hamilton for your style, and everyone at Smith and Gilmour. Neris loved illustrating the book (www.nelljohnson.co.uk is her website.)

We both want to thank Shaun Webb and all at SWD for being such a big part of the book. We didn't even mind stripping off into leotards in the middle of your office. Shaun, you really are amazing. Thank you for your input, ideas and enthusiasm.

A big thank you to Sarah-Jane Froome and to Amanda Wright for making us look our best and to Ann Hamlyn for your fabulous styling; Marks and Spencer for our clothes – especially the black Magic dresses! – WE LOVE M&S. Thank you to the fabulous shop Winnie Buswell (www.winniebuswell.co.uk) for the beautiful things you sell and allowed us to borrow. Big thanks to Amy, Sonya and Tony at the brilliant Red Chat Aveda salon in Chiswick for showing us how to blow dry.

Index

Index

Index